NATO's Eastern Dilemmas

NATO's Eastern Dilemmas

EDITED BY
David G. Haglund, S. Neil MacFarlane, and Joel J. Sokolsky

Westview Press
BOULDER • SAN FRANCISCO • OXFORD

For Kathleen Ladouceur

This Westview softcover edition is printed on acid-free paper and bound in library-quality, coated covers that carry the highest rating of the National Association of State Textbook Administrators, in consultation with the Association of American Publishers and the Book Manufacturers' Institute.

Copyright © 1994 by Westview Press, Inc.

Published in 1994 in the United States of America by Westview Press, Inc., 5500 Central Avenue, Boulder, Colorado 80301-2877, and in the United Kingdom by Westview Press, 36 Lonsdale Road, Summertown, Oxford OX2 7EW

A CIP catalog record for this book is available from the Library of Congress.
ISBN 0-8133-2064-X

Printed and bound in the United States of America

The paper used in this publication meets the requirements
of the American National Standard for Permanence of Paper
for Printed Library Materials Z39.48-1984.

10   9   8   7   6   5   4   3   2   1

Contents

List of Tables   *vii*
Preface and Acknowledgments   ix

Introduction, *David G. Haglund, S. Neil MacFarlane,*
and Joel J. Sokolsky   1

PART ONE
Eastern Challenges

1   NATO and the Quest for Ongoing Viability,
    David G. Haglund, S. Neil MacFarlane, and Joel J. Sokolsky   11

2   The Alliance Transformed: A Skeptical View,
    Christopher Conliffe   23

3   The Yugoslav Civil War, *Ernest W. Fischer*   37

4   The Great Game Revisited? The Quest for Influence in
    Independent Central Asia, *Stephen Page*   67

PART TWO
Western Interests

5   The American Response to European Nationalism,
    Kevin F. Donovan   93

6   Germany, the Blue-Helmet Debate, and the Eastern Crisis,
    Joachim Rabe   113

7   Between Eurovoluntarism and Realism: France and
    European Security in Transition, *Michel Fortmann and*
    David G. Haglund   137

PART THREE
Institutional Adaptation

8 The European Community and the Eastern Challenge,
   Charles Pentland   159

9 The North Atlantic Cooperation Council: NATO's
   Ostpolitik for Post-Cold War Europe, *William Yerex*   181

10 Discovering Westminster: The Transformation of
   Civil-Military Relations in Central Europe,
   Douglas Bland   195

PART FOUR
Conclusion

11 NATO's Eastern Dilemmas: Flexible Response Redux?
   David G. Haglund, S. Neil MacFarlane, and Joel J. Sokolsky   217

About the Contributors   223
Index   225

Tables

2.1   Scale of Force Reductions   29

6.1   Consent to Potential Missions   123

6.2   Humanitarian Aid for the Former Yugoslavia
       Since 1991: Selected Countries in Comparison   125

6.3   Intake of Refugees from the Former Yugoslavia
       as of mid-1992   126

Preface and Acknowledgments

As 1993 was drawing to a close, it seemed to some observers that so too was ending the era in which NATO enjoyed undisputed primacy among global security organizations. It was not that organizational rivals from *within* the transatlantic world were threatening to displace it from its position of *primus inter pares* (although "rivals" of a sort there were). Nor was it that there seemed to be no further need for security organizations; quite the contrary, for events in Europe and elsewhere throughout the year continued to generate an abundance of security worries.

It was rather that NATO, which came into prominence as a collective-defense organization—i.e., an alliance—was confronting a problem that was in more than a philosophical sense an "existential" one. And it was a problem that, above all, surfaced in the region from which most of the alliance's challenges had traditionally issued, the Eastern half of the European continent. NATO's existential challenge was dramatized by two Eastern "dilemmas" of the post-Soviet era: What, if anything, to do about Yugoslavia? What, if anything, to do about the former adversaries of the Warsaw Treaty Organization?

In mid-December a further note of complexity was injected into the debate, as a result of the surprisingly strong showing made in Russia's elections by the decidedly misnamed Liberal Democrats, headed by the flamboyant arch-nationalist Vladimir Zhirinovsky. While few predictions are reliable in political science, it can safely be suggested that the Russian election results will only serve to sharpen, at least over the short term, the alliance's Eastern dilemmas.

This enquiry into the varied aspects of those dilemmas began to take shape at an authors' workshop held in Kingston in May 1993. Every spring, the Queen's University Centre for International Relations arranges a colloquium on a topical issue in international security. Typically, the draft chapters presented and critiqued at the spring seminars reflect work done during the preceding academic year by the Centre's in-house research staff; as well, a few outside contributors participate in these annual endeavors. This past year's collective research project was no exception to the pattern.

Also no exception to the pattern was the source of support for this activity, always a pleasure to acknowledge. Year in and year out, the Military and Strategic Studies (MSS) Program sponsored by the Canadian Department of National Defence deserves and receives our heartfelt thanks. We would especially like to pay tribute to the dedication to that Program of Joyce Agnew, who in the past months has moved on to a new position in the federal civil service. Thanks are also owing to the NATO Office of Information and Press, and especially to Glenn Brown, Canadian Liaison Officer, for having assisted with funding for the May 1993 workshop. Manuscript-preparation costs were defrayed by a grant from the Cooperative Security Competition Program sponsored by the Canadian Department of Foreign Affairs and International Trade. We are grateful to the Department in general, and Roger Hill in particular, for this assistance.

The Centre continues to host four Visiting Defence Fellows (VDFs) from three NATO countries, Canada, Germany, and the United States. The VDFs play a key role in the Centre's work on national and international security, and it is with appreciation that we acknowledge the following: the Canadian Armed Forces, the German Ministry of Defense, the United States Air Force, and the United States Army. As always, the views expressed in the VDFs' chapters are theirs alone and should not be taken as representing those of their governments.

Our annual spring colloquia are consistently enhanced by the dedication of officials and scholars who take the trouble to come to Kingston to offer us their observations and criticisms. We are especially pleased that Hans-Jochen Peters could spare some time from his duties as head of section dealing with Central and Eastern Europe at NATO's Political Directorate to serve as our keynote speaker. We also wish to thank John Halstead, Kim Nossal, Jeanne Kirk Laux, and Arlene Idol Broadhurst for providing insightful commentary on the draft chapters.

Finally, we continue to record with delight our debt to the Centre's team of technical assistants, who have made it possible for us to produce this volume. Mary Kerr, Valerie Jarus, and Marilyn Banting remain a delight to work with. Last but certainly not least, we owe a robust "thank you" to Kay Ladouceur, who was involved with the initial phases of this project and who worked so expertly and diligently on numerous other projects over the many years she was at the Centre. It is to Kay that we dedicate this volume.

David G. Haglund, S. Neil MacFarlane, and
Joel J. Sokolsky

Introduction

David G. Haglund, S. Neil MacFarlane,
and Joel J. Sokolsky

I

One might be excused for concluding that Europe's current security funk should bode well for NATO's quest for ongoing viability. The recent relapse of part of Europe into something resembling more a charnel house than a common house should, in a macabre sort of way, be a welcome development for those who would keep NATO alive well into the next millenium. The reality of the moment, however, is that not only has the alliance's post-Cold War existential dilemma *not* been resolved by the succession of events in Europe over the past two years, it has actually been compounded. NATO's problem, one highlighted by current fighting in Yugoslavia and the general uncertainty about security elsewhere in the region from the Oder to the Urals (and even further east, as Stephen Page reminds us), does not reside on the "demand side." If the health of a club is solely a function of the number of membership applications it receives, then this institution's future has never looked brighter.[1]

Instead, NATO's troubles, though largely self-generated ones, appear almost irresoluble. They are also almost exclusively "Eastern" ones, stemming from two extraordinarily complex policy questions: (1) What is to be done about the former Yugoslavia? (2) How should the allies respond to the former adversaries of the Warsaw Treaty Organization (WTO) as *they* grapple with security challenges that had been kept in storage during the Cold War?[2] Each question, in its own way, goes directly to the most profound of NATO's contemporary challenges, namely the matter of how or even whether the alliance might transform itself and transcend its mandate of providing collective defense to the Western Europeans (and, in a different sense, the North Americans) without in the process sabotaging the internal solidarity of the current membership.

Alliances without a foe become subject to terminal decay, victims of the dual blows of lost mission and growing indifference on the part of their own members. It is in this sense that NATO's secretary general, Manfred Wörner, has rightly identified the danger of loss of credibility to which the alliance will be (if it is not already) exposed should it fail to involve itself *somehow* in a meaningful role in Yugoslavia.[3]

In the short term, NATO must respond to Yugoslavia, and in such a way that it does not end up driving wedges between the Western allies as well as losing the support of Western publics simultaneously desiring to help sort out the Balkans tragedy without in the process incurring high costs for themselves. In the longer term, NATO will also have to solve its "inclusion" predicament, encapsulated by the issue of eastward expansion. If it fails to become more of a factor in the security of Eastern Europe, it is hard to see how it can continue to be much of one even in Western Europe.[4] The two challenges, summed, constitute NATO's "Eastern dilemmas." How—or whether—it can become for the inhabitants of the continent something more than it has been (namely a collective-defense mechanism for the Western Europeans alone) is perhaps the only meaningful question one should ask about the alliance at this time. It is that question to which we turn our attention in chapter one, in which we conclude that collective defense no longer seems capable of cementing the alliance; collective security remains what it has always been—a distant promise; and peacekeeping, a possible salvational mission for the alliance, carries with it a set of risks that are not yet fully understood.

NATO officials and policymakers in the member states have assuredly been attentive to the requirements of continued alliance existence in an era when "chaos" and not the Soviet Union constitutes the threat (or, as it is more often put, the "risk"). The first significant landmark on NATO's road to its "transformation" (presumably from a predominantly military alliance to more of a "political" one) was the "London Declaration on a Transformed North Atlantic Alliance," issued by the heads of state and government in July 1990. As Christopher Conliffe's somewhat skeptical chapter demonstrates, between that time and the meeting of NATO foreign ministers in Oslo nearly two years later (in June 1992), a succession of declarations and announcements would testify to the need felt by all to make the alliance's force structure respond to the requirements of crisis management (*inter alia* by abandoning Cold War doctrines and weapons—especially nuclear ones—and embracing the logic of multinational and ostensibly rapid intervention forces and even, at Oslo, signing on to a new mission, peacekeeping).[5] A prominent accompaniment to these declarations of transformation was a significant institutional innovation, the creation in December 1991 of the North Atlantic Cooperation Council (NACC), the subject of William Yerex's chapter.

Finally, NATO has become more directly involved, almost on a daily basis, in the Yugoslav crisis since early 1993. First came the announcement in February by the US secretary of state, Warren Christopher, that America would participate in a UN/NATO peacekeeping force in the Balkans, to broker and police a ceasefire arranged under the Vance-Owen plan for dividing Bosnia-Herzegovina into a loose federation of ten autonomous provinces structured on the basis of ethnicity.[6] The peace plan engendered bitter debate both within the former Yugoslavia and in the West before it was euthanatized in late May, in favor of a carving up of Bosnia into three unequal ethnic entities.

Significantly, there was a role either for NATO or for some of the allies no matter what one's views on the merits of Vance-Owen. To the proponents, the plan could have worked if and only if a ceasefire between Bosnia's Serbs, Croats, and Muslims (i.e., the government) were preserved by a large force of peacekeepers, supplied by NATO members and other countries and under NATO operational command and overall UN authorization. Estimates of the number of troops needed for this mission ranged from as few as 40,000 to as many as 100,000. Although the Vance-Owen Plan may be dead, NATO continues, at this writing, to develop deployment plans for peacekeeping in Bosnia, in the event a peace can be arranged to keep.

For a time in early 1993 it appeared as if a more active role than peacekeeping was being envisioned. To those who denounced Vance-Owen, NATO or even just individual allies had a vital role to play, either by arming the Bosnian government forces and letting them look after their own security, or by more energetically punishing the Serbs who had been emboldened by successive triumphs in their campaign of ethnic cleansing.

Prior to the decision to let partition of Bosnia occur, the alliance had become incrementally involved in the conflict. In July 1992 NATO Airborne Early Warning (NAEW) aircraft began monitoring naval operations over the Adriatic. Three months later, NAEW aircraft began to enforce the UN ban on military flights over Bosnia-Herzegovina. NATO tactical aircraft began in mid-April 1993 to enforce the no-fly zone decreed over Bosnia at the end of 1992.

This incrementalism could never be replaced by a more forceful interventionism because the latter could only occur with American leadership and sufficient allied backing to allow the Clinton administration to convince Congress, the American public, and most importantly perhaps, itself, that the risks of military involvement were outweighed by the costs—moral, political, and strategic—of continued abstention.

As Ernest Fischer's chapter illustrates, the case for caution in Yugoslavia was and remains a strong one in Washington. In the end, the administration, with its gaze rivetted on the more important (to it) domestic agenda, decided there really were no "vital interests" of the United States at risk in Bosnia.[7]

II

Why should the Western European members of NATO be worrying so much about the security difficulties of Eastern Europe? Most broadly, two kinds of "threat" could be exacerbated if appropriate responses cannot be developed or applied. First is the threat of generalized ethnic conflict spilling over into Western Europe. Second is the possibility of Russia becoming the effective equivalent of the Soviet threat of yore.

In the first instance, there has already been a direct (and in one country, serious) impact on security created by the refugee crisis. Anti-foreign violence in Germany provides a compelling example, which Joachim Rabe's chapter explores in detail. However, one should refrain from jumping to the conclusion that the reaction to imported social problems with an Eastern provenance need lead inevitably to strains among the Western Europeans themselves. Ironically, worries about the stability of Germany could have the effect of reinforcing the desire of Germany's most important neighbor, France, to seek closer economic, political, and military integration with it—if only better to control it.[8]

There are also indirect effects of generalized chaos to the East, notably the real prospect of political conflict among the Western Europeans as a result of differential assessments both of the problem in the East and the measures required to address it. The chapter by Michel Fortmann and David Haglund discusses the tensions that were produced among the Western Europeans late in 1991 and early in 1992 as a result of a very different understanding of the need for early recognition of Slovenia and Croatia. This intra-alliance (intra-EC, really) tension over the wisdom of early recognition in turn contributed to an upturn in concern over the "renationalization" of Western European foreign and security policy.[9]

Differential "contributions" to resolving the security problems in the East can also be guaranteed to sow discord between the European allies, and between the latter and the US. A central problem here lies in constitutional limitations on German use of force for multilateral crisis management. Even Chancellor Helmut Kohl, who does believe Germany must do its share in maintaining security out of the NATO theater of operations, with armed forces if need be, draws the line at Yugoslavia, for historical reasons. Historical and moral debates aside, there remains, however, the real prospect, put on offer last February in Munich by

Senator William Cohen, that Congress will not authorize American ground forces in the Balkans unless all the major European allies—the Germans included—send troops.[10]

One of the ironies of the post-Cold War era is the refusal of that old warhorse of the alliance, the "burdensharing" debate, to amble off to the conceptual glue factory. In a new guise, burdensharing may continue to serve as a source of intra-alliance wrangling, perhaps even more so than during the period of East-West strife. No Western European country would be more affected by the resurgence of this debate than Germany, unless, of course, the US so deemphasized its interest and role in European security management as to become a less exigent *demandeur* of the European allies. This possibility is raised in Kevin Donovan's chapter.

III

Germany also figures—albeit as hopeful analogy not as source of sorrow—in the second kind of threat mentioned earlier, namely that of a spurned Russia becoming for the alliance the equivalent of the former Soviet Union. According to some, much will have been sacrificed if the current opportunity to incorporate Russia somehow into a West-facing security structure is bungled. The new, less pleasant Russia that would emerge would not generate the level of commitment to cooperative security demonstrated by its current foreign-policy shapers. Gone would be the promise of what the most prominent of these, Andrei Kozyrev, calls the "new partnership strategy."[11]

It is in this context that the German analogy is of possible utility. The prospects of democracy, prosperity, and stability in Germany and, by extension, all of Western Europe, were substantially advanced as a result of the Western embrace of Germany after its second great military defeat of this century. This contrasts starkly with the consequences of the Entente and Associated Powers' rejection of Germany at Versailles in 1919.[12] An alliance structure, in this case NATO after 1955, proved to be the vehicle not only for defending Germany against its Eastern foe, but for reassuring Germany's *Western* neighbors that they could count on and work with it to build a community of security and prosperity. NATO was in this sense an implicit collective-security structure, or at the very least a powerful and necessary "confidence-building" mechanism.[13]

For some time there has been an advocacy, in the US as elsewhere, that the West move emphatically to embrace the new Russia. The embracers have usually stressed the need for and logical merits of economic assistance, but there have been those who have argued as well that bringing Russia into an alliance with the US was a necessary precondition of any lasting rapprochement.[14]

Thus is posed, though hardly resolved, NATO's second major Eastern dilemma. For even if it could be assumed that the embracers would carry the day both in the US and in other major allied countries (they cannot), it is far from evident that the Russians themselves would welcome an invitation to join NATO. Admittedly, such unmistakable pro-Westerners as the current foreign minister, Kozyrev, have broached the thought that to consummate the new partnership strategy, an alliance with the West would have to be concluded. To Kozyrev, the path to success "lies in alliance between a strong new Russia and other democratic states. That is why we see the NATO nations as our mutual friends, and in future allies."[15] But it cannot be assumed that the foreign minister's views will prevail in the internal Russian debate, even if President Boris Yeltsin inclines toward Kozyrev's position.[16]

Apart from possible Russian objections to an expanded NATO, there is another, more philosophical, difficulty with the attempt to "solve" the Russian problem by relying on NATO as *deus ex machina*. In essence, NATO's problem is that collective defense seems to have outlived its purpose, and that collective security seems never to be able to attain its. It is for that reason that a few observers are beginning to wonder whether something in between the two conceptual poles, namely "peacekeeping," might not become NATO's new mission.[17]

IV

Because of the intractable nature of the Eastern dilemma, alliance leaders have been trying, of late, to create a halfway solution to their problem, by offering *something* to the Central and Eastern European states without extending them full membership. With time, it is thought, full membership might be proferred; alternatively, alliance leaders can always hope that the challenges of the moment will somehow have disappeared, making the membership question a moot one. In October 1993, at a NATO meeting of defense ministers at Travemünde, Germany, US Defense Secretary Les Aspin proposed that the expansion-of-membership issue be shelved, in exchange for a series of bilateral alliance agreements with the former members of the WTO.[18] Dubbed the "Partnership for Peace," this proposal would stop short of offering security guarantees as provided by article 5 of the NATO treaty, but would provide a forum for consultation, under the treaty's article 4, which states that the parties to the treaty "will consult together whenever, in the opinion of any of them, the territorial integrity, political independence, or security of any of [them] is threatened."[19] There would also be an enhanced program in this formula for some of the technical assistance measures discussed in Douglas Bland's chapter. As well, there would exist the possibility of Eastern cooperation with NATO in peacekeeping, crisis-management, and search and rescue missions.

Whether this compromise constitutes a long-term solution to NATO's Eastern dilemmas remains to be seen. Its short-term effects may well serve to smooth over some of the tensions of today *among* alliance members, albeit at some cost to the Poles, Hungarians, and Czechs—the so-called "Visegrad countries" about whom Charles Pentland writes in his chapter. Over the longer term, however, one might be permitted more than a little skepticism about the alliance's ability successfully to resolve the contradictions looming to the East.

Notes

1. For one Eastern leader's particularly eloquent case for membership, see Vaclav Havel, "We Really Are Part of One NATO Family," *International Herald Tribune*, 20 October 1993, p. 4.

2. Whether NATO should "go East" is the subject of an intriguing debate in the pages of *Foreign Affairs* 72 (September/October 1993), where the affirmative position is argued by Ronald D. Asmus, Richard L. Kugler, and F. Stephen Larrabee, "Building a New NATO," pp. 20-40; and the negative, counterthesis is presented by Owen Harries, "The Collapse of the 'West'," pp. 41-53.

3. In late April 1993 Wörner told a Canadian reporter that the many "reasons for the existence of NATO . . . will not be sufficient to prove the need for NATO in public perception if we fail to deal effectively with [this crisis] on our doorstep." Quoted in Paul Koring, "Europe's Lack of Will Condemned," *Globe and Mail* (Toronto), 1 May 1993, pp. A1, 14.

4. On this point, see William Pfaff, "If NATO Can't Guarantee Security in Europe, What Good Is It?" *International Herald Tribune*, 2 November 1993, p. 4: "NATO is a solution, or it is nothing. At present, its members are unwilling to commit the organization to anything that involves risk. But if NATO does not change and take risks, it will die."

5. NATO Office of Information and Press, *The Transformation of an Alliance: The Decisions of NATO's Heads of State and Government* (Brussels, 1992); "Ministerial Meeting of the North Atlantic Council in Oslo, Norway, 4th June 1992," *Press Communiqué M-NAC-1 (92)51* (Brussels: NATO Press Service, 1992); John Barrett, "Conflict Prevention and Crisis Management: The Approach of NATO" (Brussels: NATO International Staff, Political Affairs Division, n.d.); Hans Jochen Peters and John Barrett, "NACC and the CSCE: A Contribution in the Context of the Concept of Interlocking Institutions" (Ebenhausen: Stiftung Wissenschaft und Politik, 1993); and Jamie Shea, "NATO's Eastern Dimension: New Roles for the Alliance in Securing the Peace in Europe," *Canadian Defence Quarterly* 22 (March 1993): 55-62.

6. Hella Pick, "Enforcing the Plan," *Manchester Guardian Weekly*, 7 February 1993, pp. 1, 7; British American Information Council, "Major Powers Give Little Backing to Vance-Owen Plan," *Basic Reports* (Washington, 16 April 1993), pp. 1-2.

7. One analyst laments what he labels the "Japanization of America's foreign policy," by which is meant a policy fixated selfishly on domestic issues and only those foreign-policy ones of a primarily economic nature. See Christoph Bertram, "There Is a Foreign Policy," *International Herald Tribune*, 17 November 1993, p. 6.

8. France similarly attempted to contain Germany's apprehended eastward "drift" a decade ago. See David G. Haglund, *Alliance Within the Alliance? Franco-German Military Cooperation and the European Pillar of Defense* (Boulder: Westview Press, 1991), pp. 77-78.

9. See Jan Willem Honig, "The 'Renationalization' of Western European Defense," *Security Studies* 2 (Autumn 1992): 122-38.

10. Notes of panel discussion, "30th Munich Conference on Security Policy," Munich, 6 February 1993.

11. Andrei Kozyrev, "The New Russia and the Atlantic Alliance," *NATO Review* 41 (February 1993): 3-6.

12. The analogy is made between Western policy toward Germany in the Weimar Republic and after World War II, and the current situation regarding the proper means of aiding Russia, in George Skorov, "The West Must Decide What It Intends for Russia," *International Herald Tribune*, 25 June 1993, p. 6. Also see Gregory F. Treverton, "Finding an Analogy for Tomorrow," *Orbis* 37 (Winter 1993):1-20.

13. For this argument, see David G. Haglund and Olaf Mager, "Homeward Bound?" in *Homeward Bound? Allied Forces in the New Germany*, ed. Haglund and Mager (Boulder: Westview Press, 1992), pp. 273-85.

14. Richard Nixon, "We Are Ignoring Our World Role," *Time*, 16 March 1992, p. 72; Idem, "The West Can't Afford to Let Yeltsin's Russia Fail," *International Herald Tribune*, 8 March 1993, p. 6; Jeane Kirkpatrick, "Give Top Priority to Preserving Democracy in Russia," ibid., 25 February 1992, p. 6; Jim Hoagland, "Security, Not Economics, Is Still the Central U.S.-Russian Issue," ibid., 8 April 1993, p. 6; and Fred Charles Iklé, "Comrades in Arms: The Case for a Russian-American Defense Community," *National Interest*, no. 26 (Winter 1991/92), pp. 22-32.

15. Kozyrev, "New Russia," p. 4. For a discussion of this question, see S. Neil MacFarlane, "Russia, the West, and European Security," *Survival* 35 (Autumn 1993):3-25.

16. In late September 1993 Yeltsin seemingly indicated Russia would oppose any eastward extension of NATO; in reality, he stated it would only oppose an eastward extension that did not include it. See William Drozdiak, "NATO Likely to Slow East Europe's Entry," *International Herald Tribune*, 6 October 1993, p. 2.

17. For a critical examination, see Laurence Martin, "Peacekeeping as a Growth Industry," *National Interest*, no. 32 (Summer 1993), pp. 3-11.

18. "Aspin Tells Allies to Proceed Slowly on New Members," *International Herald Tribune*, 21 October 1993, p. 2; Steve Vogel, "U.S. Proposes Pact Nations Join NATO as 'Partners'," *Gazette* (Montreal), 21 October 1993, p. B4.

19. Quoted in Jeffrey Simon, "Does Eastern Europe Belong in NATO?" *Orbis* 37 (Winter 1993):33.

PART ONE

Eastern Challenges

One analyst describes what he labels the "provincialization" of foreign policy by which is meant a policy fixated seriously on domestic issues and only those foreign policy ones of a primarily economic nature. See Christoph Bertram, "There Is a Foreign Policy," *International Herald Tribune*, 17 November 1993.

France distinctly attempted to limit Germany's apprehended eastward drift. See David G. Haglund and Olaf Mager, eds., *Homeward Bound? Allied Military Cooperation and the European Politics of Defense* (Boulder: Westview, 1992), pp. 273-85.

See Ian William Hong, "The 'Renationalization' of Western European Defense," *Security Studies* 2 (Autumn 1992): 122-38.

Notes of panel discussion, "30th Munich Conference on Security Policy," Munich, 6 February 1993.

Andrei Kozyrev, "The New Russia and the Atlantic Alliance," *NATO Review* 41 (February 1993): 3-6.

The analogy is made between Western policy toward Germany in the Weimar Republic and after World War II, and the current situation regarding the proper means of aiding Russia, in George Skorov "The West Must Decide What It Intends for Russia," *International Herald Tribune*, 25 June 1993, p. 6. Also see Gregory F. Treverton, "Finding an Analogy for Tomorrow," *Orbis* 37 (Winter 1993): 1-20.

For this argument, see David G. Haglund and Olaf Mager, "Homeward Bound?" in *Homeward Bound? Allied Forces in the New Germany*, ed. Haglund and Mager (Boulder: Westview Press, 1992), pp. 273-85.

Richard Nixon, "We Are Ignoring Our World Role," *Time*, 16 March 1992; idem, "The West Can't Afford to Let Yeltsin's Russia Fail," *International Herald Tribune*, 8 March 1993, p. 6; Jeane Kirkpatrick, "Give Top Priority to Reviving Democracy in Russia," ibid., 25 February 1993, p. 6; Jim Hoagland, "Security, Not Economics, Is Still the Central U.S.-Russian Issue," ibid., 8 April 1993, p. 9; and Fred Charles Iklé, "Comrades in Arms: The Case for a Russian-American Defense Community," *National Interest*, no. 26 (Winter 1991/92): 22-32.

Kozyrev, "New Russia," p. 4. For a discussion of this question, see Neil Malcolm, "Russia, the West, and European Security," *Survival* 36 (Autumn 1994): 3-25.

In late September 1993 Yeltsin seemingly indicated Russia would oppose eastward extension of NATO. In reality, he stated it would only oppose an eastward extension that did not include Russia. See William Drozdiak, "NATO Likely to Postpone an Expansion," *International Herald Tribune*, 8 October 1993, p. 2.

For a counterargument, see Vladimir Baranovsky and Hans-Joachim Spanger, eds., *In from the Cold: Germany, Russia, and the Future of Europe* (Boulder: Westview Press, 1992).

Manfred Wörner, "Shaping the Alliance for the Future," *NATO Review* 41 (December 1993): 3-5; see also Ronald D. Asmus, Richard L. Kugler, and F. Stephen Larrabee, "Building a New NATO," *Foreign Affairs* 72 (September/October 1993): 28-40.

NATO, "Partnership for Peace" (Montreal), 10-11 January 1994, p. 4.

Quoted in Jeffrey Simon, "Does Eastern Europe Belong in NATO?" *Orbis*, Winter 1993: 33.

1

NATO and the Quest for
Ongoing Viability

*David G. Haglund, S. Neil MacFarlane,
and Joel J. Sokolsky*

Introduction

The collapse of the Soviet Union, the consequent disappearance of the bipolar structure of European security, and the emergence of new foci of insecurity and instability in Central, Eastern, and Southeastern Europe all raise questions about the appropriate role of the North Atlantic Treaty Organization (NATO) as an institution of regional security in Europe. The questions are all the more urgent, since NATO has served as an institutional cement tying the United States and Canada to European security. Unless the organization has a clearly defined mission in Europe relevant to the interests of the transatlantic partners, their engagement in Europe may be subject to question. Moreover, in the post-Cold War environment, a number of other organizations also claim roles related to security, raising questions about how these various institutions relate one to another in coping with emerging issues of regional security, such as ethnic conflict, migration and refugees, and nonproliferation.

In this chapter, we examine the prospects for NATO in dealing with its new security environment. We begin by focusing on collective defense (as NATO's traditional mission) and collective security as a possible alternative in the new environment. We then discuss the possibility that, failing an embrace of collective security, the less ambitious agenda of peacekeeping might provide a viable role for the organization.

The Obsolescence of Collective Defense

The initial rationale of NATO was collective defense against a perceived shared Soviet threat. In this respect, NATO was a typical alliance. It is no secret that the Soviet threat no longer exists. The basis of NATO in collective defense is, consequently, under question. Alliances generally do not long survive the demise of the threat that brought them into being. Nonetheless, a shared threat might reemerge. There is significant military capability remaining in the former Soviet Union. The current phase of positive relations between the Russian Federation and the NATO powers could deteriorate over time. The process of economic reform has not produced particularly promising results. Levels of popular dissatisfaction with the current political system are rising. Polls show increasing lack of interest in democratic development and a growing stress on the restoration of order, even if this means a return to authoritarianism.[1] Changes in Boris Yeltsin's cabinet and the slowing of the reform process suggest a rightward drift in Russian domestic politics—a drift that may have been halted, but not eliminated, by the crushing of the parliamentarians' revolt in early October 1993.[2]

In foreign policy, this has translated into increasing disillusion with the West, increasing resentment of Western policy, and a reassertion of Russian nationalism. In the former Soviet Union, the apparent rightward drift of Russian politics has already translated into greater assertiveness in relations with the non-Russian republics.[3] It is to be expected that the Russian government will attempt to reestablish a degree of hegemony within the boundaries of the former union. This has involved, and will continue to involve, Russian efforts to limit the sovereignty of these newly independent states and to secure their compliance with Russian approaches to economic and security cooperation.[4] Outside the former USSR, Russian behavior with respect to both the Gulf and the Yugoslav crises in late 1992 and 1993 suggested that it is becoming more difficult for the West to define the nature of collective international action in regional crises that impinge on Russian interests.

Although the dissolution of the Supreme Soviet in Moscow and an outcome of the crisis that ensued strongly favoring Yeltsin may allay concerns about a reassertion of Russian imperial aspirations, a return to the halcyon days of Western orientation in Russian foreign-policy seems unlikely. In the first place, Yeltsin prepared the ground for his victory by coopting large portions of the moderately nationalist center and by adopting much of the substance of their foreign policy preferences. To the extent that he remains dependent on the Russian military and moderately conservative and nationalist centrists, he is unlikely to reverse course now. For these reasons, it might be prudent to sustain the commitment to collective defense.

However, one can take such concerns too far. First, Russia itself remains in a state of near chaos, with inflation running at 2000 percent, give or take a decile or two, and industrial output continuing to drop by around 20 percent.[5] The center's control over the republic has more or less collapsed, with real power in the system shifting to regional and local authorities. The Russian Federation faces a number of deepening challenges from within to its sovereignty. These difficulties are sufficient to ensure that any regime in Russia is likely to be preoccupied with the internal crises for many years to come.

There are also serious problems relating to the Russian capacity to deploy and use force. Command and control over the armed forces remains problematic. The logistical system of Russian forces is in chaos. Commanders spend their time worrying about food and housing rather than strategy and tactics. The officer corps appears to be deeply divided on the question of reform and democratization. In the meantime, the Russian armed forces continue to shrink reasonably rapidly, as a result of deliberate national policy, but also owing to the failure of the regime to enforce its laws on conscription and to feed and properly house its troops.[6]

None of these problems is permanent. However, apart from the extreme "red-brown" fringe of the Russian political spectrum, no one seriously questions the post-Cold War settlement in Central Europe or entertains the possibility of the resumption of Cold War confrontation with the West. Those critical of what they take to be an excessively supine approach to the West by the Yeltsin-Kozyrev team argue not for a return to systemic confrontation, but for a recognition that Russia, like any other great power, has distinct interests, that these in part coincide with and in part depart from those of the Western alliance, and that, therefore, Russia should be more independent in its foreign policy behavior.[7]

This is a far cry from the resurrection of a post-Soviet Russian threat that might justify the maintenance of an alliance such as NATO in its traditional configuration. In such conditions, it is difficult to see how a continuing commitment to collective defense is necessary and, consequently, how NATO as a collective-defense organization could be maintained.

The Collective-Security Alternative

This brings us to the issue of collective security in Europe. Many associated with the alliance see NATO's post-Cold War role to lie in participation in an evolving structure of collective security in Europe. Collective security involves the construction of a structure of security cooperation among a group of states whereby the group as a whole is committed to respond collectively to an act of aggression by any of its members against any other member.[8]

Two conceptual problems are worth noting. First, the concept of collective security pertains specifically to the actions of states and relations among them. It involves the collective security of a group of states to an act of aggression committed against one of them. Collective security is not obviously relevant to matters of domestic jurisdiction. Given the nature of security problems in the former Soviet Union and East-Central Europe, it is difficult to see how a traditional collective-security system could be effective. Most of the serious security issues faced by the region are not pure interstate issues where it could be unambiguously determined when aggression was or was not occurring.

The case of Bosnia-Herzegovina is illustrative. Is this a civil war, which is a matter of domestic jurisdiction? Or is it a question of aggression by one state against another? If the former, then it is hard to see how a collective-security system could respond. If the latter, then collective security comes into play. The case in question lies in between. Civil conflict is fuelled in important ways by external intervention, both by Serbia and Croatia.

This raises the question of the level at which intervention by an external party becomes aggression. Are arms transfers sufficient? Is the cutoff at the point at which armed volunteers from the other state involve themselves? How does one reliably identify such individuals? Or is it when organized units of the other state's armed forces insert themselves? The Eastern European landscape is littered with actual or potential cases where these questions complicate the definition of a collective international response (e.g., Georgia, Azerbaidzhan, Slovakia, Transylvania, Macedonia, Kosovo).

This may seem like nit-picking. One could argue that the matter of deciding when aggression has occurred is an essentially political one and that such distinctions are at best irrelevant and at worst obstructionist. The actions of a state elicit a collective-security response when the other states in the community decide that it has committed aggression. However, states within the North Atlantic system are highly attentive to issues of risk and cost, and are consequently predisposed by their domestic politics not to use force to maintain order in the eastern part of the European region. They can be expected, therefore, to approach the definitional issues considered here conservatively.

The other side of the decision process is perceived gain or interest from participation in collective action. A collective-security response is most likely to be forthcoming when the vital interests of a large number of members of the society of states are threatened by the aggressive actions of a rogue state. States are unlikely to contemplate the combat deployment of their forces where such interests are not perceived to be at stake. The contrast between the Gulf War and the former Yugoslavia is compelling.

Second, the effective operation of a collective-security system presumes the existence not merely of a community of states, but a community of values and a community of trust. Arguably there is such a community in Western Europe, but it is not universal. There seems to be little agreement beyond the boundaries of NATO Europe on the legitimacy of the Eastern territorial settlement, on the nonuse of force in the resolution of disputes, and on the limitation of the influence of national chauvinism over state policy in the East. In this sense, there is arguably an operating de facto collective-security system in the West (where it is not necessary) already, while there is not one and probably cannot be one in the East, where it is necessary.

Turning to prospects for collective security in Europe, structures of collective security may be either global or regional. There are serious problems in eliciting a global response to threats to regional security, since the interests of many of those involved in a decision to act are not obviously affected by the issue in question. There is consequently little obvious payoff for them in acting, and normal risk aversion will dictate evasion of responsibility. One saw this in the behavior of the United States toward Yugoslavia during the Serb-Croat crisis and in the early phases of Bosnia-Herzegovina. The United States—and for that matter the United Nations—preferred that Europe handle its own problems. Similar preferences were evident in the early American response to Somalia and in the attitude of the developed states toward the Liberian civil war.

These problems are matched at the regional level. Recent experience with efforts by regional organizations to manage security in their own regions are not encouraging. On the face of it, regional approaches to collective security have considerable merit. It is the states in a region affected by conflict that have the greatest stake in its resolution. They bear the refugee burden, the economic costs, and the risk of spillover.

But it is also the states within a region that are most likely to disagree on its politics. States within a region are likely to have a high interest in conflict occurring there, but there is no guarantee that their interests will coincide. Generally, the shared interest of states contiguous to a conflict in its management and resolution is accompanied by an array of unilateral competitive interests that these states will pursue at the expense of the community interest, either because they are selfish, or because they cannot be confident that other involved parties will behave in a disinterested fashion. The former Yugoslav cases are again full of examples.

Second, regions tend to contain asymmetries of power that impede cooperation in the realm of security. Larger states tend to have a larger say in the policies of regional organizations. Smaller ones tend to be nervous about large-state aspirations to hegemony. One reason for the serious disagreement between France and Germany on the breakup of Yugoslavia was a French concern about the rise of influence of the newly united Germany in Central and Eastern Europe. This limits prospects for cooperation in the management of regional security.[9]

For all of these reasons, the ground is not well-suited to the development of elaborate systems and structures of collective security. If NATO's Eastern dilemmas are dealt with at all (and frequently they may not be), it is likely to be through less ambitious and more ad hoc approaches (e.g., peacekeeping) or through rather traditional approaches to maintaining order, such as the recognition of spheres of influence, where particular states exercise a degree of responsibility for keeping the peace in return for recognized primacy.

Peacekeeping: The Future Is Not What It Used to Be

The alliance has identified peacekeeping, including support of the United Nations, as a future role. However, the prospects of NATO transforming itself into what some are calling the UN's peacekeeping "subcontractor" are extremely uncertain. It is not just a question of the alliance lacking the political will to take a more active role.[10] It is quite simply that the very nature of United Nations peacekeeping in some of its current and proposed manifestations and the very character of NATO preclude the latter from undertaking the former.

Given its combined military power, it might seem that NATO would be especially well-suited to support the UN when the will of the world body needs to be imposed by force on states or groups within states that are not obeying Security Council resolutions. Yet there really is no combined allied force, rather a collection of national contributions, nominally under the political direction of the North Atlantic Council (NAC), but ultimately under the control of national governments. Those who contend that NATO can now act cohesively "out of area" forget that during the Cold War there were serious doubts about whether or not the alliance would be able to stay united in the face of "in-area" threats.

United Nations peacekeeping arose out of the failure of the UN to implement the collective-security provisions of its Charter. With some exceptions, multilateral peacekeeping forces did not enforce the peace. Rather they were deployed after the warring parties had agreed to a ceasefire. Forces were relatively small in number and only lightly armed and could use their weapons only in self-defense. Their role was to observe and oversee the implementation of a ceasefire provision, provide a measure of assurance, or confidence-building, to each side and thereby, in theory, help create the proper atmosphere for the peacemaking process. To this extent, the gloved hand hid a limp fist. The real power and authority of the peacekeeping force was external to it and was vested in the ability of the UN and the major powers to persuade the combatants to refrain from renewed fighting.

Peacekeeping operated within a framework of consensus and consent. In order for a force to be deployed there had to be consensus at the Security Council, especially among the five permanent members. This consensus had to include the purposes for which the forces were being deployed and the mandate. Most importantly, because of the principle of sovereignty, the deployment of a peacekeeping force could only take place with the consent of the government upon whose territory it was to operate. This might also have included the need to obtain host country consent regarding the composition of the force.

To be sure, not all of these conditions were always met, especially in cases such as Vietnam, when peacekeeping was attempted outside the UN framework or in the Congo when a UN operation became mired in a civil war. However, given the very narrow margin in which UN peacekeeping could operate, what is surprising is not that peacekeeping often failed to make peace, but that it had the successes it did. Where there was a solidly based peace to help maintain, as in the case of the Israel-Egypt-US Camp David agreement, peacekeeping forces, in this instance outside the UN framework, could provide that added measure of confidence that helped remove the risk of war.

As the Cold War drew to a close in the late 1980s, peacekeeping seemed to experience something of a renaissance. With the triumph of the coalition forces in the Gulf War, it appeared that the United Nations was poised to play more of its original collective-security role as the police commission of the new world order. This was certainly the tone of Secretary-General Boutros Boutros-Ghali's June 1992 report, *Agenda for Peace: Preventative Diplomacy, Peacemaking and Peacekeeping*.[11]

Boutros-Ghali suggested that UN operations move beyond the restricted interpositioning of lightly armed observers to include instances where the forces would actually engage in combat in order to enforce the will of the United Nations. More importantly, the introduction of forces, especially in cases of peacemaking, would not necessarily require the consent of the host country. Even where preventative diplomacy was accompanied by the deployment of UN forces with the consent of the host country threatened by a neighbor, they would have to be equipped in the event that diplomacy failed. Thus the future of peacekeeping seemed to involve in both its traditional guise and its expanded version the employment of multinational combat forces pursuant to a UN mandate and under UN control.

The world is already witnessing the expansion of UN activities beyond traditional peacekeeping. In Somalia and especially in the former Yugoslavia, operations are being undertaken where there is no consent by the host government, and, in the case of Somalia, no host government. While it has become easier to get a consensus within the Security Council, the actual implementation of the mandate on the ground appears confused. In the case of Cambodia, original consent by the rival factions gave way to open hostilities between the UN and the Khmer Rouge. Far from becoming the police force of the new world order, UN peacekeeping operations have become the fire-brigade for widespread regional and civil conflicts, trying to save the innocents from the arsonists.

In many cases, the need for a more forceful approach reflects the failure of previous efforts at traditional peacekeeping. Rather than debate what variant of peacekeeping operations is now being undertaken, it can be argued that the real distinction is between traditional peacekeeping and war. For however justified on international legal or humanitarian grounds, the imposition of the will of one country or a group of countries on another state or factions within that state by force of arms is war.

The American-led coalition achieved a relatively neat and quick victory in the war against Iraq. President Bush declared that with victory in the Gulf War the United States had "kicked the Vietnam Syndrome." But as Ronald Spector suggests in his book *After Tet*, "in a world which has recently been made safe for conventional, regional and ethnic wars, Vietnam rather than the Gulf War may be the pattern of the future."[12] A more vigorous role for the UN in dealing with such conflicts, especially those of an internal nature, may well lead to the type of quagmire America found itself in in Southeast Asia. As the Somalia experience vividly demonstrates, even the seemingly most selfless of operations can draw UN forces into the vortex of the very strife it was supposed to quell. If followed to its logical conclusion, the "agenda for peace" could become "an agenda for war," entangling the organization in a series of "savage wars of peace" around the globe.[13]

NATO: The UN's Iron Fist?

Were it a matter of expanding the scope of traditional peacekeeping operations, then NATO might well be an appropriate organization to which the UN could turn. It would be relatively easy to achieve a political consensus within NATO to support traditional peacekeeping operations in cases where there was little risk of becoming a party to a regional dispute. The allied nations have a large reserve of highly trained military personnel and the relative financial capacity to employ them over extended periods. NATO has a global reach, and 40 years of combined command and training making it easier for the forces to operate together.

Yet it is precisely because traditional peacekeeping was not working in Yugoslavia that the UN turned to NATO to supply aircraft for the monitoring of a no-fly zone and considered asking for intervention. Any intervention by the alliance might well be used to enforce a peace against the will of Bosnian Serbs and Serbia itself, to say nothing of Croatian interests.

If there was ever a situation suitable for NATO to become the UN's iron fist, the Bosnian tragedy would indeed seem to be it. Here is a test for the claim that the Soviet threat has been replaced by the threat of "instability" in Europe, an instability that might involve two NATO allies, Turkey and Greece. Here is the opportunity, through the North Atlantic Cooperation Council (NACC), to involve former members of the Warsaw Pact and Russia in collective action by having these countries contribute to peacekeeping operations. Here, in view of the failure of the European Community, the Western European Union, and the Conference on Security and Cooperation in Europe to take decisive action, is the opportunity for NATO to show that it is the central pillar of any "new European security architecture."[14] To paraphrase the popular song, "if it can't make it here, it can't make it anywhere." Indeed, if the alliance cannot bring peace to Bosnia, it is argued, it might be wise to consider ending the transatlantic compact.

The irony is, though, that any attempt by NATO to move collectively in support of the UN in Yugoslavia, or in similar peace-enforcement actions, would place such a strain on the alliance that it might well fall apart. Quite simply, NATO, despite all its apparent advantages, is not well-suited for waging war on behalf of the United Nations.

First, as already noted, the unity of the alliance was made possible by a common threat. Instability is not enough. Most instances of regional upheaval do not call into question the security of the NATO allies. As such, it is not at all clear that a consensus on the use of force can be secured within the North Atlantic Council. It is 16 separate democratic governments, not the NAC, that would have to assume the burdens of war and justify those burdens to their citizens.

Second, while NATO functioned as a strong deterrent, it never had to contend with a failure of deterrence. It never went to war. Its strategy of flexible response was very much a political agreement to disagree over strategy. There is a tendency to forget how real were the concerns as to whether or not the alliance would fall apart at the first whiff of war, whether some allies would declare neutrality in the hope of saving themselves. To be sure, the experience of the Gulf War suggests that NATO allies, acting in an ad hoc coalition, can perform splendidly. But there the alliance did not fight as an alliance under the political direction of the NAC. In reality, there is no NATO track record of success in war upon which to base optimistic expectations that the alliance could successfully mount a major military operation, as a unified actor.

Third, intra-alliance disagreements would only be compounded if NATO attempted to undertake peace enforcement (or even traditional peacekeeping) in conjunction with former Warsaw Pact members and Russia under the auspices of the NACC. The use of these forces, particularly given Russian partiality toward the Serbs and other countries' enmity, might well destroy any consensus at the diplomatic level and on the ground regarding the mandate of the UN operation.

A fourth set of considerations centers on the all-important role of the United States. If NATO is to undertake a peace-enforcement function as an alliance, such action must include the US. Otherwise, possible Canadian involvement notwithstanding, the operation might just as well be conducted under the auspices of the WEU or the EC. But this raises a host of other problems. If the initiative for NATO peace enforcement comes from the European members, will the United States and its Congress go along? If it is Washington that seeks alliance commitments on behalf of the UN, will the Europeans respond positively or will they have to be cajoled into participation?

Finally, if the alliance can indeed act on behalf of the UN in a cohesive manner under an agreed UN mandate and command arrangements, allied intervention might have the effect of turning minor wars into major ones.[15] After all, when the UN has to turn to NATO, it will mean that more resources are required. NATO intervention means escalation. The introduction of large and sophisticated NATO forces could well exacerbate the local situation into a larger, and yet still inconclusive, conflict. This would especially be the case if NATO attempted to use its force posture for large-scale conventional war to fight what would amount to an anti-insurgency campaign.

Reluctance by NATO to intervene in Yugoslavia or in other areas risks a loss of credibility and could raise doubts about the future utility of the alliance. But against this must be weighed the more likely risks of permanent damage to NATO as a result of becoming enmeshed in a bloody and expensive quagmire. This will almost certainly lead to irreparable transatlantic and intra-European acrimony.

Conclusion

NATO powers face serious security problems in Eastern Europe. However, the alliance's traditional purpose—that of collective defense—is now difficult to defend. The alternative of collective security appears unattainable. The more modest intermediate role of NATO as peacekeeper is fraught with problems and may be fundamentally corrosive of the alliance's increasingly fragile cohesiveness.

This is not to argue that NATO has no further useful role in global security. By its very existence, it could serve to stabilize the European continent and, until the United States and Canada decide otherwise, the alliance still provides the best available transatlantic link.[16] It might maintain a watching brief on the turmoil in Eastern Europe and the former Soviet Union and, if necessary, try to contain these struggles within those countries and away from allied members. Should workable settlements be reached to regional conflicts, in Europe or elsewhere, then NATO could seek to support traditional UN peacekeeping operations.

This is a modest approach to the future of the alliance, to be sure. But at this point, modesty may become NATO. Any attempt by NATO to seek a new institutional raison d'etre in collective security or in UN peace enforcement would likely not save the alliance, but might well hasten its demise. Having successfully withstood over 40 years of internal divisions and disputes over strategy, policy objectives, and burden-sharing, the allies run the risk of subjecting themselves to a new series of contentious, intractable, and perhaps fatal dilemmas.

Notes

1. See, for example, Mark Rhodes, "Political Attitudes in Russia," RFE/RL Research Report 2, 3 (15 January 1993): 42-43.

2. See Alexander MacLeod, "Yeltsin's Deal with the Russian Army Could Slow Reform," *Christian Science Monitor*, 8 October 1993, p. 8.

3. See Susan Crow, "Russia Adopts a More Active Policy," *RFE/RL Research Report* 2, 12 (19 March 1993): 1; and Raymond Bonner, "Why All Eyes Are on a Place Called Tajikistan," *New York Times*, 7 November 1993, p. 4E.

4. For some evidence that this is already occurring, see Susan Crow, "Russia Seeks Leadership in Regional Peacekeeping," *RFE/RL Research Report* 2, 15 (9 April 1993): 29. For a discussion of these trends in Russian domestic and foreign policy, see S. Neil MacFarlane, "Russia, the West, and European Security," *Survival* 35 (Autumn 1993): 3-25.

5. For a useful survey of macroeconomic trends in the Russian federation in 1992 and early 1993, see Vladimir Popov et al., *The Russian Economy in 1993: Forecast and Annual Survey of 1992* (Middlebury, VT: Geonomics, 1993).

6. See "Russia's Armed Forces: The Threat That Was," *Economist*, 28 August 1993, pp. 17-19.

7. See, for example, Sergei Stankevich, "Russia in Search of Itself," *National Interest*, no. 28 (Summer 1992), pp. 47-50.

8. This corresponds loosely to the concept of "peacemaking." For a useful discussion of the meaning of collective security, see John Ruggie, "Multilateralism: The Anatomy of an Institution," *International Organization* 46 (Summer 1992): 569.

9. The comparative merits of global and regional approaches to security issues are treated at greater length in S. Neil MacFarlane and Thomas G. Weiss, "Regional Organizations and Regional Security," *Security Studies* 2 (Autumn 1992): 6-37.

10. Paul Koring, "Europe's Lack of Will Condemned," *Globe and Mail* (Toronto), 1 May 1993, p. A1.

11. *An Agenda for Peace: Preventative Diplomacy, Peacemaking and Peacekeeping*, A/47/277, 17 June 1992, p. 20.

12. Ronald H. Spector, *After Tet: The Bloodiest Year in Vietnam* (New York: Free Press, 1993), pp. 315-16.

13. On this point see Stephen John Stedman, "The New Interventionists," *Foreign Affairs* 72 (Winter 1993): 2-16.

14. See Brigadier-General B.A. Goetze and Captain E.C. Sloan, "The New European Security Architecture," *Canadian Defence Quarterly* 22 (March 1993): 26-34.

15. On the dangers of new collective-security arrangements, see Richard K. Betts, "Systems for Peace or Causes of War? Collective Security, Arms Control and the New Europe," in *America's Strategy in a Changing World*, ed. Sean M. Lynn-Jones and Steven E. Miller (Cambridge, MA: MIT Press, 1992), pp. 199-237.

16. See Charles L. Glaser, "Why NATO Is Still Best: Future Security Arrangements for Europe," *International Security* 18 (Summer 1993): 5-50.

2

The Alliance Transformed:
A Skeptical View

Christopher Conliffe

Introduction

In 1980 the American sociologist Alvin Toffler proclaimed that the world was undergoing a transformation that, although little appreciated, would result in a new civilization.[1] Whether one accepted Toffler's theories at the time, they certainly seemed apropos by 1989, a year that unmistakably started a new chapter in modern history. The focus of this chapter is also a transformation, albeit a smaller one than that unleashed in 1989. It is the claim, made as early as June 1990, that the North Atlantic Treaty Organization was being "transformed."[2] The thrust of the argument offered here will run counter to that claim, for it is my view that not only is the alliance *not* being transformed, but that a rare opportunity to remake NATO into an instrument with a future is being missed, if not squandered.

On a theoretical plane, NATO's contemporary situation seems to be almost tailor-made for illustrating Robert Cox's contrast between "realism" and "critical theory." To Cox, the former is a problem-solving theory, suitable in periods of stability, while the latter constitutes an approach more appropriate in periods of uncertainty in power relations.[3] If one accepts his analysis, at least up to a point, then it is possible to regard the past few years as having provided ideal circumstances for the application of the methodology of critical theory to the remaking of NATO. Let us be clear, however, that critical theory as understood by most of those who subscribe to it is a Marxist construct that has, in part at least, appropriated a methodology of some seniority while passing itself off as a new invention. This is to be lamented, for there is much in critical theory that could be of value to the current debate about NATO's future. It is especially to be regretted that however much a radical approach may be required, one has been avoided like the plague by those who think and write about a "transformed alliance."

In June 1990, claims were advanced that the alliance was being changed into something new. The communiqué stemming from the London summit of 4-6 June was labelled "The London Declaration on a Transformed Atlantic Alliance." The cover of *NATO Review* in December 1991 carried the heading "The Rome Summit: NATO Transformed." Since this period, the term has been used repeatedly to characterize the changes that have been made to the alliance. Illustratively, we have heard the Canadian ambassador to NATO claiming that Canada stands at the forefront of NATO's transformation.[4] More recently, NATO's assistant secretary-general for defense policy and planning, Michael Legge, has lamented that while NATO has undergone a transformation since 1990, the general public, many members of parliaments, and even some informed commentators do not seem to realize the magnitude of the change.[5] In 1993, the secretary general, Manfred Wörner, remarked, similarly, that NATO's radical transformation was not "sufficiently appreciated even by informed public opinion in our member countries."[6]

At the risk of seeming obtuse, I must confess that, though I have been watching NATO closely since before the events of 1989, I do not detect very many of the sweeping changes that have been ostensibly made to the alliance, no matter how well-documented and publicized they might have been. What I see instead are a series of cautious, deliberate, conservative, and often unimaginative gestures. The alliance in late 1993 bears an uncanny resemblance, in its essentials, to what I and others observed in the period immediately preceding 1989. That there have been some changes is not in doubt. But are these of such magnitude to justify being called a "transformation"? I think not. Transformation, if it is to mean anything, must connote an alteration in form, shape, or appearance, and what is startling about NATO today is that it has the *same* charter, membership, purpose (viz., defense), and limitations on where it can act militarily as it had in 1989. With all of these essential features intact, how can anyone seriously claim that the alliance has been transformed? My skepticism flows from an insistence that NATO's future challenges can only be assessed in the context of the alliance's historical evolution—a context that reveals NATO to have been changing, over time, in ways redolent of the recently mooted "transformation."

The Evolving Alliance, 1949-1989

NATO came into existence on 4 April 1949 as a result of the direction taken by the USSR under Stalin. In part, it owes its existence to the

The Alliance Transformed: A Skeptical View 25

inability of the United Nations to provide a working system of collective security. Credit for the idea behind the North Atlantic treaty and NATO is usually given to the British, and in particular to Ernest Bevin, the foreign secretary. The treaty was made in the American capital, however, and to this day retains the colloquial title, the Washington treaty. NATO is the only alliance in history to have permanent institutions and a permanent staff. The two headquarters, of the secretary general and of the military commander (Supreme Headquarters Allied Powers Europe, or SHAPE), were initially located in France. There they remained until 1966, when they were transferred to Belgium. NATO headquarters is now in Evere, on the outskirts of Brussels, while SHAPE is some 60 kilometers to the southwest, in Casteau. There were 12 original members: Belgium, Canada, Denmark, France, Holland, Iceland, Italy, Luxembourg, Norway, Portugal, the United Kingdom, and the United States. The treaty may well have meant different things to different governments, and to different statesmen who had a hand in the negotiations that preceded its signing. Nevertheless, all agreed that an attack on one was an attack on all, which gave the Europeans a guarantee that American might was always available to them.

In the course of its remarkably long life, the alliance has evolved on several levels. The imperatives of many armed forces working together have led to a common strategic concept, and also to a measure of interoperability. Standardization has also been a goal, pursued with rather less success. The then commander of the Northern Army Group, writing in early 1990, was obliged to recognize that in spite of more than 30 years of integrated military structure and repeated calls for standardization "or at least interoperable equipment" since the beginning, "much of Allied Command Europe is still far from this objective."[7] A former secretary general of NATO, Lord Carrington, is reputed to have said that the only standard item in NATO equipment was the air in the tires of the vehicles.

More relevant has been NATO's strategic concept, or concepts. There had been three "strategic-concept" documents produced at various times in NATO's history prior to the one produced in 1991. Unlike the new one, these were all classified. The first, known as DC-6, was in place in December 1949. At that time, American nuclear weapons were still scarce, but by adding what few there were to the conventional resources of the alliance, nuclear "strategy" was created. This concept was in effect replaced in 1957 by document MC 14/2, which enshrined massive retaliation as the strategy, as nuclear weapons had become plentiful. It stayed in place until 1967, when MC 14/3, the strategy of flexible response, was adopted, to remain in force until 1991.

For deterrence to be credible, the strategy required adequate forces, both conventional and nuclear, and these came to be placed in three classes, composing the well-known NATO "triad" of conventional, short- and intermediate-range nuclear, and strategic nuclear weapons. Forces also had to be adequate if deterrence failed and the alliance was obliged to defend itself. The principle of forward defense called for high levels of stationed forces in the Western European theater, particularly in West Germany.

A series of events over the years has prompted a reexamination of NATO's strategy, as well as of its levels of conventional and nuclear forces. Ranking high among these have been arms-control and disarmament initiatives, in particular the Intermediate-Range Nuclear Forces (or INF) treaty, as well as the Conventional Forces Europe (CFE) agreement. Notwithstanding these, both the purpose and the defensive nature of the alliance remained unchanged. It even grew, slowly, from the original 12 members to today's 16, as West Germany, Greece, Turkey, and finally Spain joined.

With the dissolution of the Warsaw Treaty Organization (WTO) and of the Soviet empire, the future of NATO has obviously become called into question. Has the alliance come to the end of its days, and, having fulfilled its function, should it now be disbanded? Questions such as these have been raised with increasing frequency, for as George Joffe put it so well, the "problem now is that, with the collapse of the Warsaw Pact and the Soviet threat, NATO really has no obvious primary role any more."[8] Another writer, Peter Stanford, argues that NATO's strategic goals are now obsolescent, its geography arbitrary, and its command structures newly irrelevant. It has served its purpose, and while Stanford believes it would be premature to dissolve the alliance this moment, sooner or later it must go. He calls instead for an alliance with and within Europe, based on the Brussels treaty and the Western European Union (WEU). Efforts to posit future structures upon NATO are seen to be retrograde distortions; what is needed, rather, are "flexible geometry" structures that somehow manage to include a North American commitment to Europe.[9]

Dissolution of NATO on the grounds that it has done its work and is now redundant is probably the most extreme course open to the West. Whether in the longer term this option is exercised, no one can say. For the short term, NATO will be retained. But has it been transformed? And if it is not to be, can it survive past the short term? What changes should, indeed, *must* be made to the alliance if it is to avoid becoming a living dinosaur? In seeking to answer these questions, it would be well to start by looking at the external environment in which NATO now operates.

The New Security Environment

As chapter one indicated, in the Cold War context, collective defense was the alliance's principal role. The threat, and the political bloc whence it originated, were clear enough, though neither was specified in the North Atlantic treaty. With the Cold War over, security, whether national or collective, is taking on different meanings. When a state is formulating security policy, it must have a clear notion of just what is being secured.[10] Without this simple truth to inform their assessments, it becomes difficult if not impossible for governments to determine what is, and is not, a threat to their security. Once the threats are identified, appropriate armed forces can be designed to meet them. Although scientific definitions of "security" are impossible to develop, it seems unobjectionable to argue that there are three broad areas of concern to states, in which the "threat" can take varying forms: military (external), subversive (external/internal), and social (internal/external). The external and military threat is traditional in both type and provenance, and is the one that in theory shaped established foreign and defense policies as well as the composition of the armed forces that were maintained to meet it. The external threat is based on assessments that take account of capabilities as well as intentions. For more than 40 years the perceived threat to the West has been communism and the former USSR. This assessment was based on both the declaratory policy and the military capability of the Soviet Union. The collapse of the USSR as a political entity and as a superpower has made it imperative for the West to carry out a new threat assessment. This is no easy endeavor, as the current international situation is so volatile.

One early, and gloomy, attempt to forecast Western Europe's future after the Cold War came from the pen of John Mearsheimer. In two articles, "Why We Will Soon Miss the Cold War" and the expanded (and no less controversial) "Back to the Future," Mearsheimer argued that the prospect for major crises and even war in Europe was likely to increase with the end of the Cold War and the removal of the superpowers.[11] His pessimistic conclusion rested on an assumption that the distribution and character of military power are the root causes of war and peace. According to his analysis, the absence of war in Europe since 1945 has had three explanations. The first was the bipolar distribution of power on the continent, the second the rough military equality between the two poles, and the third the fact that each superpower was armed with nuclear weapons. With no common Soviet threat and no American night watchman, said Mearsheimer, Western European states would do what they did for centuries: look on one another with suspicion. The demise of the Cold War order and the emergence of multipolarity, accordingly, were likely to increase the chances that war and major crises would occur in Europe, and "local wars tend to widen and escalate. Hence there is always a chance that a small war will trigger a general conflict."[12]

To buttress his views, Mearsheimer turned to realist theory. Conflict is common among states because the international system creates powerful incentives for aggression, and this is caused by the anarchic nature of the international system. It is of more than passing interest today to contemplate Mearsheimer's 1990 trawl through Europe. With the Soviet occupation of Eastern Europe at an end, he foresaw potential trouble between Hungary and Romania over the Hungarian minority in Transylvania. The Polish-German border was also a possible trouble-maker (though less so today). The Poles and Romanians might go looking for territory formerly theirs but after World War II in Soviet possession. Civil war in Yugoslavia was distinctly possible, with consequences not yet clear; Yugoslavia and Albania, Yugoslavia and Bulgaria, Turkey and Bulgaria—all had and have potential for causing war. "The danger that these bitter ethnic and border disputes will erupt into war in a supposedly Edenic nuclear-free Europe is enough to make one nostalgic for the Cold War."[13]

Preoccupation with Europe as a whole is unsurprising, as it is there that the major changes have occurred. But is it correct to assume Western Europe must lapse from being a zone of peace? One writer who rejects Mearsheimer's pessimism is Stephen Van Evera, for whom the likelihood of a return to a warlike Western Europe is low, as the causes of previous wars in the region have disappeared.[14] The real risk is ethnic conflict in the East. To counter this risk, Van Evera proposes that the US retain a military presence in Europe, and that NATO be revamped into a collective-security system, with a new charter that allows it to deter aggression from any quarter, not just the Soviet Union. A continued American military commitment to Europe would not in itself be enough to diminish the risk of war in Eastern Europe, unless Washington were to guarantee the security of states there against attack by one another. Despite their differences, in one respect Mearsheimer and Van Evera agree: each sees nuclear proliferation in Europe as a beneficial prospect, making the continent a safer place than it would be in the absence of nuclear weaponry.

Nor is Eastern Europe the only source of concern. It almost seems as if interstate conflict is ubiquitous around the world (it isn't); nevertheless, the point hardly needs making that the optimism of many analysts in the immediate aftermath of the Cold War seems, today, curiously outdated, and not just in Europe. That being said, the security challenges facing NATO today do lack the simplicity of those of the Cold War. Most importantly, it is unlikely that states in the West will suffer direct military attacks in the near future. The situation is no longer one where defense and security are or can be synonymous, but rather one in which defense is but one constituent element of a wider security complex. However one may define security, the *context* in which NATO operates has been radically changed, and here the term "transformed" might indeed be appropriate. It is to this new setting that NATO must adapt. To date, it has not shown itself particularly successful in rising to its challenges.

NATO's Attempt to Adapt

On the national level, to be sure, a variety of responses to the new security situation have been glimpsed. A common thread even runs through the reactions of alliance members: with a few exceptions, they have been contemplating making immediate savings on military expenditure. In at least two cases, those of Britain and Canada, this quest for savings has prompted cuts that have had greater effects on capabilities than the numerically larger cuts made by the US and Germany. The magnitude of reductions in just four NATO states is given in Table 2.1, with data available from the autumn of 1992. Since then, it has become apparent that in some cases additional regular-force reductions will be made, with Germany's forces almost certain to be a case in point.

These force reductions have had important implications for the stationing policy of states. Canada completes withdrawal of its formations in Germany in 1994, though it remains a member of NATO. France initially announced that it would do the same at a different pace, but that

Table 2.1 Scale of Force Reductions

Country	Before Cuts	After Cuts
US	2,016,000	1,625,000
Germany	667,000	370,000
UK	312,000	255,000
Canada	84,000	76,000

Sources: Canada, Press release of the Minister of National Defence, Ottawa, 17 September 1991; Andrew Pierre, "The United States and the New Europe," *Current History* 89 (November 1990): 356; "Options for Change," *Parliamentary Debates* (Hansard), sixth series, vol. 177, pp. 468-71.

proved to be premature as some French forces will remain in Germany, composing a part of the Franco-German Eurocorps. British forces in Germany will be halved. For Western European and North American states, stationing is no longer as important as it was when NATO faced the WTO. But the withdrawal of the Canadian formations has posed two questions: first, can a North American state remain committed to European security without a presence in Europe? Second, if the answer is yes for Canada, would or should it be different for the US? Put differently, is it reasonable to expect North American forces to remain in Europe forever, or at least indefinitely? The end of the Cold War has accelerated plans for the reduction of stationed force levels in Germany, and in one case has led to complete withdrawal. Finally, could NATO survive the disappearance of its "stationing regime"?[15]

For a large multinational organization run by a big bureaucracy, NATO has given the impression of moving quickly with respect to the new international situation. But let us not forget that several things were in train simultaneously. The forces of change given such prominence by the dramatically changed international and strategic situation can be traced to early 1989, and have their roots in the CFE negotiations. Even if nothing else had happened in the subsequent months and years, this agreement would have led to significant troop reductions in Europe. As events unfolded, however, existing strategies such as forward defense and flexible response soon became obsolete. A strategic review was clearly necessary; this was recognized at the Defence Planning Committee (DPC) meeting in May 1990.[16] At the June 1990 meeting of the North Atlantic Council (NAC), ministers called for progress reports on the strategy review. Heads of state met in July 1990 and gave their blessing to that review.[17] At the meeting of the North Atlantic Council in Rome in November 1991, the Strategic Concept was made public. It is a comprehensive document, written in five parts, comprising the strategic context, alliance objectives and security functions, a broad approach to security, guidelines for defense, and a conclusion.[18] Let us take them in turn.

Part one deals with the new strategic environment, and reviews the political changes in Europe, as well as the progress made in arms control and force reductions (mainly CFE). It then reaffirms the defensive nature of the alliance, which will maintain security at the lowest level of defense. There is partial acceptance that the Soviet threat is much diminished, although Soviet capabilities remain. NATO forces will be reduced, but remaining formations must have a credible ability to fulfil their functions in peace and war. The alliance accepts the roles that other European security agencies will have to play, and undertakes to cooperate with them. An initiative on dialogue and cooperation with states in

Central and Eastern Europe is also included. This refers to the NACC, about which William Yerex's chapter provides further detail.

Part two covers the purpose, nature, and fundamental tasks of the alliance. NATO's purpose is "to safeguard the freedom and security of all its members by political and military means." Its nature is transatlantic and collective. Four security tasks are listed: to provide one of the indispensable foundations for security in Europe, to serve as a transatlantic forum, to deter and defend against any threat to the territory of any NATO member, and to preserve the strategic balance within Europe. The roles of the EC, WEU, and CSCE in European security are acknowledged.

Part three speaks to protecting peace in a new Europe, achieved by dialogue, cooperation, and collective defense. Management of crises and conflict prevention are seen as a part that the alliance can play, but it is through support of the CSCE, EC, WEU, and UN that this will be performed. Part four is the most substantial one. It covers principles of alliance strategy, as well as the new force posture. The alliance is held to be purely defensive, and geared to deal with an aggressor; it is indivisible; it will maintain a mix of conventional and nuclear weapons. In the new posture, forward defense is discarded. The mission remains unchanged, viz. to guarantee the security and territorial integrity of the member states. General war is now judged to have become highly unlikely, but cannot finally be ruled out. Nevertheless, the overall size, and in many cases the readiness, of allied forces will be reduced. Forces will require "enhanced flexibility and mobility." The allies, significantly, will place increased reliance on multinational forces. Finally, part five concludes that the alliance must remain defensive in nature, but can do so with a low level of forces. Other staple measures such as arms control and confidence building will be retained. The continued effort to find a European security identity is recognized.

A few months after the Rome summit, the shape of NATO's new force structure was announced. It is a three-tier arrangement, with the aforementioned Rapid Reaction Force, Main Defense Forces (which will operate in Central Europe), and a reinforcement element, known as the Augmentation Forces. To the first can be added the Immediate Reaction Force, known up to now as the ACE Mobile Force. Overall, the security of the West is seen to be linked to that of the East.[19] But the NAC also accepts that alliance security has to take account of the global context, where the proliferation of weapons of mass destruction, terrorism, sabotage, and interruptions of the passage of vital resources constitute threats of a wider nature.

Out of this elaboration of NATO's new strategic concept arise the following points. First, the alliance must change to meet new circumstances, and that change has already started. Second, a European security identity is expected to come into being. The alliance does not see this as an alternative to NATO, but as a complementary agency. Finally, NATO concedes that force-level reductions by national governments are acceptable. We must bear in mind, when reading NATO declarations, the role played by heads of state and government with respect to the alliance itself. As always, decisions at the national level are taken first, followed by decisions at the alliance level; both are made by the same people, in many instances.

The last announcement of relevance to this discussion was made in Oslo on 4 June 1992. NATO foreign ministers agreed to support the actions of the CSCE by making available alliance resources and expertise for peacekeeping in states outside the territory of members.[20] Up to now, the defensive nature of the alliance had been underscored by a limitation on NATO's operational activity to the territory of members. This departure was prompted by the civil war in Yugoslavia, which was (and is) seen as having grave destabilizing potential in Europe. Under the agreement, the assistance of NATO forces would be requested by the CSCE, an entity that, like the UN, has no integral forces. The requests would be considered on a case-by-case basis. One reason cited in explaining the decision was that UN peacekeepers were overtaxed in other regions, such as Southeast Asia (Cambodia) and the Middle East.[21] This was an intriguing announcement, for it meant that forces under NATO command could be used for peacekeeping operations, and this in addition to any other military contributions to peacekeeping missions that might already be made by the member state providing the forces to NATO.

A Transformed Alliance?

In making assessments of the claim for transformation of NATO, one must bear in mind that nowhere in the evidence is there any debate on the charter of the alliance. For the time being, it looks as though charter revision will remain a nonissue. On the other hand, NATO can, in theory at least, make forces available for use in situations not covered by the charter. It proposes to do this by responding to requests from other agencies with a stake in European security, but have no forces of their own. The territorial limitation on operations is circumvented by the same mechanism. The defensive nature of the alliance, however, remains unchanged. In view of the proliferation of missiles capable of delivering a range of warheads, and which could reach a number of member states if launched, for instance, from North Africa, the retention of credible deterrence and a defensive capability would appear to be essential. Nevertheless, focussing on these missions means that NATO will likely stand aloof from the assorted conflicts going on more or less at its doorstep. Rather than take a direct, proactive role, the alliance will only work through other agencies—if it works at all. While this may be noteworthy, it is not transformation.

Its membership has not changed either, even though several Central and even Eastern European states, including Russia, have expressed a wish to join. Poland, Hungary, and Czechoslovakia (as it was at the time) sought some form of political or associate membership as far back as 1991; they did not then ask for full membership, but were more interested in security guarantees. That was denied them. As Edward Mortimer has noted, many Western leaders have adapted to the new situation with difficulty. Used to a familiar NATO and its stability, they were relieved to find that East Germany, by being absorbed into the Federal Republic, could *ipso facto* become part of NATO and the EC without causing any great upheavals. They were content to leave the rest of East-Central Europe in a kind of "security limbo" or de facto neutrality, while negotiating rather grudging association agreements between the EC and the most advanced of Central Europe's "new democracies" —the CSFR, Hungary and Poland—which would give no definite commitment to full membership even as a long-term goal.[22] It took the Soviet coup of August 1991 to shake them out of this position of complacency. In fairness, however, it would have been foolhardy to expand the alliance too quickly. At the national level, armed forces have been much reduced and this is an ongoing process in several countries. To take on the responsibility for additional real estate, on the one hand, and incorporate armed forces so recently a part of the "other side," on the other, was an unrealistic proposition. As for the NACC, the point must be made that whatever it may be doing at the moment, it is more or less a gesture on the part of the alliance toward the states of the former USSR, and that is the best that can be said at present.

The strategic concept may be described as new, but two of its four "core security functions"—to provide a transatlantic forum and to deter and defend against any threat of aggression to a member state—are, after all, traditional functions of the alliance. Parts of the strategy are well-written and display the kind of awareness of the current security landscape that one expects of international bureaucrats of this caliber. But only one shoe has dropped, and ears keep straining to hear the second one. Previous NATO strategic concepts were hard and uncompromising; this one is soft and tentative.

NATO has kept its bureaucracy and infrastructure. There will be some downsizing but the essential structure of alliance headquarters remains unchanged. There will be some adjustments to the command structure, which will also be reduced. But there is still an American filling the position of SACEUR. No less ironic, perhaps, is the prominence of German officers in senior NATO appointments.

The strength of forces in all NATO countries that have them is being reduced, leaving those states and the alliance with much less conventional capability at a time when there may be an increasing need for forces in a growing number of theaters. The conventional third of the triad will be more flexible and mobile, we are told, although these two characteristics were always present in abundance. The ACE Mobile Force has been renamed. The Rapid Reaction Force is, to be sure, new, and has all of the characteristics of an invention created to provide a role for the reduced forces of the British Army of the Rhine. With no visible conventional military threat to NATO, it is interesting to speculate on just what this force might react to, and rapidly at that. The stationed and reinforcement tiers are hardly new. If sharp reductions in troop levels equate to fundamental change, then perhaps there may after all be some merit in the "transformation" argument.

On two other relevant aspects, the German constitution and the position of France with respect to the integrated military command, there is also no change. Helmut Kohl has certainly tried to obtain his parliament's approval to use German troops outside NATO territory, but has consistently failed to muster the two-thirds majority needed to amend the constitution.[23] Germany's deployment of peacekeeping troops to Somalia with the UN notwithstanding, the country is still seen by some as NATO's weak link. Nor have the French shown any inclination to return their forces to NATO command, at least at the time of this writing. Of all the Western European countries, they are the most ardent supporters of the concept of a European security entity with its own forces that is free of North American domination. Stripped to its bare bones, the French claim is that American might should be available to Europe whenever needed, but not in a manner that endows Washington with leadership over European security. Some observers do, it is true, detect a slight movement towards NATO on the part of France.[24]

Conclusion

In summary, it is difficult to see how the alliance has been transformed. It would be well to remember that NATO can never be more than its members allow it to be. At the moment, member states are wrestling with the same economic conditions that attended the events of 1989. It is possible that they would like to do more in terms of assistance to states in Central and Eastern Europe, but the wherewithal is simply not there. There are undoubtedly other political agendas at work, as well, and analysts are left to guess at what they might be. In fairness to the people who work for NATO, be they uniformed or civilian, one is obliged to say that they have received their directions from member governments, and are putting the best face on things. They can hardly be reproached for that. The potential problem is that while it in effect sits out the game in progress, NATO may end up as an irrelevance. As long as the US needs NATO as a credential for its presence in Europe, and a mechanism for expressing its views, the alliance will creak on. Europe will continue to subscribe to it as a means to keep the Americans in. The question then becomes, do the various countries need the full panoply of a military alliance as currently deployed in Europe?

Notes

1. Alvin Toffler, *The Third Wave* (London: Collins, 1980).
2. "London Declaration on a Transformed North Atlantic Alliance, 5-6 June 1990," *NATO Review* 38 (June 1990): 32-33.
3. Robert Cox, "Social Forces, States and World Orders: Beyond International Relations Theory," in *Perspectives on World Politics*, ed. R. Little and M. Smith, 2d ed. (London: Routledge, 1991).
4. James K. Bartleman, "Canada and NATO in Transition," *Forum* 7 (January 1993): 15.
5. Michael Legge, "The New NATO: The Political Dimensions," *Canadian Defence Quarterly* 22 (March 1993): 14-20.
6. Manfred Wörner, "The Alliance in the New European Security Environment," *NATO's Sixteen Nations* 38, 3 (1993): 8.
7. Brian Kenny, "Interoperability on the Battlefield," *NATO's Sixteen Nations* 34 (January 1990): 10.
8. George Joffe, "European Security and the New Arc of Crisis," *Adelphi Papers* 265 (Winter 1991/92): 59.
9. Peter Stanford, "NATO Must Go," *Naval Proceedings* 57 (March 1991): 36.
10. See Barry Buzan, *People, States and Fear*, 2d ed. (Boulder: Lynne Rienner, 1991), p. 15.
11. John Mearsheimer, "Why We Will Soon Miss the Cold War," *Atlantic Monthly*, August 1990, pp. 35-50; and "Back to the Future: Instability in Europe after the Cold War," *International Security* 15 (Summer 1990): 5-56.
12. Mearsheimer, "Back to the Future," p. 15.
13. Mearsheimer, "Why We Will Soon Miss the Cold War," p. 41.
14. See Stephen Van Evera, "Primed for Peace: Europe after the Cold War," *International Security* 15 (Winter 1990/91): 9. See also Idem, "Why Europe Matters, Why the Third World Doesn't," *Journal of Strategic Studies* 13 (June 1990): 1-51.
15. For a discussion, see David G. Haglund and Olaf Mager, "Homeward Bound?" in *Homeward Bound? Allied Forces in the New Germany*, ed. Haglund and Mager (Boulder: Westview, 1992), pp. 273-85.

16. Defence Planning Committee Final Communiqué, Brussels, 23 May 1990, *NATO Review* 38 (June 1990): 31-32.

17. "Ministerial Meeting of the North Atlantic Council, Turnberry, UK, 7-8 June 1990," *NATO Review* 38 (June 1990); "London Declaration on a Transformed North Atlantic Alliance."

18. "The Alliance's Strategic Concept," in *The Transformation of an Alliance* (Brussels: NATO Office of Information and Press, 1992), pp. 29-54.

19. "Rome Declaration on Peace and Cooperation," in ibid., pp. 15-28.

20. NATO press communiqué M-NAC-1(92)51, 4 June 1992, p. 4.

21. "New Mission for NATO: European Peacekeeper," *Stars and Stripes*, 5 June 1992, p. 1.

22. Edward Mortimer, "European Security after the Cold War," *Adelphi Paper* 271 (Summer 1992): 20.

23. For an analysis of the constraints on German troop deployments outside the NATO area, see the chapter by Joachim Rabe in this volume.

24. Daniel Vernet, "France Moves Closer to Nato," *Manchester Guardian Weekly*, 21 March 1993, p. 13. For a more detailed analysis, see the chapter by Michel Fortmann and David Haglund, this volume.

3

The Yugoslav Civil War

Ernest W. Fischer

Introduction

Nineteen thousand Serbs and Montenegrins died during the 1912-13 Balkan Wars. Another 325,000 Serbs, Montenegrins, and Croats perished during World War I. An estimated 1,700,000 Yugoslavs died during World War II, one million of whom died at each others' hands. Yugoslav "democide" cost another 1,067,000 lives between 1944 and 1987.[1] The current crisis has wreaked as many as 134,000 dead or missing, 500,000 refugees, and three million Bosnians driven from their homes.[2] In the region of the South Slavs, it might be best if they could forget their past.

Unfortunately, the past has only been selectively forgotten. The causes of the current crisis seem to be lost from the memory of the players external to the crisis, while the use of violence to solve the problem seems all too well-remembered by the South Slavs involved in the conflict. The international community is not succeeding at solving one of its first and most severe post-Cold War challenges: the painful dismemberment of the former Socialist Federal Republic of Yugoslavia at great cost in lives. Why?

To understand what is happening today in the states formed out of the former Yugoslavia it is necessary to understand the central issues surrounding the conflict, not the symptoms witnessed on the evening news. With the Clinton administration's search for ways to be more active, the Vance-Owen and Owen-Stoltenberg plans call for dividing Bosnia-Herzegovina, the North Atlantic Treaty Organization's search for a role in peacekeeping operations, and the threat of spillover into neighboring countries, many players have sought ways to end the crisis. This chapter will review the region's history in order to identify issues that are central to the conflict, to look at whether or not the international community has addressed those issues, and to conclude with one perspective on the future.

History

The conflict in the former Yugoslavia is an expression of national identities, particularly between the Croats and Serbs, in an environment lacking a strong central government. Over centuries, differences have developed between the combatants that have culminated in the current crisis. Key to understanding the issues central to the current crisis is understanding the region's history.

Croatia

Croats have primarily inhabited the Triune Kingdom lands of Dalmatia, Croatia, and Slavonia, but when the crisis began they also constituted almost one-fifth of Bosnia-Herzegovina.[3] Croats, along with the Serbs and Bosnian Muslims, are Slavs. They speak a language similar to the Serbs, but adopted the Latin alphabet along with Roman Catholicism.

Between the twelfth and twentieth centuries, Croatia was ruled from the north, first by the Hungarians and then by the Habsburgs. These experiences with Hungarian and Habsburg rule have left the Croats a history of constitutional autonomy within larger empires. Periodically, however, Croatia did experience movements to free it from foreign rule, ranging from the 1835-43 Illyrian movement to unite the South Slavs, to the 1848 Croatian quest for freedom from Hungarian administrative control and restoration of the Triune Kingdom, to the 1861 Party of Rights call for the formation of an independent Croatia and incorporation of Serbs into Greater Croatia.

Until the beginning of World War I, however, most Croats preferred autonomy within the Habsburg Empire. In addition to remaining within the empire, many Croats also sought control over Bosnia-Herzegovina in order to strengthen the weak geographic position of the Triune Kingdom. The Serbs desired Bosnia-Herzegovina as well, and clashes between Croats and Serbs over Bosnia-Herzegovina began in the 1890s.[4]

Serbia

To the south, in addition to Serbia itself, where they form the majority, the Serbs are minorities in the Vojvodina, Croatian Military Frontier, and Kosovo. Montenegrins and Serbs alike view Montenegrins as Serbs, and the Serbs constituted one-third of the population of Bosnia-Herzegovina when the latest crisis began.[5] Serbs profess the Eastern Orthodox faith, speak a different dialect of the same South Slav language as the Croats, but adopted the Cyrillic alphabet along with Orthodoxy. In the early nineteenth century, the Serbian language reformer, Vuk Karadzic, attempted to define Serbs by their use of the central South Slavic dialect, which included many Bosnian Muslims and Croats.[6] The Croats and Muslims have not accepted this definition and have held to their insistence that the dialect spoken by a community does not, by itself, define its nationhood.

Unlike the Croats who were oriented northward, the Serbs found themselves facing south, either for territorial acquisition or in rebellion against the Ottoman Empire. At one point during the fourteenth century, Serbia commanded an empire ranging from the Danube to central Greece, and from Albania to western Thrace, which included current Macedonia.[7] The subsequent Ottoman conquest of Serbia subjugated the Serbs to 500 years of Ottoman rule and led both to Serbian insurrections against the Ottoman occupation and to migrations to avoid Ottoman reprisals.

The Serb migrations are especially important for understanding the current crisis because they brought Serbs, Croats, and Muslims together at the village level. Following Serbia's conquest by the Ottomans in the fourteenth and fifteenth centuries, tens of thousands of Serbs migrated northward, out of Old Serbia and away from the Ottomans. In 1690 alone, about 70,000 Serbs migrated to and populated the Military Frontier between the Habsburg and Ottoman Empires. In the wake of seventeenth and eighteenth century Serb migrations, Albanians occupied the depopulated Kosovo-Metohija, Sandjak, and western Macedonia regions.[8] In the end, the migrations resulted in Serbs intermixed with the Bosnian Muslims and Croats in the north, while in the south Serbs came into conflict with the Muslims who had occupied the areas vacated by the Serbs leaving Old Serbia. These are the areas in contention today.

Unlike Croatia's search for autonomy within the Habsburg Empire, Serbia sought independence from Ottoman rule and control over territory lost to the Muslims. The uprisings of the 1830s, 1878, and 1912-13 gave rise to a Serb national identity that led first to Serbian autonomy and autonomy of the Orthodox church in 1830, and then to recognition of Serbia as an independent state in 1878, and the election of Peter Karadjordjevic as king in 1903.

Serbia, however, wanted more than autonomy or independence within the boundaries that existed during the nineteenth century. In 1844, the Nacertanije Plan was prepared for Prince Alexander Karadjordjevic that called for an autonomous Serbia joined by Bosnia, Herzegovina, Montenegro, northern Albania, portions of the Vojvodina, and an outlet on the Adriatic.[9] In 1876, Serbia and Montenegro fought against the Ottomans in support of the Bosnia insurrection; Serbia wanted Bosnia and Montenegro wanted Herzegovina. Contrary to the Serbs' desires to control Bosnia-Herzegovina, though, Austria-Hungary was awarded the right to administer Bosnia-Herzegovina by the 1878 Treaty of Berlin. Then, between 1908 and 1909, Austria and Russia agreed to Austrian annexation of Bosnia-Herzegovina. Under a weakening Ottoman control, the Serbs perceived that they had a chance to control Bosnia-Herzegovina, but under Habsburg control, Bosnia-Herzegovina seemed lost. Serbia and Croatia both desired Bosnia-Herzegovina and both were denied it.

Yugoslavia

Twice Yugoslavia was created and twice it has been torn apart. The spark that ignited World War I was lit by Bosnian Serbs, supported by a Serbian Army officer, trying to rid Bosnia of Austrian rule in order to reunite Bosnia with Serbia.[10] Throughout the war, Serbia retained its focus on Bosnia-Herzegovina. During the French, British, and United States attempts to negotiate a peace with the Habsburg Empire in 1918 Serbia sought Washington's assistance in obtaining Bosnia-Herzegovina. Upon gaining freedom from foreign occupation on 1 November 1918, Serbian forces took Bosnia-Herzegovina and the Vojvodina from the Habsburgs.

The Kingdom of Serbs, Croats, and Slovenes, created on 1 December 1918, was a patchwork of states united for various reasons under a government unable to fulfill the expectations of the various nationalities. Croatia and Slovenia joined because they were members of a defeated empire and sought a way to maintain their national identities, Slovenia against Germanic and Italian influences and Croatia against Hungarian. Slovenia also sought association with a larger state for protection of the one-third of its population that lived in Italy, Austria, and Hungary, and Croatia was searching for a way out from under Hungarian rule.[11] The Serbs, as part of the forces victorious over both the Habsburg and Ottoman Empires, saw Yugoslavia as a means to unite "peoples who were the same as themselves in an expanded Serbia."[12] Bosnia did not like being ruled by Austria; Montenegro, as a Serb enclave, followed Serbia; and Macedonia remained part of Serbia. In essence, the nationalities joined together to support their national goals rather than to support one common Yugoslav goal.

Ultimately the two major groups, the Serbs and the Croats, came into conflict over the issue of autonomy. Serbia had achieved independence as a kingdom and saw the new state as the culmination of events leading to national unity under a strong Serb leader. The Croats' experience with Hungary and the Habsburg Empire, on the other hand, led them to seek a federal system within which Croatia would remain autonomous. In the end, the 1921 constitutional monarchy under the Karadjordjevic

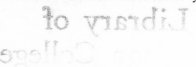

dynasty supported the Serbs' goal of a strong government in Belgrade, but failed to provide the autonomy sought by the Croats and Slovenes. The government struggled for eight years and came to an end when King Alexander, frustrated with the inability of the Serbs and Croats to work together, dissolved the parliament in 1929, suspended the constitution, proclaimed a royal dictatorship, and renamed the country Yugoslavia.

In the turmoil created following King Alexander's actions, independence groups developed among the Yugoslav nationalities. One of the most extreme was the Croatian fascist movement, Ustasha, founded by Ante Pavelic, which was involved in the assassination of King Alexander in 1934. From the time of Alexander's death until World War II, the Serbs continued to view Yugoslavia as a Greater Serbian monarchy. In the end, the first Yugoslavia failed largely because it represented "the Serb vision of a South Slav state,"[13] which was contrary to the self-determination concept held by other Yugoslavs.

In April 1941, it took the German army a little over one week to defeat the Yugoslav army and drive the government into exile. The Ustasha collaborated with the Nazis, established the independent state of Croatia, which included Bosnia-Herzegovina, and began a campaign against the Serbs, Jews, and Gypsies. In Serbia, Draza Mihailovic led the Chetniks, who remained loyal to the government-in-exile, and fought both the Croatian Ustasha and Tito's Partisans. The Partisans, Yugoslavia's only supranational party, fought the Germans, Chetniks, and Ustasha. They offered relief from Serb supremacy and their promise of equality made it possible for the Partisans to draw support from all ethnic groups, mobilize heterogeneous populations, and rise to postwar power.[14]

Following the war, Tito took advantage of the support for his Partisans and centralized power under the Communist Party of Yugoslavia.[15] He established a federation of six republics and two provinces. Macedonia was made a separate republic, contrary to the Serbs' desire to retain it as southern Serbia. Likewise, Montenegro was created as a separate republic, again contrary to Serb desires. The borders for Croatia, Slovenia, and Bosnia-Herzegovina were based on traditional boundaries. Serbia was given control over the provinces of Vojvodina and Kosovo. Because of the impact of migrations, however, many Yugoslavs found themselves living as ethnic minorities within the borders of the several republics, especially in the Croatian Military Frontier and in Bosnia-Herzegovina. Tito faced the same challenge that the first Yugoslavia faced: creating a government that would protect minority rights and attain an acceptable balance between central control and republic autonomy.

Tito imposed a centralized bureaucracy over the federation in an attempt to reduce the effect of the republics' nationalistic goals. During the war, he had promised that equality among nations would be honored. When he came to power, he promoted his wartime slogan of Brotherhood and Unity, which focused on maintaining central power at the expense of republic freedom of action.

Power centralized at the national level was favorable to the Serbs who saw this as an opportunity to increase the economic position of the less well-developed southern republics at the expense of the richer northern republics, as well as an opportunity to revive Serbian influence through a unitary form of government.[16] On the other hand, Slovenia and Croatia sought a greater degree of decentralization to reduce their economic burden and stymie the growth of Greater Serbia. In 1962, at the sixth plenum of the League of Communists of Yugoslavia central committee, Tito ultimately fixed the course that Yugoslavia would follow until after his death with his position that "we have to take decentralization as our point of departure." This connected the problems of economic reform and national unity, increased the autonomy of Croatia and Slovenia, and reduced Serbia's influence.

The issue came to a head with the 1974 constitution. Supported by Edvard Kardelj, a Slovene, and Croatian delegates, this constitution decentralized many of the powers held by the central government and formed a confederation. Most powers, except those in the areas of defense, foreign affairs, and joint economic concerns, were shifted from the federal government to the six republics and two provinces. A collective federal presidency was created; Bosnian Muslims were recognized as a Muslim nation; and Vojvodina and Kosovo were given status as autonomous provinces within Serbia, rather than as provinces directly controlled by Serbia. The result was a fragmented government consisting of eight units competing against each other within a decentralized confederation. It did not provide guarantees for the rights of minorities and opened opportunities to create nation-states. The greatest loser was Serbia, which ceded control over two provinces and the influence it exerted under the unitarian structure of the federal system. From a Serb perspective, the losses could be attributed to a Croat, Tito, and a Slovene, Kardelj.

After Tito's death in 1980, the confederal structure proved too weak to deal with the pressures within. The charismatic leader who had held the system together was gone. The Partisans who had supported him were mostly dead and replaced by nationalistic leaders at the ever increasingly independent republic level. Unemployment increased, production fell, foreign indebtedness grew, and inflation raged. There was no authority at the center of the state and the central government was unable to stop the disintegration of the economy or to achieve cooperation among the political leaders of the republics and provinces.

Out of the confusion reemerged nationalism, the first sign of which occurred in 1981 when the ethnic Albanians revolted against the Serbs in Kosovo.

Relations between the two groups were still tense when Slobodan Milosevic was elected president of the League of Communists of Serbia in 1987. He came to power as a nationalist who favored the rights of Serbian and Montenegrin minorities living in Kosovo, and as a socialist who favored a strong central government in Belgrade. The Croats and Slovenes saw Milosevic moving away from the decentralized confederation and toward a unitary Greater Serbia.

There then began a series of events that led directly to the current crisis.[17] Between 1988 and 1990, Milosevic forced through amendments to the Serbian, Kosovan, and Vojvodinan constitutions that ended autonomy for Vojvodina and Kosovo, and in July 1990 he dismissed Kosovo's provincial parliament, banned the Albanian press, and shut down the Albanian language television in Pristina. This was followed by the 7 September 1990 Albanian Yugoslav deputies proclamation of a separate constitution and independence for Kosovo, which was abolished by Serbia on 28 September 1990. In October 1990, fearful of stronger militias in the republics, the Yugoslav Peoples' Army (JNA) began impounding weapons designated for use by territorial forces in republics other than Serbia. On 14 January 1991, the federal constitutional court annulled Slovenia's 26 December 1990 declaration of sovereignty.

Yugoslavia was left without a head of state on 15 May 1991 when Serbia blocked Stipe Mesic, a Croat, from becoming president.[18] Concerned over Milosevic's repression of Albanians in Kosovo, his drive to retain socialism, and his interest in maintaining a state-controlled economy, Slovenia and Croatia declared their independence on 25 June 1991. Macedonia followed with a declaration of independence on 18 September 1991 and Bosnia-Herzegovina voted for independence on 29 February 1992.[19] Montenegro passed a referendum favoring union with Serbia in a Yugoslav state on 1 March 1992, and the Federal Republic of Yugoslavia was proclaimed on 27 April 1992. Finally, on 24 May 1992 Kosovo voted to secede from Yugoslavia. The vote was deemed illegal by Belgrade and on 24 June 1992 Serbian police prevented the Kosovar parliament from assembling.

Complicating the disintegration along republic lines was the search for autonomy by minorities that cut across republic borders. As early as 28 February 1991, the Serbs in Croatia had declared themselves independent. This was followed by the Serb declaration of the autonomous region of Krajina on 17 September 1991, and a vote for autonomy on 27 October 1991 by the Muslims in the Sandjak. On 7 April 1992, the Serbian Republic of Bosnia-Herzegovina was declared independent.

This was countered on 3 July 1992 by the creation of the autonomous Croatian Community of Bosnia-Herzegovina. Lastly, on 12 August 1992, the Serb republics of Krajina and Bosnia-Herzegovina announced their intention to unite.

By the fall of 1992, the former Yugoslavia had not only divided along republic lines, but the minorities within Croatia, Serbia, Kosovo, and Bosnia-Herzegovina had also demonstrated desires for independence or autonomy. The solution to the crisis rested in negotiations or use of force. Negotiations failed and the Serbs initiated conflict, first in Borovo Selo, Croatia, in May 1991 to protect Serb minority rights, then in Slovenia on 27 June 1991 to prevent the breakup of the federation, and finally in Bijeljina, Bosnia-Herzegovina, on 1 April 1992 to protect Serb minorities and to carve out a corridor to the Krajina.

Central Issues

Historically, there are a number of differences among the republics of the former Yugoslavia: north-south orientation, religion, language, degree of autonomy desired, impact of migrations, and goals of territorial acquisition. Which of these need to be addressed to solve the conflict and prevent spillover to neighboring areas?

The republics on the periphery, Slovenia and Macedonia, withdrew from the former Yugoslavia comparatively easily. Slovenia was the most homogeneous republic in terms of language, religion, and cultural identity.[20] As a result, Slovenia has been spared much of the disruption caused by transplanted ethnic minorities and competition with other republics over territory. Slovene goals for uniting with the first and second Yugoslavia were primarily for protection from their more powerful neighbors. Over time, the Slovenes sought greater economic freedom from the southern republics and economic integration with the West. Eventually, the Slovenes seceded out of fear of Milosevic's policies of political and economic centralization. The JNA intervened on 27 June 1991 and the federal government in Belgrade voted to withdraw the JNA from Slovenia on 18 July 1991, just three weeks after the intervention commenced. During the war, an estimated 63 deaths occurred[21]—few compared to the 134,000 or so since the dismemberment began. One argument for the relative ease of Slovenia's successful withdrawal is that Serb actions in Slovenia were oriented more to sending a message to the Croats than in retaining Slovenia in the state.

At the southern end of the former Yugoslavia, Macedonia seceded even more easily than Slovenia. Macedonia was created as a republic by Tito in 1945.[22] As was the case with Slovenia, it was small and needed Yugoslavia to protect it from its neighbors. During the period leading to the Slovenian and Croatian withdrawal from Yugoslavia, Macedonia attempted to maintain a balance between them and Serbia. As in Slovenia and Croatia, Macedonia's 1990 elections brought in a non-communist, nationalist government, which sought a balance between the interests of Slovenia and Croatia on one side and Serbia and Montenegro on the other. Macedonia sought an economic course that would protect Macedonian interests but not alienate Serbia and, along with Slovenia and Croatia, Macedonia favored a confederal system.

The collapse of the federal state placed Macedonia in an alliance dominated by Serbia, which in the past had viewed Macedonia as part of southern Serbia. With Slovenia independent and Serb attention focused on fighting in Croatia, Macedonia declared independence on 18 September 1991, and by 27 March 1992 the JNA had completed evacuating from Macedonia, without casualties. Macedonia's concern over Serbian centralism appears to be the major reason for its secession.[23]

The actions of the remaining four republics of the former Yugoslavia are intertwined. Serbia and Montenegro are aligned in opposition to Croatia, and Bosnia-Herzegovina is caught in the middle. Serb-Croat interests conflict in three areas: minority rights, particularly for Serbs who live in Croat lands; territorial goals in Bosnia-Herzegovina; and the amount of local governmental autonomy.

Minority Rights

At the root of the conflict are the rights of minorities living outside the control of their parent nation, a carryover from the earlier migrations. Serbs constitute approximately 12 percent of Croatia's population and, while they are spread throughout the Military Frontier, they are concentrated in areas that border Serbia, such as eastern Slavonia in the Baranja and Western Srijem, and in the Krajina, which is separated from Serbia by Bosnia. In Bosnia-Herzegovina, Serbs comprise 33 percent of the population and are concentrated in the rural areas around western and northern Bosnia and eastern Herzegovina.[24] Under a federal government, the Serbs felt that the rights of these minorities could be protected.[25] Under a confederation, autonomy would devolve to the republics and Serbia would have less control over Serb minorities, and Serb minorities would have less control over their own fate. Following dismemberment of the state, Serbia would have no control over Serb minorities and no way to protect them. Especially fearful to the Serbs living in Croatia was the rise to power in April 1990 of the nationalistic Croatian Democratic Union. In the Serbs' minds, Jasenovac, the Croat-run death camp during World War II, still loomed ominously.[26]

To protect themselves, Serb minorities have sought a Greater Serbia or autonomy within their new states. The latter has led to the formation of the Serb Autonomous Region of Krajina, the Serb Autonomous Region of Western Slavonia, and the Serb Republic of Bosnia-Herzegovina. Whereas the largely Slovene state of Slovenia was able to secede, ethnically mixed Croatia and Bosnia-Herzegovina could not secede without a fight because Serb minority freedoms would not be guaranteed.

Territorial Acquisition

A second major issue is competition for territory, especially between the Serbs and Croats. Bosnia-Herzegovina is the point where Roman Catholicism, Eastern Orthodoxy, and Islam meet; where the borders were drawn between the Habsburgs and Ottomans; and where peasants need to be better fighters than farmers. Since at least 1878, Serbia has coveted Bosnia-Herzegovina, but its desires have been frustrated first by the Habsburgs and then by successive Yugoslav governments. Tito considered Bosnia-Herzegovina important to the extent that he placed 60 percent of the military industries and installations there. For the Serbs, territorial acquisition in Bosnia-Herzegovina remains important for several reasons: the heavy investment in military infrastructure makes Bosnia-Herzegovina important to the Serb-dominated JNA; Serbs constitute one-third of the Bosnia-Herzegovina population; and they desire a land route across Bosnia to reach the Serb enclave in the Krajina.[27] Although the federal army and air force withdrew from Bosnia-Herzegovina in the spring of 1992, the fighting has been continued by the Bosnian Serbs as members of the army of the Serbian Republic of Bosnia-Herzegovina or as members of irregular units, with external support provided from Serbia. One interpretation of the Serbs' goals in Bosnia-Herzegovina is that they entered the war with the "stated aim of establishing an independent enclave stripped of all non-Serbs."[28]

Croats are fighting in Bosnia-Herzegovina to stem the loss of territory to Serbs, to prevent the development of Greater Serbia, and to make territorial acquisitions that Croats deem necessary to strengthen Croatia. The presence of Croatian forces in Bosnia-Herzegovina is of no little significance and, according to Canadian Major General Lewis MacKenzie, former United Nations Protection Force (UNPROFOR) commander in Bosnia-Herzegovina, the Croatian army has a greater presence there than the Yugoslav army.[29] Since coming to power, Croatian President Franjo Tudjman has alluded to making Bosnia-Herzegovina part of Croatia and there are indications that the Croats intend to annex portions of Bosnia-Herzegovina.[30] These overtures have been unsettling for the Serbs who recall Austria's and Croatia's attempts to control Bosnia-Herzegovina.

While the two antagonists compete for Bosnia-Herzegovina, there are signs that they have also collaborated in attempts to secure their respective interests. In March 1991, Tudjman and Milosevic met at Karadjordjevo in northern Vojvodina and struck a preliminary agreement on how to divide Bosnia-Herzegovina between them. This was followed by an agreement in early May 1992 between Croatian and Serbian military leaders Mate Boban and Radovan Karadzic in Graz, Austria, that called for splitting Bosnia-Herzegovina between the Croats and Serbs. Subsequent Croat and Serb actions have supported their desires to carve up Bosnia-Herzegovina and to pen the Muslims into an area of central Bosnia.[31] The Serbs' actions in Bosnia-Herzegovina have received considerable notice in the press. The Croats' actions, on the other hand, have not been as well publicized, yet they have been active militarily. Among other places, Croats have fought Muslims at Novi Travnik, Vitez, Zenica, and Mostar. According to one Croat government spokesperson, "Croats would no longer fight Serbs on the Muslims' behalf."[32]

Agreements between the Serbs and Croats, however, have not stopped them from competing with each other to control as much of Bosnia-Herzegovina as their respective military capabilities will permit. On 3 July 1992, the Croats established the autonomous Croatian Community of Herceg-Bosna that gave Croats, with only 18 percent of the population, control over almost 30 percent of Bosnia-Herzegovina. A look at the map shows that the Serbs, with 33 percent of the population, control about two-thirds of the territory. The Bosnian Muslims, with 40 percent of the population, are being squeezed into an area that is bordered by Tuzla, Sarajevo, and Zenica, which is about 5 percent of the former republic.

Central Control Versus Local Autonomy

A third issue is the degree of governmental control. Periods of nonviolence between the members of the former Yugoslavia during the twentieth century existed when strong central governments held power. As discussed above, between the turn of the century and World War I, Serbia and Montenegro were separate kingdoms, Croatia and Bosnia-Herzegovina were part of the Habsburg Empire, and Slovenia was a province of Austria. Following the First World War, the Kingdom of Serbs, Croats, and Slovenes functioned under a parliamentary democracy and later a royal dictatorship. Under Tito, disputes between the antagonists were controlled with resolve. Violence has erupted only when there was not a strong central government during 1941 to 1945, and since 1991.

Twentieth-century violence stems largely from the Croats' fears of a hegemonistic Greater Serbia, and Serbs' concerns that Serb minorities living under Croat control will again face Ustasha-type treatment. The Bosnian Muslims are positioned in the middle of the Serb and Croat quest for territory.

At the heart of the issue is the conflict between the Serbs and the Croats over the degree of central control. The Serbs have sought a federal government with the republics subordinated to protect Serb minorities living outside Serbia and to strengthen Serbia's position relative to the other republics. Croatia has sought a federation or confederation that gave greater autonomy to the republics. The dilemma was finally brought to a head by the 1974 constitution, which began the decentralizing process that led to the summer 1991 demise of the central government and opened the door for the antagonists to pursue their national interests. Because no one was in charge, everyone could do as they pleased.

Spillover

Should a solution to the causes of the conflict in Bosnia-Herzegovina not be found, there is a good probability that the conflict will spill over to Kosovo for the same reasons: Serbia's search for protection of a Serb minority and control over territory populated largely by another nationality in an environment lacking central control. Less likely, but still of concern, is the threat of spillover to the Hungarian minority that constitutes 21 percent of the Vojvodina and the Muslim population in the Sandjak that represents as much as 2 percent of the Serbian population.

The crux of the issue is that the conflict in the former Yugoslavia centers around minorities left in the wake of migrations who fear their physical safety and access to political power are not protected, competition for territory in Bosnia-Herzegovina, and failure to sustain a balance between central control and republic autonomy. These issues must be addressed to work toward a solution to the current conflict and to prevent the conflict from spilling over into bordering areas. What has been the international community's response to these issues?

International Community Actions

Perhaps rivaling the confusion of what is going on inside the former Yugoslavia is the confusion over what is happening outside the country in response to its demise. There is little doubt that the international community has good intentions toward solving the crisis, as can be determined from the literature produced by various organizations.[33] Yet, the conflict goes on. Why?

National Positions

Competing national interests have hampered efforts to solve the crisis both for individual states and organizations. For instance, Italy is tied to the European Community position. It first supported keeping Yugoslavia a single state, then reversed its position. Its concerns focus on sustaining the lines of communication through the former Yugoslavia, protecting Italian minorities living there, and containing the spread of refugees. Hungary was supportive of Slovenian and Croatian independence, but has concerns over the 500,000 Hungarians living in the former Yugoslavia, many in Serbia-controlled Vojvodina. Austria supported recognition of Slovenia and Croatia, but is concerned over the potentially large number of refugees. Austria and Hungary have had their borders violated by federal aircraft and Austria at one time placed its military on alert, but both countries lack the military power to intervene.

Germany was the strongest proponent of Slovenian and Croatian independence, but its relations with Serbia continue to be affected by the memories of World War II. It has been a strong supporter of the idea of a European buffer force, but has been prevented from participating by its constitution.[34] France has historically enjoyed good relations with Serbia, favors deploying a European buffer force, and prefers limited United States involvement. Great Britain favors a negotiated settlement without military intervention.

Romania has been supportive of Serbia, and Bulgaria has been in agreement with Turkey against Serbia and still covets part of Macedonia. Greece has been openly supportive of Milosevic, which brings the Greeks into conflict with the Turks who support the Bosnian Muslims and Albanians in Kosovo. Turkey and other Islamic countries have supported intervening on behalf of the Bosnian Muslims. Albania is concerned for the welfare of the two million Albanians living in Kosovo, but as with Hungary and Austria it lacks the military capability to be a threat to Serbia. The best Albania can do is guard its borders and offer limited relief to refugees.

All of this created difficulty in developing a common European position on recognition of the new states, which in turn led first to an ultimatum to Serbia on 28 October 1991 to transform Yugoslavia into an association of sovereign republics and ended with European Community recognition of the independence of Slovenia and Croatia on 15 January 1992. Even at that, the United States did not act in concert with its allies and held to the Vance recommendation not to recognize the new states until 7 April 1992. And the confusion grew. France and Germany favored the introduction of forces as buffers, while Germany could not and Great Britain did not want to deploy forces to the area. France sought a European solution to the problem while Great Britain wanted a UN or NATO-based approach that would involve the United States. Boris Yeltsin was pressured by Russian conservatives to use the Security Council veto to prevent UN action against the Serbs, while President Bush made isolating Serbia "economically and politically" one of the steps that the United States had "underway to help defuse and contain the crisis."

The confusion among players external to the conflict continued into the spring of 1993. France was prepared to send reinforcements to UNPROFOR; Great Britain was wondering if it should withdraw; Germany remained constrained by a debate over constitutional issues; the United States questioned whether Bosnia's Muslims should not have arms and why the no-fly zone should not be enforced; and the Russian Supreme Soviet voted to urge the UN to impose sanctions on Croatia or lift them from Serbia.[35] There simply was no agreed strategy or demonstrated collective will among states.

Responses of Regional Organizations

Regional organizations have fared no better. The European Community brokered the Brioni Declaration for the peaceful resolution of the crisis, but this agreement was undermined when Slovenia reneged on demobilizing its forces and lifting blockades against federal army barracks. The European Community has been unable to attain a lasting ceasefire and its 28 October 1992 ultimatum to Serbia failed because it lacked the collective will necessary to be enforced. The Conference on Security and Cooperation in Europe (CSCE) has been as feckless. It has passed arms embargoes, introduced initiatives to conduct its own peacekeeping operations, and held meetings to discuss humanitarian aid. Yet, once the armed conflict began the CSCE had essentially failed.[36]

The two military organizations, the Western European Union (WEU) and NATO, have likewise been searching for their roles. The WEU determined early on that "a return to the status quo ante bellum seems out of the question." When faced with the essential military issue of the use of force to end the conflict, the WEU posed the question of whether Europe was prepared to accept significant losses "in the hope, but not the certainty, of restoring peace between the Yugoslav peoples?" The answer was No. Of the two cases considered for the use of force, guaranteeing a ceasefire was rejected because one neither existed nor had been agreed to, and imposing peace by force was generally not supported among WEU members.[37] All that the WEU was able to contribute was a flotilla in the Adriatic to assist in sanction enforcement against Serbia and Montenegro.[38]

NATO, with greater ability to provide a security system, likewise has ruled out massive use of ground forces in Bosnia-Herzegovina. It has, however, undertaken limited support for the UN. In response to the UN secretary general's request, NATO deployed a headquarters from NORTHAG and approximately 5,000 troops to Croatia and Bosnia to protect convoys of food and medicine, and to escort detainees.[39] These troops are serving as Blue Helmets, not as a NATO force, and will remain as long as their parent countries elect to sustain them financially. NATO has also provided AWACS to identify violations of Bosnian-Herzegovinan airspace and contributed ships to enforce the sanctions in the Adriatic. Yet, as the organization best qualified to render military support, NATO has remained on the margin because of French opposition to its involvement and because NATO's members agreed with the WEU analysis that the potential loss of life outweighs the potential gain.[40]

International Organizational Responses

At the international level, the UN has focused its attention primarily on the symptoms of the conflict. The 34 Security Council resolutions passed from UNSCR 713 of 25 September 1991 through UNSCR 821 of 28 April 1993 tended to fall into four categories: military supply and arms embargoes, peacekeeping operations and support for UNPROFOR, humanitarian aid and relief operations, and sanctions against the belligerents.

The military supply and arms embargo was put into effect on 25 September 1991 and applied to the whole of the former Yugoslavia. Its purpose was to prevent further proliferation of weapons throughout the former Yugoslavia. Subsequent to its passage, members of the Islamic Conference Organization have favored supplying arms to Bosnian Muslims, Russia has mentioned lifting the embargo to Serbia, and the United States has discussed lifting the embargo on Bosnia. For their part, the then chief UN and European Community negotiators, Cyrus Vance and Lord Owen, opposed lifting the arms embargo.[41] The arms embargo will remain an issue of contention among players external to the crisis as long as there is conflict in Bosnia-Herzegovina.

Eight thousand UNPROFOR I peacekeeping forces were deployed to Croatia in March 1992 in response to the Vance Plan that called for peacekeepers in UN protection areas to protect Serb and Croat minorities living in Croatia. An additional 15,000 UN forces were approved in September 1992 under UNPROFOR II to protect aid convoys in support of the UN high commissioner for refugees, to provide preventative peacekeeping forces in Macedonia, and to monitor the ban on flights from airfields in Serbia, Croatia, Montenegro, and Bosnia. The UN force headquarters was situated in Sarajevo, 400 kilometers in front of the peacekeepers, where it had no mandate. When the Bosnian government failed and the Serbs withdrew to Pale, the Sarajevans expected UNPROFOR to protect them from Serb attacks, which it could not do.[42] As a result, the UN found itself unpopular in the very city that it was trying the most to help because it could not bring in adequate supplies to offset the need, was preventing Sarajevans from leaving Sarajevo to limit the number of refugees, and was ineffective in ending the Serb shelling.[43]

Further reducing the UN's effect in Bosnia-Herzegovina has been the lack of resolve of its constituent members. On 30 May 1992, the UN imposed economic sanctions on the Federal Republic of Yugoslavia, yet it was not until 16 November 1992 that it authorized stop and search operations on the Danube and Adriatic. In a similar vein, on 9 October 1992, the Security Council imposed a ban on military flights over Bosnia, except for UNPROFOR flights, but did not provide for enforcement of the resolution until 31 March 1993. While the Serbs did reduce their number of flights in response to the October 1992 ban, they remained at liberty to violate the ban for almost six months. United Nations actions that can be violated at will seem of questionable value and beg the question: Have such UN actions contributed to ending the crisis?

On 15 May 1992, the UN identified the need for humanitarian aid and relief operations to assist Sarajevo. To provide the 270 tons of food needed daily, the UN high commissioner for refugees oversees the transportation of supplies both by land and air assets. In terrain as rugged as Bosnia, however, the stream of supplies can be stopped almost at will by the combatants. In September 1992, an Italian aircraft carrying supplies to Sarajevo was shot down by an unknown force and, in March 1993, Serb forces refused to allow relief convoys to cross into Bosnia. Difficult as these missions are, they are likely the most important actions taken by the UN because they save lives and deflect criticism.

With regard to the sanctions imposed on the Federal Republic of Yugoslavia, criticism has come both from the former Yugoslav prime minister, Milan Panic, who felt that the sanctions unify the Serbs behind Milosevic, and the latter himself, who warned that efforts to stop the fighting in Bosnia are endangered unless the sanctions are lifted. Nevertheless, the sanctions have had an effect.[44] The monthly inflation rate for March 1993 was 225 percent; unemployment is 50 to 70 percent; and the oil embargo has caused four-mile long gasoline lines in Belgrade, although petroleum continues into Serbia from Greece, through

Macedonia, and petroleum and arms arrive from Russia.[45] The United Nations has said that the sanctions will remain in effect until Belgrade recognizes the pre-conflict borders. This stipulation may have been intended to show resolve, but it places the UN in the position of backing off if new borders are accepted under the process started by the Vance-Owen Plan.

The disjointed nature of the international community's response to the Yugoslav crisis is evident in the proliferation of monitoring missions proposed by various organizations. Besides UNPROFOR's presence in Croatia, Bosnia, and Macedonia, there are NATO and WEU ships in the Adriatic, and monitoring missions from the European Community and CSCE in Kosovo, Vojvodina, and Sandjak, as well as six other neighboring countries. For instance, the CSCE has early warning and human rights monitoring missions in Kosovo, Vojvodina, the Sandjak, and Macedonia; the European Community Monitor Mission Yugoslavia (ECMMY) established ceasefire teams along the lines between Serbia-Croatia, and Croatia-Bosnia, and the European Community is working with Albania, Hungary, Bulgaria, Romania, and Greece to put into place early warning teams; the European Community and CSCE are working to establish sanctions assistance missions in Romania, Hungary, Bulgaria, Albania, Macedonia, and Ukraine to advise these countries on how to tighten sanction controls; and UNPROFOR has established teams to monitor the flight ban at some airfields in Serbia, Montenegro, Croatia, and Bosnia-Herzegovina, as well as placing an early warning team in Macedonia.[46]

Among the monitoring missions, forces subordinate to UNPROFOR communicate through UNPROFOR channels, including the NATO forces in the former Yugoslavia and the AWACS over central Eastern Europe and the Adriatic. The NATO and WEU flotillas have established an informal ad hoc communication channel to forward information to UNPROFOR. The other missions appear not to fall under an UNPROFOR central reporting system and are communicating through their parent organizations, which reduces or eliminates the UN decision-makers' ability to sort out conflicting reports or capture the information from all of the reporting agencies into one coherent picture.

One final area of interest is the international community's consideration of solving the crisis by force. Peacekeeping forces in the former Yugoslavia can only use force for self-defense. The problem is that "peacekeepers cannot keep a peace that no one else wants."[47] Given the inability so far to prevent the Serbs, Croats, and Bosnian Muslims from killing each other with the superb peacekeeping forces in place, military intervention would seem the most likely military mechanism should a solution by force be attempted.

Because the fighting is at the village level, with neighbor fighting neighbor, fighters mixed with civilians, and atrocities by extremists having turned neighbors into implacable opponents, peace attained by intervention appears doubtful. According to British Foreign Secretary Douglas Hurd, "I don't think you can impose peace by military force." There is no front line, rather many pockets of fighting. To stop the fighting would require forces scattered throughout the entire country to separate the warring factions and to negotiate with local commanders, some of whom lack control over their own forces. From the perspective of introducing thousands of American troops into the argument, former Secretary of State Eagleburger responded "I'd rather watch than do that."

Even the selective use of armed force most likely would not end the conflict. Enforcement of the no-fly zone will ground Serbian aircraft, but will do little to end the fighting since most Serb combat aircraft have already ceased their missions. Moreover, an enforcement provision serves to support the Serb contention that the international community is aligned with Serbia's opponents, which may strengthen Milosevic's position with his Serb followers instead of weakening it. Further, use of air attacks against Serbian artillery positions may prove ineffective as well. According to one expert, "air power is least effective in a civil war."[48] General Colin Powell, former chairman of the United States joint chiefs of staff, has identified several problems: it would be difficult to locate and destroy all Serb artillery; it might indicate that Washington was taking sides; and it might result in a response against the UN relief effort by warring parties.

While frustration at finding a solution to the problem has led to consideration of the use of force, there is little hope that force would gain anything other than deeper involvement by members of the international community and greater loss of life. The best solution is one attained through negotiations where all parties agree to the solution. Solutions imposed by force run the risk of bringing new problems and new conflicts.

In the end, the international community's responses have been hampered by a lack of consensus among the individual states and a focus on symptoms by organizations. These have been compounded by holes in the arms embargo and sanctions, a perception of UN ineffectiveness, and redundant monitoring missions lacking central control. These efforts have been, to a degree, disjointed and ineffective. While the humanitarian relief efforts are worthwhile and helpful, none of the efforts will solve the crisis because they do not address the central issues, i.e., minorities, territorial acquisition, and loss of central control.

Focus on the Central Issues

Given the complexity of the situation in former Yugoslavia, there is little surprise that finding a solution has been difficult. The combined UN-EC approach taken by the Vance-Owen team, however, pointed in the right direction. As early as December 1992, Cyrus Vance and Lord Owen identified the need to find peace through a negotiated settlement and outlined several steps to be pursued in order to arrive at a settlement: negotiate a permanent ceasefire; do not enforce the UN flight ban because of reprisals against relief operations; do not lift the arms ban against the Bosnian Muslims; and discuss a territorial settlement.[49]

The subsequent Vance-Owen Plan of January 1993 consisted of three elements: military accords for a ceasefire, removal of heavy weapons, and lifting of the siege of Sarajevo; constitutional principles that set up a decentralized governmental structure with a nine-member presidency, consisting of three members from each ethnic group, and ten provinces within which most governmental functions would rest; and a redrawn map of Bosnia-Herzegovina.

In May 1993, Croatia, Bosnia-Herzegovina, and the Bosnian Serb president, Radovan Karadzic, agreed to the Vance-Owen Plan.[50] Their acceptance was short-lived, however. Negotiations and fighting continued throughout the summer of 1993. By the fall, discussions had moved away from the Vance-Owen proposal for ten provinces toward the tripartite division preferred by the Serbs. But plans that provide for an immediate ceasefire, a negotiated settlement followed by mechanisms to address minority rights, install a government and resolve the Bosnia-Herzegovina territorial dispute, while uncertain, nevertheless address the central issues of the conflict.

It has been estimated that it will take 50,000 troops to enforce a settlement and there is a risk that if a plan is accepted and ends the present fighting, it will eventually fail, trapping peacekeeping forces in the midst of a renewed conflict. These are risks that the international community needs to recognize and accept. Intervention against Serbia could take between 300,000 and 500,000 troops, result in a prolonged conflict, and risk Russian intervention.[51]

Further complicating the use of troops, whether for peacekeeping or intervention, is the fact that Europe is unwilling to deploy the substantial forces needed unless there is American participation. But according to Senator William S. Cohen, a large United States presence in peacekeeping is unlikely unless Germany participates in the process at the "foxhole" level. Such a suggestion usually brings the debate to a full stop.

But there is a need for Washington to assert itself in support of a negotiated settlement. The Clinton administration must let the Bosnian Muslims know that they should hope for no unilateral United States military help and that they will have to continue to support a negotiated settlement; to influence members of the Islamic community, particularly Turkey, Iran, and Saudi Arabia, not to violate the arms embargoes or to intervene; to seek Russian assistance in pressuring the Serbs not only to accept the plan, but also to comply with it, and to understand that spreading the conflict to Kosovo might well bring to an end the West's noninterventionist policy; to seek German pressure on Croatia to remain behind the plan; and to pressure Germany to promote actively troop commitments in support of peacekeeping efforts. Without firm United States support, the peace process will unravel.

Spillover Control

A final area of attention for the international community is the containment of the conflict within its current borders. As costly as has been the fighting to date, it will be far more costly should it spill over into Kosovo. Kosovo is not just another piece of land; it is sacred to the Serbs. It is where they lost their empire to the Ottomans and, in their minds, the battle of Kosovo has never been finished.[52]

The risk of conflict in Kosovo has progressively increased since 1989. Milosevic placed Kosovo directly under Serbian control abolishing the autonomy it enjoyed under Tito, an estimated 100,000 Kosovars have lost their jobs, and the Serbs have closed schools taught in the Albanian language. Serbian oppression continued throughout 1992: in September, the Serbs removed art treasures from the monasteries in Kosovo; in October Serbian police clashed with Kosovar demonstrators in Pristina; in November Serbs armed Serbian civilians; and, in December Serbian police fired into a crowd of Kosovars, killing at least one.[53]

There are an estimated two million Albanians living in Kosovo. Should the conflict expand, they have a natural tie to the Muslims in Albania, as well as the 400,000 Albanian Muslims living in the western portion of the former Yugoslav Republic of Macedonia. The refugees would certainly spread to those areas and there is a high probability that the conflict would follow. The Turkish prime minister, Suleiman Demirel, has publicly offered military support to Albania in the event spillover occurs as a result of conflict with Serbia.[54] This would align Turkey, Albania, Bulgaria, and Macedonia, backed by the Islamic Conference Organization on one side, and Serbia, Greece, and Romania, backed by Russia, on another side.

Actions taken to avoid a spillover include European Community monitoring teams in Kosovo and a UN Nordic battalion in the Former

Yugoslav Republic of Macedonia to police crossing points with Kosovo. Both the United States and Great Britain have warned that military force may be used against the Serbs, should the fighting spread to Kosovo.[55] Perhaps, though, the greatest contribution to peace in Kosovo has been the peaceful opposition offered by the Kosovars. Although the environment for conflict exists, the catalyst for conflict has been kept in check. The question is how much longer will the Kosovars restrain themselves. As they witness other groups in the former Yugoslavia gain freedom or autonomy, they can be expected to reach a point where their demands will take a more forceful approach.

Future Prospects

The range of imaginable options for addressing the current crisis extends from doing nothing on one hand, to intervening militarily, disarming the combatants, and establishing a government of occupation on the other hand. Since the international community has already been involved for two years, it would be difficult to extricate itself and do nothing. With regard to conquering and governing portions of the former Yugoslavia, as has been stated earlier, Western states have been unwilling to support the use of military force for intervention and it is doubtful that Western populations will support a prolonged presence of forces in the region. Where does the West go from here?

History shows us that minority rights and territorial ambitions have been frustrated for centuries. To expect, after two years of bitter fighting, a resolution that will roll back the territorial gains to the prewar borders and return refugees to villages where their families have been killed is unrealistic. The fighting will stop completely only when the combatants exhaust themselves or the Serbs, Croats, and Bosnian Muslims consolidate what they perceive are acceptable objectives. At that point, the international community must have in place a plan that will address the situation's central issues in order to prevent a recurrence of combat later.

Near Term

The first requirement is to retain the concentration on a political solution and not seek a military one. Officials such as Douglas Hurd, Colin Powell, and Lawrence Eagleburger have argued against seeking a solution via military means. Is the conflict in Bosnia-Herzegovina limited from the perspective of Serbs and Bosnian Muslims? Of course not. Then, should the West expect to solve the conflict with a limited application of force, such as enforcement of no-fly zones, bombing Serbian artillery positions, or attacking Serb airfields? No. The destruction of a few Serb transport aircraft will have little or no political or military impact and attacks on Serb artillery may prove embarrassingly ineffective, while attacks on airfields in Serbia could well steel the Serb will. Can the West expect its population to support a long-term major concentration of force in Bosnia-Herzegovina with the attendant casualties? Doubtful. The Western states' expectations for conflict, short of a threat to their national survival, run more along the lines of rapid solutions with few casualties as experienced in the Gulf War, not prolonged conflicts with the potential for mounting casualty rates. The use of external force in a civil war is not the answer for peacemaking, but it will have a role in peacekeeping once a peace is achieved.

Peacekeeping forces under the UN should remain in Croatia to separate the Croats and Serbs, and they should also continue to support humanitarian relief operations in Bosnia-Herzegovina. As frustrating as these missions have been, they keep peacekeeping experts on the ground who will be ready to provide guidance when the time arrives for the use of peacekeepers in Bosnia-Herzegovina. The history of peacekeeping operations shows that peacekeeping will not work until there is both peace and the belligerent forces' acceptance of peacekeepers. When the fighting ends in the former Yugoslavia and the combatants agree to accept peacekeepers, then the peacekeeping force can be expanded to include members from other nations, including the United States.

The international community should continue to push hard to plug the leaks in the economic sanctions against Serbia, because they are having an immediate impact on the Serbs' daily life. The passage of UNSCR 820 that stiffened sanction enforcement against Serbia and Montenegro was a significant move in the right direction. While the Serbs are not the only guilty party in the conflict, they are the most important party and must agree to a settlement. Sanctions are a means to influence the Serbian people to bring pressure on Serb leaders to end the conflict. At the same time, the arms embargo against all parties to the conflict, not just the Serbs, should be kept in force. The solution to the problem is not more means of destruction, but a political settlement.

Humanitarian relief operations must be continued. They are visible demonstrations of the West's will to help the Bosnians and they save lives. Relief operations could well be the greatest loser should a military solution be pursued that results in reprisals against the humanitarian aid organizations.

Spillover control will remain vitally important for an indefinite period of time. International observer missions and UN forces should be maintained in Kosovo, the Sandjak, and the Vojvodina to limit sanction and embargo violations and to deter spillover of the conflict. Along the same line, the sanctions-assistance missions in neighboring states should be continued to keep an international presence in areas external to the former Yugoslavia where spillover might occur, especially in Albania and Macedonia. Because of the extremely serious threat to peace in the event that spillover were to involve Russia, Greece, Turkey, or other members of the Islamic community, the international community should follow the lead of the United States and Great Britain and be prepared to use force against any member of the former Yugoslavia that spreads the conflict outside its current boundaries.

As the international community continues these efforts, its operations need to be unified under one command and control headquarters. With elements of UN, NATO, and WEU forces, as well as CSCE and European Community monitoring missions in the area reporting through different channels, there is a need for an overarching headquarters to receive these reports. While the interaction of these organizations can be very helpful, coordination among them is essential if there is to be a common will or unity of purpose. The UN has demonstrated noticeable shortfalls in its handling of the crisis so far, but with its experience in conflict resolution it should nonetheless take the lead and be the umbrella organization under which these other organizations operate. Until there is central control, there will be no clear picture of what is happening, which will negate any hope of developing unity of purpose, political will, and guidance for future operations.

In a similar vein, when planning for the use of military forces the best approach is to lead with the longest and strongest suit. That means NATO, with firm United States support, should take the lead in whatever military planning and execution the UN secretary general requests. NATO has the planning and operational experience, and the United States can provide the strategic lift, communications, intelligence, and logistical support required. No other organization can match these credentials.

Finally, the major world players need to work together. The Western states need to continue pressure on the Bosnian Muslims and Croats to abide by the negotiated solution. Likewise, Russia has to pressure the Serbs to accept the negotiated settlement and not to spread the conflict to Kosovo. The Islamic states need to be encouraged not to provide assistance to the Muslims in violation of UN sanctions and embargoes. And, Greece, Romania, and Ukraine need to be pressured to plug the holes in the sanctions and embargoes.

Long Term

While near-term efforts are extremely important in working toward a ceasefire and negotiated settlement, we should not count on them achieving lasting effects. In the long term, economic sanctions against Milosevic may prove as ineffective as sanctions have proved against Saddam Hussein. Embargoes on military related equipment may impede a nation's war-making abilities, but may not have much impact on the daily lives of the citizens. Peacekeeping forces between combatants who do not desire peace risk loss of life for very little gain. Experience in Cyprus tells us that the democratic states, upon whom responsibility to separate combatants will fall, are generous and patient, but unwilling to remain forever.

To obtain a solution to the current crisis that will reduce the likelihood that another conflict will occur again, a negotiated settlement must be attained that will resolve the dispute at the village level. The ongoing negotiations are a step in the right direction. The ultimate goal must be a Bosnia-Herzegovina that provides security for the people of all major ethnic groups. This means that Bosnia-Herzegovina will be divided, that population relocations will occur, and that each of the three sides will have to make territorial concessions. Serbia cannot expect to create a Greater Serbia with fingers of land extending into Croatia and most of Bosnia under Serbian control. Bosnian Serbs will have to relinquish some of the territory they currently hold. The Bosnian Muslims will have to yield some of former Bosnia to control by the Serbs and Croats. Likewise, Serbs living in Croatian held lands will have to be integrated into the political process and granted autonomy within their region. Monitoring teams, operating under one headquarters, will be required to ensure that minority rights are protected.

Unless areas are provided where ethnic groups feel that they can reside in relative safety and exercise political power, conflict will continue, lives will be lost, refugees not only will not return to their homeland, but will also increasingly flee and burden neighboring states. The international community will continue to anguish over what should be done and an indefinite international force presence will risk increased loss of lives by the peacekeeping countries.

Even with provinces established that provide safety for the ethnic groups, a government consisting only of representatives from the three ethnic groups most likely will not work. Bosnia-Herzegovina has had peace only during periods of outside rule, e.g., 500 years of Ottoman rule, four decades of Habsburg rule (1878-1914), the Royal Dictatorship (1918-1941), and Tito's Yugoslavia (1945-1991). Between 1941 and 1945, and since 1992 savagery has reigned throughout Bosnia-Herzegovina. Until the ethnic groups learn to work together, the governmental structure with the best chance of maintaining order will be one that places most governmental functions at the province level and installs over the provinces a provisional government consisting of representatives of the three ethnic groups and international advisers, perhaps from the CSCE or European Community. As confidence grows among the ethnic groups, the provisional government can phase out the international advisers and develop into a national government.

Lastly, once the conflict ends all parties will need time to recover from the shock, reestablish ties with the outside world, and with the other former republics of Yugoslavia, make repentance, and try war criminals. During this process, an international presence will be needed. Monitoring teams from the regional organizations and UN peacekeeping forces will be needed to keep the peace. This will not be attainable, however, until the combating groups in Bosnia-Herzegovina exhaust themselves, agree to the process, and willingly accept the monitoring teams and peacekeeping forces. In the final analysis, we cannot ask the warring ethnic groups to forget the past, but they will have to ignore it if they want a future that is not simply the past happening over again.

Notes

The views expressed in this chapter are those of the author and do not reflect the official policy or position of the Department of the Army, Department of Defense, or the US Government.

1. Samuel Dumas and K.O. Vedel-Petersen, *Losses of Life Caused by War* (Oxford: Clarendon Press, 1923), p. 59; although many figures have been published for Serb and Montenegrin losses in WWI, data for Croatian losses are less exact because they participated as part of the Austro-Hungarian army. The figures listed here are for order-of-magnitude purposes only, not exact counts of battle or battle-related deaths. They have been estimated from data in B. Urlanis, *Wars and Population* (Moscow: Progress Publishers, 1971), p. 64: Col. H.L. Gilchrist, *A Comparative Study of World War Casualties* (Washington: United States Government Printing Office, 1928), p. 7; Stanko Guldescu, "Croatian Political History, 1525-1918," in *Croatia: Land, People, and Culture*, ed. Francis H. Eterovich (Toronto: University of Toronto Press, 1970), p. 70; Gil Elliot, *Twentieth Century Book of the Dead* (Great Britain: Hazell Watson & Viney, 1972), p. 83; John Zametica, "The Yugoslav Conflict," *Adelphi Papers* 270 (London: IISS, 1992), p. 8; R.J. Rummel, *Power Kills: Absolute Power Kills Absolutely* (Hawaii: Haiku Institute of Peace Research, 20 October 1991), p. 4. In democide, Rummel includes genocide, politicide, and mass murder; see p. 1.

2. For data on dead and missing see: Lee Michael Katz, "U.N. Tries Warplane Diplomacy," *USA Today*, 12 April 1993, p. 9A. Data on refugees were offered by Robert Gates, former CIA Director; see Anthony Lewis, "Pressure on Serbia," *New York Times*, 18 December 1992, p. A39. Reasons why the casualties may be as high as they are rest in the revenge sought by Croats, Serbs, and Bosnian Muslims, intermingled at the village level, against real or perceived perpetrators of atrocities against family members or friends, as well as the purge of the Yugoslav Peoples' Army of non-Serb commanders in June 1991, which placed

undisciplined irregulars and reservists in command positions who either lacked the training or the will to control their forces.

3. James Gow, "Deconstructing Yugoslavia," *Survival* 33 (July/August): 293.

4. Peter F. Sugar and Donald W. Treadgold, eds., *A History of East Central Europe*, 11 vols. (Seattle: University of Washington Press, 1977), vol. 8: *The Establishment of the Balkan National States, 1804-1920*, by Charles and Barbara Jelavich, pp. 251-55.

5. The Military Frontier, known as the Military District (Vojna Krajina), was a defensive zone created by the Habsburg emperor in the sixteenth century around the borders of Bosnia and Turkish-occupied Serbia, eventually ranging from Dalmatia to Transylvania. It was created to stop the northern expansion of the Ottoman Empire and was heavily populated by Serbs who migrated from what is today southern Serbia and Kosovo. The emperor granted the land to soldier-peasants, who were free from feudal obligations in return for military service. The portion called the Krajina in today's press represents the crescent of land running along eastern Dalmatia through southern Croatia along the Bosnian border; see Ivo Banac, *The National Question in Yugoslavia: Origins, History, Politics* (Ithaca, NY: Cornell University Press, 1984), p. 44.

6. According to Ivo Banac, old eastern Stokavian was spoken in the Vojvodina, eastern Bosnia, eastern Herzegovina, Montenegro, and most areas of Serbia. Ibid., p. 47. Serb migrations carried Stokavian-speaking Serbs into portions of Croatia and Bosnia-Herzegovina adding to differences between the nationalities.

7. The extent of Serbian pre-Ottoman expansion and the Serbs' sense of possession of the lands in and adjoining southern Serbia are captured by the 1346 crowning of Stephen Dusan as Tsar of the Serbs and Greeks in the Serbian capital located in Skopje, the current capital of the Former Yugoslav Republic of Macedonia.

8. One of the keys to understanding partially the cause of the current conflict and the violent nature of the warfare rests in understanding the impact of the population's redistribution. By the twelfth century, Serbs had settled in two areas, Zeta (corresponding roughly to Montenegro), and Rashka, which included the land northwest of the River Morava, including Serbia, Kosovo-Metohija (Kosmet), and the Sandjak. The Serbs refer to the Kosmet and Sandjak areas as Old Serbia.

9. Jelavich and Jelavich, *Establishment of the Balkan National States*, p. 63.

10. Archduke Franz-Ferdinand and his wife were assassinated by Gavrilo Princip on 28 June 1914, the anniversary of the Battle of Kosovo and St. Vitus day, the day of Serbia's patron saint. Princip was one of six Bosnian conspirators whose goal was to eliminate the archduke as a perceived obstacle to uniting Bosnia-Herzegovina with Serbia. They were assisted with weapons and munitions by Colonel Dimitrijevic of the Serbian Army.

11. Michael G. Roskin, "The Bosnian-Serb Problem: What We Should and Should Not Do," *Parameters* 22 (Winter 1992-93): 24.

12. Gow, "Deconstructing Yugoslavia," p. 292.

13. Ibid.

14. George and Patricia V. Klein, "Nationalism vs. Ideology: The Pivot of Yugoslav Politics," in *The Politics of Ethnicity in Eastern Europe*, ed. George Klein and Milan J. Reban (New York: Columbia University Press, 1981), p. 247.

15. The Communist Party of Yugoslavia was renamed the League of Communists of Yugoslavia (LCY) at the 1952 Sixth Party Congress to reflect the Party's role change under self-government from the ruling party to the leading role of the Party. See Zagorka Golubovic, "Yugoslav Society and Socialism: The Present-Day Crisis of the Yugoslav System and the Possibilities for Evolution," in *Crisis and Reform in Eastern Europe*, ed. Ferenc Feher and Andrew Arato (New Brunswick, NJ: Transaction, 1991), p. 398.

16. Ivo Banac, "The Fearful Asymmetry of War: The Causes and Consequences of Yugoslavia's Demise," *Daedalus* 121 (Spring 1992): 145.

17. See Timothy L. Thomas, "Ethnic Conflict: Scourge of the 1990s?" *Military Review* (December 1992): 21-24.

18. The Serbs most likely refused to seat Stipe Mesic as the chairman of the presidency because the government controlled the ministry of defense, but the presidency controlled the general staff and the Serbs were concerned over Mesic's control over Serbian commanders. See "Yugoslavia Tells Army to Back Off," *New York Times*, 1 July 1991, p. C1.

19. Slovenia, Croatia, and Bosnia-Herzegovina have received international recognition. Because of Greek pressure against recognizing a state with the same name as its northern province, Macedonia did not receive wide recognition immediately after it declared independence. It was not admitted into the UN until April 1993, and then only under the name of the Former Yugoslav Republic of Macedonia. Prior to that, Macedonia was recognized only by a few states, including Turkey, Bulgaria, Albania, and Russia. Rump Yugoslavia has not been recognized and, in fact, lost its seat in the UN on 22 September 1992.

20. For instance, of the 10 percent minorities in Slovenia, only 2 percent are Serbs and 3 percent Croats, and Slovenes speak a western Slavic language not readily intelligible to most Serbs and Croats. See Gow, "Deconstructing Yugoslavia," p. 293; and Jelavich and Jelavich, *Establishment of the Balkan National States*, p. 236.

21. "Yugoslavia Tells Army to Back Off."

22. While Macedonia is not homogeneous, it has a relatively small Serb population and a large (anti-Serb) Albanian population: 67 percent Macedonian, 20 percent Albanians, 2 percent Serbs, 11 percent others. See Gow, "Deconstructing Yugoslavia," p. 293.

23. WEU, "Document 1293: European Union and Developments in Central and Eastern Europe," *Proceedings of the Assembly of the WEU, 37th Session*, 27 November 1991, p. 334.

24. Greg Englefield, "Yugoslavia, Croatia, Slovenia: Re-emerging Boundaries," *Territory Briefing*, no. 3 (Durham, UK: International Boundaries Research Unit Press, 1992) p. 14.

25. Misha Glenny, "Yugoslavia: The Revenger's Tragedy," *New York Review of Books*, 13 August 1992, p. 41.

26. Between 1941 and 1945, Jasenovac was the pro-Nazi death camp run by

the Ustasha where hundreds of thousands of Serbs, Jews, and Gypsies were exterminated.

27. Since the fighting began in Bosnia in the spring of 1992, the Serbs have cut a corridor along northern Bosnia from Serbia to the Krajina. It runs east to west generally along a line from Bijeljina, through Brcko, Bosanski Brod, Derventa, Banja Luka, Omarska, Kozarac, Bosanski Novi into Croatia to Pletvice, and then south to Knin. It is doubtful that the Serbs will forfeit this corridor because it is the lifeline between Serbia and the Serb minority living in Croatian Krajina.

28. Chuck Sudetic, "U.N. Expulsion of Yugoslavia Breeds Defiance and Finger-Pointing," *New York Times*, 24 September 1992, p. A14.

29. Lewis MacKenzie, "Perils of U.N. Military Action in Balkans," *Toronto Star*, 6 February 1993, p. B1.

30. Sudetic, "U.N. Expulsion of Yugoslavia Breeds Defiance and Finger-Pointing," p. A14. The importance of Bosnia-Herzegovina to Croatia has its roots in history: "Croatians consider that the twin provinces of Bosnia and Hercegovina are old Croat lands." Stanko Guldescu, *History of Medieval Croatia* (The Hague: Mouton and Co., 1964), p. 242.

31. "Serbs Continue Offensive," *New York Times*, 9 October 1992, p. A10.

32. George Rodrique, "Sources: Croats Fighting Muslims," *Philadelphia Inquirer*, 24 October 1992, p. A4.

33. For example, see: WEU, "Document 1293," pp. 329-58; "London Conference Documents" (text of statements approved 26-27 August 1992, at the London Conference on Yugoslavia), *US Department of State Dispatch Supplement*, vol. 3 (September 1992), pp. 3-6; and "UN Security Council Resolutions on the Former Yugoslavia," ibid. (16 November 1992), pp. 833-34.

34. For an elaboration, see the chapter by Joachim Rabe, this volume.

35. "How Many Little Wars Make a Big One?" *Economist*, 30 January 1993, p. 46; Steven Erlanger, "A Yeltsin Setback on Bosnia," *International Herald Tribune*, 19 February 1993, p. 2.

36. Theresa Hitchens, "Role in Yugoslavian War Sidetracks CSCE Summit," *Defense News*, 13-19 July 1992, p. 6.

37. WEU, "Document 1293," p. 335.

38. Theresa Hitchens, "Yugoslavia Dispute Disrupts CSCE Summit," *Defense News*, 13-19 July 1992, p. 1.

39. Paul Lewis, "U.N. Will Add NATO Troops to Bosnia Force," *New York Times*, 11 September 1992, p. A1.

40. Theresa Hitchens, "NATO Questions Role in Yugoslavia," *Defense News*, 29 June-5 July 1992, p. 38.

41. Frank J. Prial, "U.N. Tightens Curbs on Belgrade by Authorizing a Naval Blockade," *New York Times*, 17 November 1992, p. A3; Elaine Sciolino, "U.S. Names Figures to be Prosecuted over War Crimes," ibid., 17 December 1992, p. A1.

42. Address by Major General Lewis MacKenzie, 5 February 1993, Queen's University, Kingston, Ontario.

43. John F. Burns, "At the Bottom of Desperation, Sarajevans Join Refugee Line," *New York Times*, 28 October 1992, p. A8.

44. Sanctions include oil, gasoline, coal, iron, steel, rubber, chemicals, tires, aircraft, and motors. See Eric Schmitt, "A Naval Blockade of Belgrade Seen Within a Few Days," *New York Times*, 18 November 1992, p. A14.

45. Joseph Fitchett, "Russia's Pro-Serb Line is Growing Factor in Balkan Conflict," *International Herald Tribune*, 2 February 1993, p. 2.

46. See "London Conference Documents," p. 4; David Shorr, "CSCE Tries Preventive Diplomacy in Several Hot Spots," *Basic Reports*, no. 26 (Washington: British American Security Information Council, 9 November 1992), p. 1; idem, "Monitor Missions for Yugoslavia Slow to Be Sent," *Basic Reports*, no. 25 (Washington, DC: British American Security Information Council, 21 September 1992). p. 1; and UNSC Resolutions 795 and 786.

47. Desmond Morton, "Peace-Keeping, Peace-Making, War-Making: Making a Distinction," *National Network News*, 17 (15 October 1992): 3.

48. "Air Power Alone Is Powerless in this War," *Los Angeles Times*, 2 September 1992, p. 11.

49. David Binder, "Vance Asks Bush for More Time for Bosnia Talks," *New York Times*, 19 December 1992, p. 6. Subsequently, Vance and Owen agreed to enforcing the no-fly zone against Serbian aircraft. While UNSCR 816 calls for using "all necessary measures in the airspace of the Republic of Bosnia and Herzegovina, in event of further violations," it stops short of calling for attacks against ground targets and targets in Serbia.

50. Under the plan, the Serbs with 33 percent of the population receive about 43 percent of the territory, down from approximately 70 percent that they control now. The remainder of the territory most likely would have been divided equally between the Croats at 18 percent of the population and the Bosnian Muslims at 40 percent of the population. See John Darnton, "Bosnian Serbs Set to Reject Peace Plan," *New York Times*, 26 April 1993, p. A8; and Jonathan C. Randal, "Croats Press Fight in Central Bosnia," *International Herald Tribune*, 4 February 1993, p. 2.

51. Daniel Williams, "U.S.: Bosnian Policy puts American Prestige on the Line," *International Herald Tribune*, 12 February 1993, p. 2; A.M. Rosenthal, "Their Plan Could Bring an Honorable Peace," ibid., 6-7 February 1993, p. 6.

52. Ivo Banac, "Post-Communism as Post-Yugoslavism: The Yugoslav Non-Revolutions of 1989-1990," in *Eastern Europe in Revolution*, ed. Ivo Banac (Ithaca, NY: Cornell University Press, 1992), p. 174.

53. Kitty McKinsey, "There Is Trouble Brewing in the Heart of Serbia," *Whig-Standard* (Kingston), 15 October 1992, p. 25; "Albanians, in Enclave, Battle Serbian Police," *New York Times*, 14 October 1992, p. A10; Elaine Sciolino, "Bush Asks France and Britain to Back Force of Monitors in Kosovo," ibid., 25 November 1992, p. A6; and "Police Fire into Crowd," ibid., 4 December 1992, p. A13.

54. Jason Feer, "Disorder within Serbia Could Elevate War in Region," *Defense News*, 22-28 June 1992, p. 43.

55. David Binder, "Bush Warns Serbs Not to Widen War," *New York Times*,

28 December 1992, p. A6; and "U.K., In Shift, Will Consider Use of Force in Balkans," *International Herald Tribune*, 1 January 1993, p. 1.

4

The Great Game Revisited? The Quest for Influence in Independent Central Asia

Stephen Page

Introduction

The recent acquisition of independence by the former Soviet republics of Central Asia has led some to speculate that the "Great Game" is being resurrected. This is, no doubt, tongue-in-cheek for the most part; there is no longer a Russian or a British Empire to thrust itself into the Afghan mountains, either to expand or defend its frontiers. However, it is generally accepted that Iran and Turkey are engaged in a serious contest for influence over these ancient societies.

This is not a contest for territory or buffer zones, in the old sense of geopolitical competition. It is, however, very much bound up in national security considerations as they are being conceptualized since the end of the Cold War. Although it seems mostly a regional contest, there are global elements to it, as the United States anxiously watches for signs of the spread of its new ideological enemy, Islamic fundamentalism (Iranian-style). Moreover, although the USSR has disintegrated, Russia is still a global player at the nuclear level, and one of the region's new states, Kazakhstan, possesses nuclear weapons.

If indeed there is a version of the Great Game being played, what are the stakes? First, and potentially most important, at the global and regional level, there is the question of who will control the nuclear weapons of Kazakhstan. Second, at the same levels but in a higher realm of speculation, is the question of the impetus given to anti-Western Islamic fundamentalism by Iranian advances in the region, not to mention the question of the significance of such. Third, of concern at the regional and extraregional levels, violent conflicts such as the

Azerbaidzhan-Armenia war or the festering civil war in Tadzhikistan could suck in other players (Russia, Turkey, Iran, other Central Asian states) and destabilize the whole region and beyond.

Fourth, at the local level, but spilling over to the regional and extra-regional, are issues of political and societal security. The new states of Central Asia are all experiencing rapid and discomfiting change. They harbor the grievances of decades, if not centuries: borders that were drawn by a conqueror, more to divide and rule than to reflect the intricacies of ethnic distribution; the imposition of language and anti-religious rules that ignored the customs of centuries-old civilizations; and a modernization process that involved the imposition of new economic and political structures with large-scale in-migration of the conquerors, and the oppression of the indigenous peoples by both outsiders and new indigenous elites. The cross-border linkages, both within the region and between the region and its neighbors, ensure that if these grievances break out in violence, they cannot but have a broader impact.

Fifth, again at local, regional, and extraregional levels, are questions of economic security. The new states require massive amounts of economic assistance in every conceivable form in order to have a chance at prosperity. For their neighbors and others, delivery of assistance is not only essential to reduce the chances of instability in the region, it also provides access to raw material resources and opportunities for lucrative trade and contracts that will enhance their own economic well-being.

Finally, at a more abstract level, the whole region is an ecological disaster area. Much of it is contained within the region, and is not likely seriously to affect neighbors (except thinly populated regions of Russia). The security question raised is unlikely to be perceived as urgent by outside states, and regrettably is unlikely to be addressed in the short- to medium-term future.

Characteristics of the Region

The "region" here, "Central Asia," is a large and highly diverse area. For this chapter it will include not only Uzbekistan, Kyrgyzstan, Tadzhikistan, Turkmenistan, and Kazakhstan, but also Azerbaidzhan. Other than their conquest by the Russian Empire and subsequently by the Bolsheviks, the only characteristic they have in common is that they are inhabited mainly by Muslims. However, this is no more a unifying factor than elsewhere; the Uzbeks, the Kyrgyz, the Turkmens, the Tadzhiks, and the Kazakhs are Sunni, while the Azeris are Shi'a. In their indigenous languages and cultures they have slightly more in common; the Uzbeks, Kyrgyz, Turkmens, Kazakhs, and Azeris speak Turkic dialects, while the Tadzhiks speak a Persian dialect. While these facts indicate two indigenous groupings with affinities toward Turkey or Iran, in fact the Bolsheviks in the 1920s divided them into "national" (and in some cases artificial) ethnic groups, each with its own republic, with the trappings and the facade of sovereignty.

The creation of republics changed the landscape in a number of ways. With a titular nationality, a culture (and in some cases a language) could be created that set the major groups apart.[1] Although visible ethnic nationalism was suppressed, titular elites were allowed to grow, and to develop interests that they then had to protect against other national groups and republics. Age-old economic systems, like irrigation networks, became the subject of interrepublic bargaining, in which each had every incentive to maximize its take. At the same time, a USSR-wide politico-economic system was being formed, in which decisionmaking was centralized in Moscow, and in which to a large extent ethnic elites were forced to negotiate, not with each other but with Moscow for economic resources. The result was that by the time of their independence in 1990 and 1991, the possible affinities between the titular ethnic groups were much weaker than the differences in their interests.

Economically, all of these republics were poorly developed, although they are rich in natural resources. Azerbaidzhan was one of the earliest sources of oil in the USSR, but by the 1980s its fields were largely depleted (by incompetence and outdated technology as well as years of exploitation); oil-related and other industries are also situated there. Turkmenistan is rich in oil and gas; 14 percent of the USSR's natural gas originated there, but was not backed by much industry.[2] Raw cotton was the mainstay of Uzbekistan's economy; virtually all of the crop was shipped to Russia and Ukraine to be processed. Turkmenistan and Kazakhstan also have substantial irrigated agricultural sectors, along the Amu Darya and Syr Darya rivers. The waters of these rivers are now overused, creating a major ecological disaster in the Aral Sea; overuse of chemical fertilizer has created another ecological disaster in these states. Since agricultural production is apparently fairly efficient here, there is little prospect of growth in this sector.[3] Tadzhikistan and Kyrgyzstan are also agricultural economies, with some raw materials; Kyrgyzstan was one of the USSR's major producers of uranium concentrate (from ores mined elsewhere).[4] Kazakhstan has a large agricultural sector, but the mainstay of its economy will likely be the giant Tenghiz oilfield that in 1990 provided 7 percent of the USSR's oil production.[5] It has significant amounts of other raw materials as well, including uranium. Kazakhstan has more and varied industry than the other new states, but could by no means be called industrialized.

Until the late 1980s, all production was directed into the USSR economy; all pipelines ran into Russia. This was never a great advantage, as the raw material and energy products of the region were consistently undervalued. As the USSR disintegrated and then Russia's economy collapsed, there has emerged a double disadvantage: there is a smaller market (and that not for hard currency), but there are few alternatives, since the infrastructure does not exist to ship goods to foreign markets where they would command hard currency. Furthermore, with the collapse of the USSR, the transfer payments from Moscow to the Central Asian republics, which provided as much as 40 percent of their revenues, disappeared. Thus, the new states are desperate for economic assistance, trade agreements, and investment.

Economic weakness seems certain to be their major problem for the coming decade, as they struggle to make the transition to market relationships. However, these problems will inevitably exacerbate other, social, problems, the most serious of which is likely to be hostility between ethnic groups. This has already broken out into outright war between Azeris and Armenians, in a struggle since 1988 over the fate of Nagorno-Karabakh, an Armenian enclave in Azerbaidzhan, and to a lesser extent over Nakhichevan, an Azeri enclave separated from Azerbaidzhan by Armenia. There have also been limited outbursts of ethnic violence in other parts. In June 1990, Kyrgyz and Uzbeks in the Kyrgyz border district of Osh engaged in bloody clashes, with casualty figures said to number in the hundreds before the Soviet armed forces were called in to halt the fighting (with further casualties); by then, Uzbeks from Uzbekistan had crossed the border to help their brethren. The fighting was precipitated by Kyrgyz anger at the economic position of the Osh Uzbeks.[6] Elsewhere, there exists long-standing resentment at the treatment of Tadzhiks in Uzbekistan, at the assignment (in the 1920s) of the ancient Kyrgyz cities of Samarkand and Bukhara to Uzbekistan, and at the Uzbeks' appropriation as their own of various Tadzhik cultural heroes.[7]

In 1992, violence erupted in Tadzhikistan, as the Tadzhik opposition, grouped around Muslim organizations but also around specific clans and tribes, forced the resignation of President Rakhmon Nabiev, the former first secretary of the Tadzhik Communist Party. Fighting raged over several weeks, until the old guard, supported by its clans and tribes as well as forces from the CIS, was restored to power. This fighting illuminated three essential conditions about Central Asia: the extent to which clan, not nation, is the vital unit; the continued hold on power of the old guard (in Kazakhstan, Uzbekistan, Turkmenistan, and Tadzhikistan) communists now in the protective coloring of nationalists; and the growth of Islam as a unifying opposition force—although it is still largely a religious and cultural phenomenon, not a political force, and "fundamentalism" is not yet a factor.

Potentially the most dangerous ethnic situation, but one that has caused surprisingly little trouble in the region thus far, is the presence of substantial numbers of ethnic Russians. Numbering 10 million in total, their weight is felt unevenly in the region; they comprise 38 percent of Kazakhstan's population, and 22 percent of Kyrgyzstan's, but 10 percent or less of the others'.[8] However, they comprise a disproportionately large share of the technological-economic elite, and thus are likely to be increasingly resented (as well as for their past colonialist mentality toward indigenous peoples who are now aggressively reclaiming their lost linguistic and cultural heritage). Their reduced status (now as "foreigners") and dispersion in three of the states is increasing their nervousness about their fate; on the other hand, the concentration of Russians in northern Kazakhstan and northeastern Kyrgyzstan is making the governments of those states nervous about Moscow's reactions to Russian minorities' complaints, whether these are well-based or not. The conditions and feelings of the ethnic Russians play back into Russia's domestic politics.

The External Players: Turkey

Since the beginning of the Cold War, Turkish foreign policy had been based on two principles: pointing Turkey in the direction of Europe while building a secular and pluralist political system; and promoting Turkey as a bridge between Europe and the West on the one hand and the Middle East on the other by joining West European institutions while maintaining nonantagonistic relations with neighbors and avoiding involvement in regional disputes. The end of the Cold War and the collapse of the USSR found Turkish foreign policy at a certain impasse. Its bid to join the European Community was being stonewalled, and showed little chance of being successful. The economy was suffering. Islamic sentiment was on the rise. At the same time, Turkey's participation in NATO, obvious to all since 1950, could be questioned both in Europe and in Turkey. If there was no longer a USSR to be contained from expanding into the Mediterranean and the Middle East, would NATO too begin to view Turkey without enthusiasm? Would NATO, in redefining itself, shift its focus away from its southeastern perimeter? With the old threat gone, would Turkey be better off to court its old enemy Russia and look to new relationships with its eastern neighbors?

Turkey's president, the late Turgut Ozal, sought a partial remedy to the impasse by strong support for the US-led actions against Iraq: first by cutting the Iraqi oil pipeline, and then by allowing US aircraft to fly from Turkish bases. This uncharacteristic partisanship supplemented a strong appeal for the West to remember Turkey's value as a bridge to the

Islamic world. The disintegration of the USSR proved a boon to this message, as new and impoverished entities appeared in regions where the United States had little presence let alone expertise, and where Iran appeared to have an inside track because of its contiguity, anti-communism, and Islamic credentials.

Ankara could make an excellent case for suggesting Turkey as a more attractive partner for these new states in their search for assistance and transition models. Central Asia, in the eyes of many Turks, is their ancestral home. Most Central Asian languages are Turkic dialects. Their populations, while nominally Muslim, are accustomed to a secular state, and are mostly Sunni.[9] Their societies, and particularly their elites, are Westernized, and want to be more so; and their economic elites want training in Western industrial skills. It seemed that if Turkey were provided with the resources, it could lead Central Asia into the Western world.

This was a message that Washington wanted to hear (and one that Secretary of State James Baker delivered vigorously on his trip to the region in February 1992). But it was also a message in tune with new Turkish realities, and it survived the failure of the West to provide much in the way of resources. For some, the invocation of the (mostly mythical) Greater Turkestan[10] and pan-Turkism[11] in general was satisfying to their vision of a greater role for Turkey in the region and the world. Turkish politicians were not immune: Prime Minister Suleiman Demirel, during his Central Asian tour in May 1992, said that Ankara was prepared "to assume political responsibility for the destiny of the region from the Adriatic to the Great Wall of China;" afterwards, he declared: "we saw there is a Turkish world, at least in people's intentions, . . . a commonality that can't be denied;"[12] and Foreign Minister Hikmet Cetin wrote that Turkey has a "special historic responsibility towards the Turkic republics in the trans-Caspian region."[13]

However, even without the rhetoric, it is clear that, particularly if Turkey is not allowed to join the European Community, it would be useful and prestigious to have an economic hinterland and a region of which it feels an organic part. None of its neighbors will give it such a role. Central Asia, however, needs the goods, services, and expertise that the Turks can supply; in return, Turkey would benefit from increased markets for its manufactured goods and labor, and from supplies of Central Asian raw materials, especially oil and gas, which would reduce its dependence on regional rivals for these goods.[14]

Furthermore, the development of Central Asia as a region of secular democratic states with strong connections to the West and to international institutions like the Conference on Security and Cooperation in Europe (CSCE) would enhance Turkey's security. In the long term, it is presumed that such states would overcome their internal difficulties and settle their external problems peacefully. It is further presumed that this would deny the region to forces of Islamic fundamentalists whose target one day would be Turkey.

Ankara has no choice but to operate on these assumptions, but it must be recognized that in the short term the result of Turkish involvement might be to endanger the country's security. The road to stability is bound to be difficult, and the pressure for Turkey to become involved in local disputes is mounting; the continued successes of Armenia against Azerbaidzhan have put the Turkish government in a very difficult situation. Its public is broadly in support of the Azeris, but intervention would arouse the suspicions of both Iran and Russia, and would likely not be viewed with favor in the West. In the rest of Central Asia as well, anything more than diplomatic, economic, or cultural involvement could involve the Turks in local conflicts, and would certainly antagonize Russia or Iran, or both.

Turkey was very quick off the mark in Central Asia. In March 1991 while the republics were just starting to talk about sovereignty, Ozal visited Azerbaidzhan and Kazakhstan. Turkey was the first to recognize Azerbaidzhan's independence, in November 1991, and the independence of the others in December. Almost immediately the presidents of Turkmenistan, Uzbekistan, and Kyrgyzstan visited Ankara.[15]

A debate over language in all the former republics gave the Turks another immediate opening. After the revolution, the Bolsheviks had forced the Central Asians to switch from the Arabic script to the Latin alphabet; in 1934 they forced another shift to Cyrillic.[16] Independence was accompanied by a vociferous demand to revert, and the combination of their Turkic dialects, Turkey's use of the Latin alphabet, its greater utility in rendering their languages, and the desire to open themselves to the West, made the Latin alphabet the choice of all but Tadzhikistan. Azerbaidzhan was the first to decide, and Turkey's parliament sent its old printing plant to Baku; one Istanbul firm finally found a use for a basement-full of old manual typewriters.[17] Ankara also signed agreements with all the new states on providing 10,000 student spaces in Turkish schools and universities, and on creating a few Turkish-type schools in some. Agreements were also quickly negotiated in the telecommunications field. By the end of 1992 Turkish television was broadcasting 24 hours a day into Central Asia, and their telephone systems had been hooked into the Intelsat network. Turkish books and various other publications were being published in the local languages and distributed.

These agreements were important, both for establishing Turkey's immediate positions, and for creating long-term systemic links.

However, the expectations of both sides were fixed on economic ties. Over the first few months, culminating in Demirel's tour in May 1992, agreements were signed with all the states totalling more than $1 billion in credits.[18] This was clearly beyond Turkey's ability to sustain, but Baker's visit to Central Asia and Demirel's visit to Washington in February, along with an American relief program channeled through Turkey (PROVIDE HOPE), provided an apparently clear message of American backing. It seemed that this was what the Central Asian leaders were looking for.

At the same time, Iran sent signals of discomfiture at Turkey's inroads and at the involvement of the United States, which made no secret of its anti-Iran motives. As Iran moved to create a regional economic organization, Turkey acted on Ozal's six-year-old proposal for a Black Sea Economic Cooperation pact (whose membership would encompass a region from the Adriatic to the Caspian and possibly beyond). The centerpiece of the pact is undoubtedly the Turkey-Russia tie, which builds on the surge in Turkey-Soviet economic relations at the end of the 1980s based on Soviet supplies of oil and gas and Turkish manufactured goods and services; 90 percent of this trade was with the Russian Republic. The pact would stimulate investment, trade, and pollution control.[19] By contributing to Russian economic recovery, it would also enhance Turkey's prestige in the larger region and its popularity as a partner in Central Asia, where the legacy of the Soviet centralized economy ensures that the health of Russia's economy will be influential for years and even decades. Bringing the pact to fruition might also provide its members with a way station on their desired road to the European Community.

Ankara also made sure it was involved in the creation of the Economic Cooperation Organization. Based in Teheran, it was intended to be Iran's vehicle for regional development (see below). Turkey's status as a founder nation has allowed it too to claim a leading role in the organization and to prevent Iran from completely dominating it.

The impact of Turkish economic initiatives thus far is difficult to evaluate, because, aside from the highly publicized initial credits and agreements, it has been left to private business to follow up. Private business has been active, especially in Baku, and there seems to be a great deal of declaratory meeting of minds, but as yet little result. This is not surprising. The Central Asian states have a long way to go in creating the legal and societal stability necessary to attract private investment and long-term commercial activities. After that, it will be a long time before it becomes clear that a "Turkish model" has prevailed.

It is not surprising either that, after the initial excitement of the appearance of these new states died down, attention has increasingly focused on the substantial oil and gas reserves of Kazakhstan, Turkmenistan, and Azerbaidzhan. Much of the development and redevelopment of these fields will be put in the hands of Western and Arab oil companies.[20] However, Ankara has taken a great interest in the question of how to get the resources to market. Over the past year it has thrown its diplomatic resources behind Turkish companies that propose to build pipelines by a variety of routes, all of which end at the eastern Mediterranean Turkish port of Iskenderum.[21] The benefits for the Turkish economy are obvious; the difficulties, however, are enormous, and the benefits for the producing countries somewhat questionable. To get to Iskenderum, pipelines would have to cross the Caspian Sea to Baku, and then transit either Armenia or Iran before reaching Turkish territory. (Turkey's only territorial contact with Central Asia is an 11-kilometer frontier with Nakhichevan, which is separated from the rest of Azerbaidzhan by a stretch of Armenia.) On the other hand, a pipeline from Kazakhstan to a Black Sea port would have to pass only through Russian territory, and would have relatively easy access to networks serving Russia, Ukraine (which is searching for a non-Russian source), and eventually Europe. For Turkmen gas, the shortest route to an ocean port is through Iran to the Gulf.

It is doubtless these considerations (but possibly also some resentment at perceived Turkish condescension and paternalism) that led to some "digging in" of heels. Turkmenistan in particular has declared its neutrality in the "model" competition; as a secular but authoritarian president, Separmurad Niiazov has little interest in being tied to either Turkey or Iran, and sees Turkmenistan as being rich enough in resources to stand on its own.[22] Uzbek President Karimov also let it be known that he saw nothing useful in the model of Turkey's multiparty democracy.[23] The others as well, when they gathered in Ankara at the end of October 1992, were prepared to resist Ozal's urgings for closer Turkic economic cooperation under Turkey's leadership.[24]

The exception to this distancing was Azerbaidzhan; in fact, after the October meeting, Baku initialed an agreement with Ankara for the construction of an oil pipeline to Iskenderum, with a short portion in Iran.[25] Part of the reason for this was the strongly pro-Turkish government, under Abulfaz Elchibey; it not only had expectations of Turkish economic and technical assistance, but also hoped that Turkey would involve itself more deeply (diplomatically if not militarily) in the conflict with Armenia. Indeed, Turkey found it difficult to keep its distance; Azerbaidzhan is culturally the closest to Turkey. However, outside the main centers the people are mostly Shi'a, and in the south identify more with their ethnic cousins in Iran. (The ethnic ties prompt Iran to be interested in Azerbaidzhan, both proactively and defensively, lest the independence of Azerbaidzhan give Iranian Azeris ideas. In addition, the ancient enmity between Armenians and Turks provides an opening to Teheran, competing with Turkey in the region.)

Mindful of the consequences of a wider war, destabilizing not only the Caucasus but Turkey's relations with Europe, Russia, and Iran, Turkey for the most part acted as a moderating influence. It attempted, sometimes with Russian help, to arrange a ceasefire. It allowed grain and other Western aid to reach Armenia, thus breaking the Azeri blockade; it did not do this consistently, but tried to use its ability to cut land access to put pressure on Armenia to end the fighting. In addition, Ankara tried to deter Armenia, or force the West to pressure the Armenian government, by threatening active military intervention.[26] These threats became much more serious after Armenian advances began in April 1993, the fall of Elchibey, and Iran's threat of intervention. Turkey began to supply arms, and Ozal, during his Central Asian tour, warned that Turkey might be forced to intervene as it had in Cyprus.[27] He quickly moderated that stance, but as Armenian advances continued, Turkish forces were moved to the border. Turkey's new prime minister, Tansu Ciller, threatened to ask her legislature for a declaration of war against Armenia in September 1993.[28]

Iran

Like Turkey, Iran found that the end of the Cold War and the disintegration of the USSR had left it with new uncertainties and new opportunities. The old, stable (if at times uncomfortable) modus vivendi with Moscow had gone, and with it the threat of attack and the intense ideological hostility. In their place appeared an opportunity to escape the isolation that fundamentalist proselytizing had brought, particularly among its Islamic neighbors. Tadzhikistan was Persian in ancestry and Azerbaidzhan was Shi'ite, and they might be expected to be sympathetic (although there was the danger that Azerbaidzhan's independence might have a greater impact on Iran than the reverse). In the Sunni Central Asian states, Teheran could hope that it was the anti-communism of the Khomeini era broadcasts that would be remembered, not the Shi'ite fundamentalism. It could also hope to benefit by the Persian legacy that pervades all these societies, below the more recent Turkic and most recent Russian influences.[29] Contiguity also seemed certain to favor Iran; both Turkmenistan (with its large energy reserves needing a route to world markets) and Azerbaidzhan share borders with Iran (again, a source also of concern in the case of Azerbaidzhan, in which nationalist elements apparently believe that the Azeri province in Iran should join Azerbaidzhan).

For Iran, then, there was an opportunity to create a hinterland based on religious affinity, or if not that (and that declined in importance with the moderation of the post-Khomeini Islamic Republic), on economic grounds. The Iranian economy was not as well suited as Turkey's to this type of relationship, especially after the devastation of eight years of war with Iraq; Iran's ability to grant even credits is noticeably smaller than Turkey's.[30] Nevertheless, it was assumed by Teheran no less than Ankara that the state that successfully "imprinted" these new states would reap the economic and other rewards of patronage. For Iran, that also meant an opportunity to keep the West, especially the United States, out of the region, now the northern frontier of Iran's "natural" sphere of influence.

It is not clear that political instability in the whole region favors Iran. In Azerbaidzhan, Armenian successes have led to increased popularity for Iran-oriented political organizations, but the resulting unrest might play back into Iran in unacceptable ways; Teheran would probably prefer to see an end to that conflict. Similarly, instability in Sunni Turkmenistan would not necessarily benefit Teheran, and could destabilize the Turkmen areas in Iran. In Tadzhikistan, political instability favors the further growth of the Islamic opposition which is aligned toward Iran; however, any overt Iranian involvement would alarm and alienate the other states, which are economically more important to Iran.

In terms of Iran's military security, the independence of Central Asia reduces whatever tenuous threat from the USSR that existed. It is difficult to see any threat from the region, with the important exception of spillover of civil conflict. In another sense, however, the region has become more significant. It contains reserves of uranium, and nuclear weapons (long-range Soviet missiles in Kazakhstan), and presumably expertise in nuclear weapons technology. It is widely accepted in the West that Iran covets all of these, and there have been reports that it has acquired uranium and nuclear warheads from Kazakhstan, although none of these have been corroborated.[31]

Iran was somewhat slow off the mark before the Central Asian republics declared their independence because of concern about Azeri sentiment and about Moscow's reactions. From mid-August 1991, however, the Iranian government made it clear that the development of economic relations with Azerbaidzhan and Turkmenistan was of primary importance; communications links and energy supplies were a particular focus of attention.[32]

By February 1992, however, Iranian regional policy was paralleling Turkey's. On Iran's initiative, the Regional Cooperation for Development Organization, a long-dormant parallel organization to the Central Treaty Organization which had been meant to create a common market, was resurrected as the Economic Cooperation Organization (ECO), and expanded to include all the Central Asian states except Kazakhstan. The result, it was claimed, was the second-largest common market after the EC, and one that had the potential to be expanded to take in the whole Islamic world.[33]

At the founding meeting, where agreements were signed to cut tariffs, and declarations were made on the importance of developing cooperation in various fields, Turkish-Iranian tension was evident. Ozal, fresh from his success in creating the Black Sea Economic Cooperation group, insisted that all ECO members pledge to create a free-market system; this brought a rejoinder from Iranian President Ali Akhbar Hashemi-Rafsanjani that Turkey was trying to impose an alien system on Islamic states. Rafsanjani also was reported to have said that the participants "came to the conclusion that Central Asia's main outlet to the world market was via Iran."[34] Ozal was apparently also nettled by Rafsanjani's surprise announcement on the eve of the conference that Iran, Azerbaidzhan, Russia, Turkmenistan, and Kazakhstan would form a Caspian Sea organization for cooperation in shipping, fisheries, pollution control, and related issues, with headquarters in Teheran. This, said Ozal, was "superfluous."[35] (Since Iran has signed agreements on oil and gas development and transport with Kazakhstan, Turkmenistan, and Azerbaidzhan, these subjects may also be dealt with in this organization, to which Turkey does not belong.)

At ECO's second summit, in May in Ashgabat, the capital of Turkmenistan, Iran again played a leading role. The main agreement signed was to connect Uzbekistan and Turkmenistan by rail to Iranian Gulf ports. Throughout the summer, Iranian-Turkmen relations seemed to grow stronger. However, the first summit meeting of the Caspian Sea organization, in October, demonstrated that the bloom was off the rose.[36] Azerbaidzhan, Kazakhstan, and Turkmenistan reacted coolly to Iran's draft organizing document, which they felt concentrated only on Iran's interests. In November Kazakh President Nursultan Nazarbaev visited Teheran (straight from the Turkic summit in Ankara, where he voiced his disapproval of the idea of "Greater Turkestan"), but refused to sign a cultural cooperation agreement with Iran because he apparently believed it would further the growth of fundamentalist attitudes in Kazakhstan.[37] He did, however, sign a number of other agreements that would involve Iran in helping to restructure and develop Kazakhstan's economy.

Central Asian leaders were also worried by the end of 1992 about the deteriorating political situation in Tadzhikistan. In September, the old-guard president, Rakhmon Nabiev, was ousted by opposition forces grouped around Islamic organizations. After a brief but vicious bout of fighting, ex-communist forces with the help of the Uzbek military restored one of their own, Imomali Rakhmonov, as head of state. The Iranian government proclaimed its noninvolvement and called for a peaceful settlement; its neighbors were not convinced, but there was no evidence of Iranian (as opposed to Afghan) support for the Tadzhik opposition, and overt Uzbek support for the old guard did not affect a state visit by Karimov to Teheran in November to sign trade and transportation agreements.

The most difficult relationship for Iran, as it is for Turkey, is that with Azerbaidzhan. In the first days of Azeri independence, Iran signed agreements to cooperate in a number of vital areas, including oil exploration, oil refining, supply of oil and gas and its transit to outside markets, communications, and training for Azeri clerical students. Outside the CIS, Iran has become Azerbaidzhan's largest economic partner.[38] It has also undertaken to supply and aid Nakhichevan. However, after the election of Elchibey, Azerbaidzhan leaned strongly toward Turkey. Teheran is thus not only concerned about the effect that Azeri independence might have on "Southern" (i.e., Iranian) Azerbaidzhan, but also about the "balance of influence" in Central Asia. This led it to work very hard at mediating a solution to the Armenian-Azeri war over Nagorno-Karabakh, mediation that has achieved only the occasional evanescent ceasefire. It has also led it to respond on occasion to Armenia's probes for support. This is presumably to confound Turkey, or to register disapproval at Baku's relationship with Ankara, or to demonstrate its desire to maintain good relations with Moscow, which has allowed the sale to Iran of a variety of weapons systems. However, Armenian victories in the spring and summer of 1993 forced Iran to take a much harder line, as Azeri territory was occupied and a wave of refugees moved to the border with Iran. Teheran, obviously concerned about the destabilizing effect of this situation on Iran's Azeri population, moved troops to the area and risked confrontation with both Turkey and Russia by threatening intervention.[39] Two positive results for Iran have been Elchibey's replacement by Gaidar Aliev, who has sought better relations with Teheran, and a much greater Russian interest in improved cooperation with Iran.

Russia

The disintegration of the USSR left Russia with more dilemmas than opportunities in its security environment. At the end of 1991, it was faced with the task of having to formulate "foreign policy" toward entities that it had in large measure controlled for 70 years. The republics had become the *"blizhnee zarubezhe"* (the "near abroad").

In the economic sphere, it appeared there might be some advantage to the loss of the southern republics. For years, Russia had (at least on the surface) been subsidizing them; in 1991 it was the main provider of Soviet subsidies covering over 40 percent of Tadzhikistan's and Uzbekistan's expenditures, over 30 percent of Kyrgyzstan's, and over 20 percent of Kazakhstan's and Turkmenistan's, a total of 23.5 billion rubles.[40] However, the interconnectedness of the Soviet economy,[41] and the distortions generated by a central planning system that was created by and for the benefit of Moscow (i.e., the Russians), make figures like these very suspect. The Central Asian republics (excluding Azerbaidzhan) accounted for the production of 90 percent of the USSR's raw cotton, 25 percent of its copper, 50 percent of its gold, 60 percent of its uranium, 25 percent of its natural gas, and 50 percent of its agricultural produce; together they were the third-largest producers of oil and coal in the USSR.[42] At the same time, these republics were all located at the bottom of tables indicating per capita and absolute economic development in the country.[43] Clearly, the terms of domestic economic exchange did not favor them; the main beneficiary was Russia.

Even now, it is not apparent what the balance was between subsidies and uneven development. In the short term, however, both sides suffered from the breakup of the system. For Russia, uneven development meant that many of its factories relied on Central Asian raw materials that were relatively cheap; independence brought with it demands for hard currency (particularly for goods like energy that had alternative markets), and in some cases competition for supplies. Restructuring of Central Asian economies also disrupted supplies; in the case of cotton, of which 90 percent of production was delivered to textile factories outside Central Asia, disruptions in deliveries have contributed to the latter working at only 25 percent of capacity.[44] The maintenance of the ruble zone has helped to reduce the impact on both sides. However, should Russia's economic chaos continue, and if Central Asia can reorient a significant part of its economy to hard-currency markets and attract foreign investment (no small "if," but possible), they will abandon the ruble. (Turkmenistan, with its marketable raw materials and the planned pipelines, will likely do so.) In this case, Russia's economic security will be put at further risk.

In terms of its security at the strategic military level, Russia is presumably better off. The end of the Cold War enabled Moscow to pursue cooperative relations with its enemies. Despite the grumblings of conservative and military critics that strategic weapons and the strategic threat still exist,[45] Russian President Boris Yeltsin has followed the arms control/arms reduction path of Soviet President Mikhail Gorbachev. Tensions between Russia and the West have not been lower since 1945, and the risk of a nuclear confrontation is very slight indeed; moreover, if continued, the reduced levels of tension should pay off with the reduced militarization of the Russian economy, and greater economic security.

There are two caveats to this picture of greater strategic security that relate to Central Asia. The first of these is the continued possession of nuclear weapons in the hands of Kazakhstan. Although relations between Russia and Kazakhstan are now arguably the closest of any members of the CIS, the presence of large numbers of ethnic Russians in Kazakhstan (38 percent of the population, versus 40 percent Kazakh, concentrated in the northern half of its territory) sets up a possible conflict. Russian voices have been raised suggesting annexation of the Russian-populated areas.[46] Shortly after the August 1991 coup, Yeltsin himself talked of redrawing Russia's boundaries in the event of the breakup of the USSR.[47] The Kazakh government might well think of nuclear deterrence. The other Central Asian-related caveat is the deleterious effect on Russian security if Kazakh nuclear warheads or Central Asian enriched uranium were to be sold to a third party. The "Islamic bomb" is feared no less in Moscow than it is in Western capitals.

It was at the level of regional security that Russia faced new difficulties. By the time the USSR had disappeared, military conflict between Azerbaidzhan and Armenia was already well entrenched, and other parts of the Caucasus were equally prone to ethnic violence. In the new states east of the Caspian, colonial borders had been drawn without excessive concern for ethnic communities, and one of the effects of *glasnost* and *demokratizatsiia* had been to heighten awareness of real and imagined ethnic grievances. The resurgence of Islam reflected in part the rejection of Bolshevism, and in part a popular reclamation of culture; whether fundamentalist or not, it threatened the interests of entrenched ruling groups, and was likely to be anti-Russian (both within those states and toward Russia as neighbor and former hegemon). It seemed bound to generate instability, as did economic transformation. There was a real possibility of conflicts feeding back into Russia, itself undergoing painful transformation, either through the unhappiness of its own Muslim minorities or through appeals for help from newly expatriate Russians. They are a new form of "protracted regional (Third World) conflict" in which the USSR involved itself in the past; Russia is in no position to do so.

Finally, there is the problem of the insecurity of the collective Russian psyche caused by the disappearance of the inner and outer empires, and the dramatic reduction of the Russians' world role.[48] This is an unpredictable and ephemeral factor; nevertheless, it has had a real effect on Russian domestic politics.[49] The conservative and reactionary factions have recognized its potency for Russians disaffected by change, and have used it as a pillar of their attack on the Gorbachev and Yeltsin reforms. It is not inconceivable that a Russian leadership could be forced into (or might even willingly join in) an adventure on the southern frontier (for example, to protect a Russian minority),[50] in order to assuage such disaffection.

The position of the Russian minorities (25 million in the territories of the former Soviet Union, of whom about 10 million reside in Central Asia) in fact has become a significant factor in the development of Russian foreign policy, both generally and specifically in regard to relations with the CIS (of which all Central Asian states except Azerbaidzhan are members). In the first months of independence, Russian foreign policy seemed focused primarily on the maintenance of close cooperative relations with Western countries, especially the United States. Although Russia's foreign minister, Andrei Kozyrev, declared that relations with the CIS were his main foreign policy priority, his opponents seemed to have considerable justification for doubting that.[51] Eventually, however, after a sustained attack on him in the Supreme Soviet, Russian foreign policy did in fact begin to distance itself from the West. The attack was helped by statistics that demonstrated that Russians were leaving Central Asia in significant numbers and that more would leave if they could.[52] It also benefited by ethnic Russian actions in Moldova, and Latvian and Estonian actions regarding their Russian minorities—actions that forced Yeltsin to take a hard line against those countries, even at the risk of damaging relations with the West.

There are no doubt many variants of the opposition to Kozyrev's "Atlanticism." With the possible exception of reactionary dreams of restoration of empire, most of them are related to a belief in the Eurasian nature of Russia. Eurasianists (and this included the center-right Civic Union grouping in the Supreme Soviet, which Yeltsin had tried on occasion to court) believe that Russia constitutes a natural bridge between the West and the East-South. While not rejecting the West, they fear that too close association with it will unnecessarily alienate the Muslim world and China, the parts of the world where they see not only a natural affiliation but also economic advantage.[53] According to Sergei Stankevich:

> These states are attempting to accomplish historical tasks similar to ours: integration into the world economy without losing their identity and defending their own interests; transition to a new technology structure; implementation of comprehensive reforms encompassing both industry and agriculture; acquisition of financial, food, and other self-sufficiencies.[54]

(Stankevich also articulates a more mystical strain that sees Russia as having a mission "to initiate and support a multilateral dialogue of cultures, civilizations, and states." This is feasible because Russia "emerged and grew strong as a unique historical and cultural amalgam of Slavic and Turkic, Orthodox and Muslim components.")[55]

Eurasianist thinking obviously requires an active Russian policy in Central Asia. Such a policy is not all that far beneath the surface of Atlanticist thinking either, and Yeltsin must also have been influenced by the strong support that Kazakhstan's president, Nursultan Nazar-baev, was lending to the idea of an effective CIS (as opposed to the Ukrainians' determination to keep it a very weak forum for consult-ation). Moreover, violence in the Caucasus was on the verge of spreading into Russian territory. Thus, sharpening the focus on the CIS and on Central Asia in particular was a necessary and easy concession to the Eurasianists.

It was necessary also because of economic realities, something most of the Central Asian states east of the Caspian recognized very quickly. Each side needed the other still. In fact, Russians were (and are) so embedded in the Central Asian economies, as managers, technicians, planners, and advisors, that it was (and is) probably impossible for Central Asian governments to disengage their economies from Russia's even if they had other suppliers and markets available. Their inability to do so is evidenced by their continued presence in the ruble zone, despite the disastrous record of the Russian economy since inde-pendence; their economic policies are being heavily influenced, if not directed, by Russia's.

Nazarbaev, recognizing the realities,[56] and also the dangers attached to Kazakhstan's hosting a large Russian population, was instrumental in the extension of the CIS beyond the Slavic republics; he has persist-ently called for a greater degree of economic integration in the CIS, including regulatory bodies with some teeth to ensure compliance with agreements signed. He has also supported a degree of political reinte-gration, in the form of a body like the European Parliament.[57] The others are not as enthusiastic; Kyrgyzstan, Uzbekistan, and Tadzhikistan accept the long-term economic ties; Turkmenistan, buoyed by its perceived economic prospects, is keeping as much distance as is currently possible. Azerbaidzhan refused until recently to join the CIS; Azeris have bitter memories of the Soviet military intervention in Baku in January 1990, and many are convinced that Russia has sided with Armenia over Nagorno-Karabakh.

As violence continued or threatened to break out in several parts of the CIS, ten of the eleven member states (not Turkmenistan) agreed in March 1992 to the idea of establishing peacekeeping and military observer groups. These would be sent on the request of conflicting parties to keep apart warring parties who had already reached a cease-fire. In a further development, a collective security treaty was signed at the Tashkent CIS summit meeting in late May.[58] This agreement provided for noninvolvement in military alliances, for joint consultations in a permanent Collective Security Council of the presidents in response to a threat, and collective action in accordance with the UN Charter. The list of signatories is instructive: Russia, Armenia, and four Central Asian states (Kazakhstan, Kyrgyzstan, Tadzhikistan, and Uzbekistan). The latter states were undoubtedly reacting to the outbreak of riots in Dushanbe, the capital of Tadzhikistan, where opposition forces, mainly Islamic groups based in the eastern part of the country, were demanding the removal of the old-guard government of Rakhmon Nabiev (the government that signed the collective security treaty). It is also instructive that these agreements have not been brought to fruition.[59]

The Tadzhik violence intensified throughout the summer, and in September Nabiev was ousted. This ushered in a small-scale civil war until December, when old-guard forces again returned to power. The Tadzhik events frightened the leaderships of the neighboring states. All believed (or professed to believe) that this was the first manifestation of the Islamic fundamentalism that wanted to sweep into power throughout Central Asia. Although it was not evident whether this really was the case, and there is no evidence that Iran had any involvement, it was clear that well-armed Afghan Tadzhiks had been moving freely back and forth across the border, and had some hand in the events. (It is also known that Tadzhik opposition groups had close ties to Gulbuddin Hekmatyar's Hezb-i Islami.)[60] In Uzbekistan, where Islam is becoming a force even though Islamic parties are banned, the presence of a substantial Tadzhik community with grievances makes it impossible to halt the conflict at its borders. The economic situation in Kyrgyzstan is bad enough that any unrest in the region could spark trouble. The spread of Islamic radicalism to Kazakhstan would likely cause concern among the Russian population.

Consequently, Russian forces which had been posted along the Tadzhik-Afghanistan border were reinforced. The 201st Motor Rifle Division, which was stationed in Dushanbe, was reported to have supported the return of the government, and afterward patrolled the city.[61] Moscow declared that the Tadzhikistan-Afghanistan border remained Russia's external border "for the time being."[62] CIS border guards (mostly Russian) took on the burden of closing the border; as clashes and casualties multiplied, the 201st and other Russian forces were sent in to help. Foreign Minister Andrei Kozyrev, on a visit to Teheran—aimed at establishing a "strategic partnership" to secure stability in Central

Asia—made it clear that Russia was claiming a legitimate right to defend the Tadzhik government.[63] Uzbek President Karimov clearly agreed, and moreover declared that Russia was the chief guarantor of Uzbekistan's security as well.[64]

Thus, the Russian government has moved into a foreign policy that had at least elements of Eurasianism. It seems clear that Moscow has decided that its interest lies in having the military and legal capability to respond to unrest in the territories of the former Soviet Union. As well as the collective-security agreement, it has concluded bilateral security agreements with Kazakhstan, Uzbekistan, Kyrgyzstan, and Turkmenistan.[65] Most recently, both Kozyrev and Yeltsin have suggested that NATO and the UN should recognize that "the entire geographical area of the former USSR is a sphere of vital interest" to Russia, which, "historically destined to be great,"[66] should be granted by the world community "special powers as a guarantor of peace and stability" in the region.[67]

Conclusion

Is there a version of the "Great Game" underway in Central Asia? To use that term seems exaggerated; however, there is a competition among outside parties. Russia, Turkey, and Iran are clearly the major players, but Pakistan, Saudi Arabia, the smaller Persian Gulf states, and even Israel have been actively seeking a role in the region.

The goals of the competition are clustered around one minor and two major objectives: the minor objective is to provide the "model" of development in Central Asia; the major objectives are to gain economic advantage and to ensure stability in the region.

In early 1992, becoming the model for Central Asian economic and political development was considered to be the major objective, since the other two could flow from it. However, it has become clear that the development process is no more ahistorical or flexible in the Central Asian states than elsewhere. It can perhaps be nudged in one direction or another, but to do more would require resources that are not available to any of the outside players, who all have different objectives.

On the other hand, the Central Asian governments have shown that they are eager to receive assistance from, and to establish trade relations with, all parties. In this competition to get in on the ground floor, as it were, each of the major players has certain advantages. Iran has some cultural affinity to Tadzhikistan; it also has an Islamic identity that, while foreign to all save the Azeris because it is Shi'ite, is bound to attract attention because of the persecution of Islam in the Soviet period. It has territorial contiguity and the shortest transportation routes to market.

However, it does not have large economic resources, or the financial backing of the West; indeed, opposing Iran's activities is a major motivation for others getting into the "game."

Turkey's major advantage initially was the perception in Central Asia that Ankara was the best gateway to and from the West, the best channel for assistance, investment, and know-how. It also benefited from cultural affinity, and its status as a modern, capitalist, industrialized Middle East state, a secular state in an Islamic society. Turkish business has been very active in the new states; however, it is hampered by the instability in some of them, and the uncertainty of investment protection. Unless it is heavily backed by Western business, there seems no reason to assume it has much advantage over Iranian or other companies. Thus far, with the exception of the energy sector, there has not been much Western interest, either from the private sector or, more importantly, from governments; this has contributed to a lessening of interest, perhaps in both directions.

Russia is in a somewhat different situation from the others. It is already in a position of economic advantage, because of the organization of the Soviet economy. It must therefore attempt to keep its position by urging the Central Asian states (except Azerbaidzhan) not to allow the further disintegration of the old economic ties. In this, other than the continuing importance of the *nomenklatura*, the "old guard network," in those economies, it really has only negative incentives: it has goods that can be bought for rubles, and it has markets for goods that are not competitive on outside markets.

The three outside players' activities regarding regional stability appear to be complementary. The possible exception here is Iran's interest in the growth of Islamic politics, which in the current political climate is almost bound to be destabilizing; nevertheless, no evidence of Iranian involvement in the Tadzhik unrest, or of the promotion of "fundamentalism" elsewhere, is available. All have borders with Central Asia that are permeable to the spillover of ethnic and/or religious unrest; all have problems that might be manipulated from outside, should they meddle.

Russia appears to have the most at stake here. Its loss of empire has left a well of resentment on which conservative forces have capitalized. This is unlikely to dissipate quickly, and active Russian involvement in Central Asia would probably assuage it somewhat. This is also a feasible policy since Russian forces remain stationed east of the Caspian, and those governments have need of them. In general, Russia, in turmoil itself, fears a spread of instability that could threaten its own cohesiveness.

If there is a Great Game under way, what have been its results? Have any of the contestants gained a significant amount of influence in the region? It is hard to see that they have, although one should not ignore the possibility that structural influence is being built very gradually through economic activity. If this is the case, and if some degree of prosperity can be achieved, then Central Asia will likely gravitate to "the West," perhaps through the mediation of Turkey.

The most obvious exercise of immediate influence, however, would be the resolution of conflict in the area. If this is the standard, then it is clear that Russia is the only state that has the potential for influence. Its intervention in Tadzhikistan (at the request of the putative government and of neighboring states) has demonstrated that. In the case of Nagorno-Karabakh, however, none of the players has been able to exert the necessary degree of influence. All have tried, using diplomacy and in the case of Turkey economic threats. It is a measure of how little leverage they each have, and of the concern with which they all view the stability of the region, that Russia has been forced to appeal to the international community for permission to intervene, and that neither of the other players protested.

Notes

1. Shireen Hunter, "The Muslim Republics of the Former Soviet Union: Policy Challenges for the United States," *Washington Quarterly* 15 (Summer 1992): 59-60.

2. William Fierman, "The Soviet 'Transformation' of Central Asia," in *Soviet Central Asia: The Failed Transformation*, ed. William Fierman (Boulder: Westview Press, 1991), p. 20.

3. *Economist*, 26 December 1992, p. 45.

4. Fierman, "The Soviet 'Transformation' of Central Asia," p. 20.

5. *Economic Review: Kazakhstan* (Washington: International Monetary Fund, May 1992), p. 1.

6. Gene Huskey, "Kyrgyzstan: The Politics of Demographic and Economic Frustration," in *Nations and Politics in the Soviet Successor States*, ed. Ian Bremmer and Ray Taras (New York: Cambridge University Press, 1993), p. 406.

7. Ann Sheehy, "Tadzhiks Question Republic Frontiers," *Radio Liberty Research*, RL366/88 (11 August 1988), pp. 2, 4; Ann Sheehy, "Tadzhik Party First Secretary Addresses Concerns of Local Intelligentsia," *Report on the USSR* 1, 3 (1989): 21.

8. *Economist*, 26 December 1992, p. 44. *Pravda*, 19 January 1993, claims that there are 12 million Russians in Central Asia.

9. Shireen Hunter, "Turkey's Difficult Foreign Policy Options," *Middle East International*, 17 May 1991, pp. 18-19.

10. Greater Turkestan existed as a governorate in the Russian Empire from 1867, and as an autonomous republic of the RSFSR until 1924. Fierman, "Soviet 'Transformation' of Central Asia," pp. 12, 17.

11. Pan-Turkism, the belief that there existed a broad Turkic community that could and should be united, was sustained in the early part of the twentieth century by Central Asian-born Turkish intellectuals. Philip Robins, *Turkey and the Middle East* (London: Pinter, 1991), p. 6. Currently, Turkish ultranationalists envisage Turkic lands from the Mediterranean to the Himalayas, presumably taking in not only Central Asia, but also the Azeri parts of Iran. Shireen Hunter, "Muslim Republics of the Former Soviet Union," p. 71, fn. 7.

12. *Kommersant*, no. 18 (27 April 1992), p. 22, in Foreign Broadcast Information Service, *Daily Report:Central Eurasia* (hereinafter cited as *FBIS/CE*), 27 May 1992, p. 12.

13. Hikmet Cetin, "The Security Structures of a Changing Continent: A Turkish View," *NATO Review* 40 (April 1992): 12.

14. *Middle East Economic Digest* (hereinafter cited as *MEED*), 30 October 1992, p. 4.

15. For examples of agreements signed, see *FBIS/CE*, 10 March 1992, pp. 105-9; and 17 March 1992, pp. 99-103.

16. Fierman, "Soviet 'Transformation' of Central Asia," p. 30.

17. *Middle East International*, 21 February 1992, p. 13.

18. *Economist*, 12 September 1992, p. 18.

19. *The Middle East*, August 1992, p. 29; *Commonwealth of Independent States and the Middle East* (hereinafter cited as *CIS&ME*), January 1992, p. 18.

20. *MEED*, 17 April 1992, p. 8.

21. Ibid., 26 June 1992, p. 28; 13 November 1992, p. 72.

22. With a tiny population, a large desert area, and huge reserves of natural gas, Turkmenistan (the largest exporter of natural gas in Eurasia after Russia) is being called the "Kuwait of Central Asia." *MEED*, 17 April 1992, p. 8; *Turkmenskaia Iskra*, 2 August 1992, in *CIS&ME*, August 1992, p. 33.

23. *Pravda Vostoka*, 13 March 1993, in *CIS&ME*, March 1993, p. 11.

24. See reports in *CIS&ME*, November 1992, pp. 1-2, 9-10; *MEED*, 13 November 1992, p. 72.

25. Ankara TRT television, 7 March 1993, in Foreign Broadcast Information Service, *Daily Report: Western Europe* (hereinafter cited as *FBIS/WE*), 8 March 1993, p. 57; and 9 March 1993, p. 43.

26. *Bakinskii rabochii*, 3 March 1992, in *CIS&ME*, March 1992, p. 4; *The Middle East*, July 1992, p. 8; *New York Times*, 18 April 1992, p. 46.

27. *Kazakhstanskaia Pravda*, 15 April 1993, in *CIS&ME*, April 1993, p. 10; *Gunaydin* (Istanbul), 8 April 1993, in *FBIS/CE*, 12 April 1993, p. 37.

28. *Globe and Mail* (Toronto), 9 September 1993, p. A12.

29. Graham Fuller, "The Emergence of Central Asia," *Foreign Policy*, no. 78 (Spring 1990), p. 50; Shireen Hunter, "Muslim Republics of the Former Soviet Union," p. 60.

30. *MEED*, 20 March 1992, p. 22; 10 July 1992, p. 15; *Narodnaia gazeta* (Dushanbe), 1 July 1992, in *FBIS/CE*, 19 August 1992, p. 62.

31. *Washington Post*, 10 October 1992; Bess Brown, "Central Asian States Seek Russian Help," *RFE/RL Research Report* 2, 25 (1993): 84.

32. *The Middle East*, March 1992, pp. 33-34.

33. *Middle East International*, 21 February 1992, p. 13; *Izvestiia*, 30 November 1992.

34. *Bakinskii rabochii*, 13 May 1992, in *CIS&ME*, May 1992, p. 3.

35. *Izvestiia*, 18 February 1992, p. 5.

36. *Turkmenskaia iskra*, 21 October 1992, in *CIS&ME*, October 1992, p. 2.

37. *Moskovskie novosti*, 22 November 1992, p. 14.

38. *Kommersant*, 15 January 1993, in *FBIS/CE*, 5 February 1993, p. 11; *Teheran Times*, 22 February 1993, in Foreign Broadcast Information Service, *Daily Report: Near East & South Asia* (hereinafter cited as *FBIS/NESA*), 5 March 1993, p. 60.

39. *Globe and Mail*, 3 September 1993, p. A7.

40. *Economist*, 26 December 1992, p. 45.

41. "Decades of . . . central planning have left just one or two factories supplying the entire Soviet market. . . . Economists . . . have worked out that, of 5,884 product lines, 77% were supplied by just one producer." *Economist*, 13 July 1991, p. 23.

42. *Christian Science Monitor*, 21 March 1991, p. 19.

43. *Economist*, 21 September 1991, p. 58.

44. Information supplied to author by Russian economist Vladimir Popov, 25 April 1993.

45. *Krasnaia zvezda*, 20 March 1992; *Voennaia mysl*, July 1992, p. 7.

46. John Dunlop, "Russia: Confronting a Loss of Empire," in *Nations and Politics*, p. 61. Vladimir Zhirinovsky won 7.8 percent of the Russian vote in June 1991 with the message that the Russians should take back the empire and put the minority peoples in their place. Ibid., p. 68.

47. *Manchester Guardian Weekly*, 1 September 1991, p. 7. Yeltsin later retracted the statement.

48. "We are no longer 1/6 of the earth's surface. . . . But we continue to carry within ourselves 1/6 of the globe. . . . It is a scale we have become accustomed to." S. Razgonov, *Moskovskie novosti*, no. 45 (1991); "Today we are deprived of everything. . . . The most important thing Russia has had to forfeit is its status as a great power that used to fill the rest of the world with awe." Aleksander Kazintsev, *Nash sovremennykh*, January 1992, p. 180. Both quoted in Igor Torbakov, "The 'Statists' and the Ideology of Russian Imperial Nationalism," *RFE/RL Research Report* 1, 49 (1992): 10.

49. See Vera Tolz, "The Burden of the Imperial Legacy," *RFE/RL Research Report* 2, 20 (1993): 41-46 for a discussion of the impact of the USSR's dissolution on the democratic camp in Russia.

50. "Where people who regard themselves as belonging to Russian civilization live, there is Russian territory, protected by Russian might." Eduard Limonov, *Sovetskaia rossiia*, July 1992. Quoted in Ibid., p. 12. "Defending the rights and interests of Russians 'and those identifying ethnically and culturally with Russia' on the territory of the former USSR is deemed to be a particularly important task in the Russian General Staff's draft military doctrine." John Lough, "The Place of the 'Near Abroad' in Russian Foreign Policy," *RFE/RL Research Report* 2, 11 (1993): 22, quoting *Voennaia mysl* (special edition), nos. 4-5, 1992.

51. Andrei Kozyrev, "Russia: A Chance for Survival," *Foreign Affairs* 71 (Spring 1992): 10; *Rossiiskaia gazeta*, 21 January 1992. Foreign Minister Kozyrev did not visit Central Asia until April; only then did Russia establish diplomatic relations with Turkmenistan and Tadzhikistan. Suzanne Crow, "Russia's Relations with Members of the Commonwealth," *RFE/RL Research Report* 1, 19 (1992): 10-11.

52. John Dunlop, "Russia: Confronting a Loss of Empire," pp. 47, 67.

53. Alexander Rahr, "'Atlanticists' versus 'Eurasians' in Russian Foreign Policy," *RFE/RL Research Report* 1, 22 (1992): 17-22.

54. Sergei Stankevich, "Russia in Search of Itself," *National Interest*, no. 27 (Summer 1992), p. 51.

55. Ibid., pp. 47, 39.

56. When Kazakhstan tried to establish a degree of financial autonomy for itself, Russia engaged in a crippling boycott that forced Nazarbaev to sign an agreement for the full coordination of financial and trade policies. Martha Brill Olcott, "Central Asia's Catapult to Independence," *Foreign Affairs* 71 (Summer 1992): 117.

57. Alexander Rahr, "Russia: The Struggle for Power Continues," *RFE/RL Research Report* 2, 6 (1993): 4; *Argumenty i fakty*, February 1993, p. 2; Ann Sheehy, "The CIS: A Progress Report," *RFE/RL Research Report* 1, 38 (1992): 3-4.

58. *Kazakhstanskaia pravda* (Alma-Ata), 23 May 1992, in *FBIS/CE*, 4 July 1992, pp. 59-60.

59. Suzanne Crow, "Russia Seeks Leadership in Regional Peacekeeping," *RFE/RL Research Report* 2, 15 (1993): 31.

60. Alexandre Bennigsen and Marie Broxup, *The Islamic Threat to the Soviet State* (London: Croom Helm, 1983), pp. 111-13. However, Muriel Atkin points out that Hezb-i Islami is predominantly Pushtun; the largely Tadzhik Jamiat-i Islami is more moderate on the role of Islam in the society. Muriel Atkin, "Tadzhikistan: Ancient Heritage, New Politics," in *Nations and Politics*, p. 377.

61. *New York Times*, 21 February 1993, p. 12.

62. *Izvestiia*, 19 February 1993, p. 4.

63. *Izvestiia*, 1 April 1993, p. 3; Interfax, 31 March 1993, in *CIS&ME*, March 1993, p. 3.

64. Cited in Bess Brown, "Central Asian States," p. 86.

65. Ann Sheehy, "The CIS," p. 5; *Nezavisimaia gazeta*, 20 May 1992, in *FBIS/CE*, 3 June 1992, p. 92; *Turkmenistan* (Ashgabat), 6 August 1992, in ibid., 27 January 1993, p. 113.

66. Andrei Kozyrev, "The New Russia and the Atlantic Alliance," *NATO Review* 39 (February 1993): 3, 4.

67. Boris Yeltsin, quoted in *Globe and Mail*, 1 March 1993, p. A1. Sergei Rogov, deputy director of the Russian Academy of Sciences' Institute of the USA and Canada, calls this "the Brezhnev Doctrine, Yeltsin style." The Supreme Soviet's committee for international affairs and foreign economic relations, in formulating a similar idea earlier, referred to a "Russian Monroe Doctrine." *Izvestiia*, 7 August 1992, p. 4.

PART TWO

Western Interests

5

The American Response to European Nationalism

Kevin F. Donovan

Introduction

Packs of hungry dogs roam the streets, attacking people too caught up in their misery to notice the danger. Prime Minister Khosrov Harutyunian conducts interviews by kerosene lamp, his office joining tens of thousands of other dwellings without electricity or heat. Desperate for warmth against the winter chill, a family feeds a small stove with the works of V.I. Lenin, on whose pages undoubtedly rest the promises of communist utopia.[1]

In Armenia as in many other areas of the former Soviet empire, the guarantees of stability and order provided by the center have been erased. Just as if the warden and his staff had unlocked the cells and abandoned the prison to its inmates, the inchoate nations of Eastern Europe struggle for survival in a regional microcosm of international anarchy. While the collapse of communism is well understood as a catalyst for these conflagrations, less apparent are the underlying causes that reinforce the splintering of nations and define the options available to the United States in formulating policy to address these problems. This chapter confronts these issues and argues that although near-term diplomatic, military, and economic policies may provide an illusion of resolution, they must be accompanied by a long-term strategy that addresses the fundamental role that elites play in determining the nature of ethnicity and the role of nationalism within their society.

Ethnicity and Security

Current literature on the problems of Eastern Europe and the former Soviet Union (FSU) is liberally laced with references to resurgent

nationalism. The twentieth-century articulation of this historic phenomenon, often traced back to Woodrow Wilson's postwar call for
self-determination of nations, is usually condemned as dangerous and
anachronistic in the modern world of interdependent economies and
global information exchange. Yet, regardless of its alleged detrimental
effects, nationalism and the forces of ethnicity that drive it are crucial
concerns for the immediate security of the entire region.

It is important to begin the discussion by distinguishing between
ethnicity, ethnocentrism, and intra- and trans-border nationalism, particularly with regards to the threats they pose for regional security.
Ethnicity is a difficult concept. If an ethnic group was defined by language, the United States would be considered a homogenous people. If
ethnicity was defined by skin color, there would be no "ethnic conflict"
between Serbs and Croats. If religion formed the basis for ethnicity,
Catholicism would create a truly "universal" ethnic identity. If common
culture dictated ethnicity, how did the distinctions between Sunni and
Shi'ite Muslims come about?

Certainly, ethnicity draws from all of these elements. It will be defined
here as a form of internally presumed and/or externally imposed self-
and group identification, derived from elements of race, language, culture, religion, and economic class.

In the absence of a contaminating political environment, ethnicity is
intrinsically benign. Switzerland is often offered as the quintessential
example of various ethnic groups living in harmony under a consensual
government. Indeed, Ernest Gellner conceives of the idea of *nation* as a
politically neutral extension of ethnicity: "Two men are of the same
nation if and only if they share the same culture, where culture in turn
means a system of ideas and signs and associations and ways of behav-
ing and communicating, [and] they recognize each other as belonging
to the same nation."[2] Ethnicity begins to become a problem when political discrimination among groups is perceived to exist or when one group
chauvinistically exalts the characteristics of their culture while con-
demning the ethnicity of others. Such ethnocentrism may give rise to the
political expression of nationalism, wherein aggrieved nations (self-
conscious groups of peoples) seek separate political structures as the
only equitable method of guaranteeing cultural freedom and preserva-
tion. When nationalist sentiment seeks to extend this "imagined community" to perceived cultural compatriots in other countries, the specter
of transborder nationalism is born.

Should the US Care?

From the US perspective, each of these manifestations of ethnicity gives rise to different sets of security concerns. Ethnocentrism, seen as an internal struggle for political power and legitimacy, is best dealt with as a local/regional problem (especially where democratic institutions prevail, such as in Canada), or through international diplomatic and economic pressure where illiberal regimes impose immoral practices (South Africa). Where violence between ethnic groups has impoverished innocent citizenry (Armenia), diplomatic and economic pressure might be accompanied by humanitarian assistance to help alleviate suffering.

Although violent and nonviolent intrastate ethnic conflict may exert varying degrees of influence on the human-rights agenda of US policy-makers, nation building through transborder nationalism, as typified by events in the former Yugoslavia, will *always* entail special security concerns for the United States. This is so not because of the threat to US "vital interests" (Secretary of State Warren Christopher views Bosnia as a "humanitarian concern" for the United States, not a "vital interest"),[3] but rather because the consequences of volatile nationalism may create conditions that place the vital interests of America's European allies at risk. The split between the Czech and Slovak nations does not directly affect US economic concerns, nor does it present a threat to US territorial integrity. Neither does a possible Serbian program of ethnic cleansing in Kosovo. Fighting in the Georgian Republic would seem of extremely marginal concern to the United States. While the direct consequences to the United States of these nationalistic struggles are minimal, any general armed conflict in Europe resulting from an uncontainable buildup of pressures stemming from violent nationalism would necessarily dictate US military assistance to beleaguered allies.

Scenarios leading to such a general European conflict are not far-fetched. Foremost among these is an ethnic-cleansing campaign of Kosovars by the Serbs. Presumably, the ethnic Albanian majority would seek assistance from Albania, which signed a military cooperation agreement with Turkey in November 1992. Turkey's return to the Balkans would conjure up old passions among the countries of this region that Turkey once ruled, not the least of which would come from Greece (which, along with Romania, has openly supported Milosevic's Serbia), which remains antagonistic toward the nationalism of its northern neighbor, Macedonia, despite the latter's recent admission to the United Nations. Macedonians, with their 400,000-strong ethnic Albanian population, would likely ally with Albanian Kosovars. Furthermore, the Macedonians could expect assistance from their eastern neighbor, the Bulgarians, whose strong historic and cultural affinities toward

Macedonia lead some to envision a combined state.[4] Together with the historic connections between the Serbs and Russians (despite a weakened President Yeltsin's assurances of nonsupport for *Bosnian* Serbs), the danger of a polarizing Balkan conflict, involving a coalition of Turkey, Albania, Bulgaria, and Macedonia on one side, against Greece, Romania, and Serbia, with perhaps tacit Russian support, on the other, quickly arises. The pernicious implications for European security are evident. In addition, given the United States' World War I and II experiences and the fact that it remains the world's de facto international patron, the ability for the United States to remain aloof from such a conflict is virtually nil. The plausibility of the spillover argument has convinced the Clinton administration to deploy roughly 300 US ground troops to Macedonia as part of a multinational peacekeeping force.

While the world's attention is focused on the most visible ramifications of nationalism's violence and separatism, even the most outwardly stable countries of the former Soviet empire are not immune to the problems of ethnicity. Jan Zielonka argues that Poland and Hungary are far from stable democracies: economic problems, weak political institutions, ineffective executive bodies, and poorly developed civil societies characterize the struggle for democracy and European integration. These problems exacerbate unresolved ethnic questions—tensions have flared over declarations of autonomy by Polish minorities living in Lithuania and concern has been raised over Hungarian Prime Minister Jozsef Antall's declaration that he is the leader of all 15 million Hungarians, although nearly 5 million of these live in surrounding countries.[5] While economic calamities will continue to harbor the most danger for Central Europe, Zielonka cautions that ethnic violence cannot be ruled out: "Although ethnic animosities in Central Europe have as yet produced no major violence, there are nevertheless several places where the classic recipe for such violence exists. This recipe includes the awakening of a frustrated minority, often with a link to an outside power, trying to assert itself against a xenophobic, unstable, and over-suspicious majority. Moreover, the rise of ethnic conflicts against a background of economic misery and political chaos can prove particularly explosive."[6]

Economic pressures resulting from the migration of refugees create a potential for military involvement by countries saddled with the task of absorbing these immigrants. Countries such as Germany, Austria, Italy, Greece, and Turkey are forced to provide housing, social services, jobs, and infrastructural improvements at the expense of other economic priorities. The extremely high costs of supporting this refugee flood, on top of painful efforts to recover from an economic recession, may induce European leaders to rethink their reluctance to commit military forces. In an acknowledgement of its desire for stability within the Central

European region, Germany has provided more than 90 percent ($905 million) of the 1990-91 economic aid to Czechoslovakia. Again, although not directly saddled with debilitating economic effects from transient refugees, the United States would be hard pressed to ignore a request for military assistance as one of its allies was being swept into the vortex of an economic whirlpool.

Finally, the siren song of an interventionist foreign policy based on morality and human rights is proving incredibly hard to resist. The ability of CNN and the mass media to set the political agenda with wrenching depictions of brutality and atrocity produces a galvanizing effect on the American psyche. These altruistic incentives are reinforced by formal American acceptance of institutionalized international principles set forth in the 1975 Helsinki Accord and built upon by the 1990 Conference on Security and Cooperation in Europe (CSCE) Charter of Paris, wherein the signatories agree that "all of the Euro-Atlantic region must be governed by the same standards of international and domestic conduct. Security for individuals, groups, nations and states within Europe's eastern half cannot be regarded as less vital than elsewhere from the Atlantic to the Urals."[7] Although the lack of concrete action to redress ethnic-rights violations in Moldova and Georgia, let alone Bosnia, may seem to paint the Paris Charter as unsubstantiated rhetoric, the media have used human rights proclamations to set the political agenda and bring the West to the brink of military intervention in the Balkans. The present focus on Bosnia precludes the same intensity of debate regarding Western options in the strife-ridden territories of the former Soviet Union. Obviously, the perceived "righteousness" of the cause is a powerful motivating force—the call for action based on alleged "moral, historical and cultural responsibility"[8] may only be muted by the return of body bags carrying America's young.

US Military Capabilities

The fact that the United States may be forced, by virtue of its "entangling alliances," to provide military assistance to defend its *allies'* vital interests is only one of several paradoxes confronting US security planners. While alliance and historical affiliations may initially favor US military commitment in European nationalist conflicts, the American people will resist and extract themselves from a long-term, open-ended, bloody hostilities involving American soldiers. Following Vietnam, the Gulf War experience has left a legacy of expectation regarding the commitment of US military power: future warfare must be short, relatively casualty-free, and decisive—a formula not well-suited to the lingering animosities characteristic of deep-seated ethnic strife.

Moreover, even as US military planners resist involvement specifically for these reasons, they possess one of the world's largest military organizations, and certainly its most capable. Following the collapse of the Soviet Union, an initial draft of a US policy for post-Cold War strategy sought to justify a security structure that would dissuade emerging rivals from challenging the US role as the remaining superpower. After an international uproar, the official policy statement signed by Secretary of Defense Dick Cheney in May of 1992 greatly toned down these official aspirations.[9] Undoubtedly, concerns remain regarding the persistence of this US hegemonic mentality (although others might be alarmed if it disappeared).

Regardless of whether military superiority was intentional or not, the US military remains the most capable in the world. In terms of numbers and readiness (quantity and quality), the United States is unrivaled. Even *after* the current rounds of prodigious defense cuts, the United States should be able to field 20 percent more tanks with 60 percent more capability than Russia. US fighter jets will have 24 times the capability of the Iraqi air force, 22 times that of North Korea, and five times that of China. The US Navy's superiority over its nearest rivals is a quantum leap beyond the air and land advantages.[10]

This lack of peer competition has not been lost on US strategic planners. Drawdowns notwithstanding, Secretary of Defense Les Aspin's recently completed "bottom-up review" proposes a force structure that could almost simultaneously respond to two major regional contingencies (such as a Persian Gulf threat and a North Korean incursion), a capability no other country even contemplates. The National Military Strategy calls for "strategic agility" and "power projection"—the rapid movement of forces from "wherever they are to wherever they are needed."[11] Obviously, the capability inherent in these strategies is not required for the protection of US borders or territory; rather, it is designed to ensure the ability to project power worldwide in an effort to secure perceived US vital interests. Thus the US security community finds itself confronting the paradox of resisting calls for intervention while at the same time sizing its force and designing overarching military strategies specifically for that purpose.

Despite these paradoxes, America's geopolitical position, economic power, and international prestige allow it the unique opportunity to choose (or not choose) among many arrows in its diplomatic quiver. Of George Liska's three S's, "security and sustenance in society,"[12] President Clinton's successful candidacy was based on the domestic imperative, the notion that an economically powerful and rejuvenated America provides the best hope for national security and a humanitarian international order. Together with the aforementioned rules for military commitment drawn from the Gulf War, the arms-length treatment of ethnic conflict in Eastern Europe is understandable. Moreover, a strong sentiment exists in the United States that the European Community is much better placed financially, institutionally, and geographically to deal with the problems of ethnic conflict in its own backyard.[13]

Of course, the institutions of European security may have been less the solution and more the problem in dealing with the issues of violent European nationalism. Even with a European consensus on how violent nationalism affects the Community's vital interests (a dubious assumption and perhaps the heart of the problem in prompting European action), the redundancy and overlap among a plethora of institutions that include the European Community and its security arm, the Western European Union (WEU), NATO organizations (to include the North Atlantic Cooperation Council), and forums provided under the auspices of the Conference on Security and Cooperation in Europe, create the potential for institutional paralysis in determining the manner in which European crises should be managed.[14] Ratification of the Maastricht treaty may do little to alleviate the institutional bottleneck; procedures for European Union policy approval may actually prove to be more tedious that those currently in place elsewhere.[15] Although the United States is showing signs of increasing impatience with the Europeans' inability to formulate a workable security structure, it is unlikely that the Clinton administration will give up on the idea of European leadership for European problems.[16]

Within these constraints, the following near-term framework for US involvement in European ethnic conflict will likely guide US policymakers. Ethnic strife resulting from economic tensions could become a primary catalyst for European conflict. The United States will not be able to resist inclusion in any such conflict that involves its NATO allies. Washington will continue to emphasize that, despite the abysmal European response to the problems of the Balkans, ethnic conflict resulting from the breakup of the Soviet Empire is primarily a European problem and that the Europeans are financially and institutionally capable of addressing it. The rapid conclusion of the European Union and endorsement of WEU and European-based security solutions will be advocated. Washington will not disengage completely, but rather will continue to be actively involved in the CSCE process particularly regarding human rights and economic development. Because of its undeniable military power, projection superiority, and leadership role in the world community, America's security assistance will be provided to the WEU directly or through UN-sponsored efforts with low-risk air and naval assets when military instruments are required.

The US military contribution to rising European ethnic strife will likely remain limited and highly contingent upon the nature of the conflict. Where the crisis is characterized by intrastate ethnocentrism involving intensive media coverage of the oppression of innocent civilians, humanitarian food and medical relief operations, such as PROVIDE HOPE to the former Soviet Union and PROVIDE COMFORT to the Kurds in Iraq, will likely key the response. Where ethnic-driven separatist movements, although not a direct threat to US vital economic or security interests, have implications for countervailing alliance formations (typified by current conditions in the Balkans), the United States might augment regional or United Nations-sponsored military ground forces with high-tech surveillance and intelligence assets as well as air force and sea-based combat systems. Not unless the problems of ethnicity (to include expansionistic religious fundamentalism) cross international borders wherein threats to US vital interests or historic commitments are at stake (scenarios involving Mideast oil fields) will the US resort to a coalition-based, full-blown ground commitment on the order of Desert Storm.

Nonmilitary Strategies for Dealing with Nationalism

The foregoing discussion has concentrated on some near-term problems of nationalism and their implications for security policy in Europe. Yet, military options will not resolve problems associated with ethnicity; they are merely individually designed containment cells forged to constrain the newest in an inevitable series of explosions. Although, in the short term, contemporary leadership may be forced to attend to this wearisome strife through military responses or some novel "security" arrangement, it will require enlightened leadership, both in the West and in the affected regions, to develop a program that neutralizes the foundations of competitive ethnic conflict. An effective long-term strategy must deal with the roots of nationalist sentiment.

The theoretical underpinnings of nationalism as a natural right can be traced back to Thomas Paine's *Rights of Man*: "A nation has at all times an inherent right to abolish any form of government it finds inconvenient and establish such as accords with its interest, its dispositions, and its happiness."[17] The proclivity to equate Paine's "nation" with an ethno-cultural unit of one's choosing gives rise to claims of moral sanctity for the nationalist's cause. However, most observers of the nationalist phenomenon are convinced that such an outlook is dangerous and perverted.

Gellner argues that there is nothing "natural" about nationalism at all—it necessarily resulted from the division of labor associated with the

Industrial Age. Cultural groups, aware of the need to have access to the basic literary and computational skills (high culture) required to ensure their economic viability in the modern world of labor specialization, push for the political power necessary to ensure that access when it is perceived to be threatened. Threats to this access can take the form of linguistic, racial, and religious discrimination restricting social and economic mobility.

Palestinians living in Israel provide a good example. In his book, *Sleeping on a Wire: Conversations with Palestinians Living in Israel*, David Grossman foresees a coming explosion to rival the intifada in the occupied territories resulting from a denial of access to the high culture necessary for economic viability. If Palestinians living in Israel are truly "integrated first-class citizens" of the state, Grossman asks "where among the Palestinian minority are the VCRs and the computers that you can find in almost every Jewish school? Where are the laboratories, the workshops, the sports facilities? Where are the counselors?" Cultural exclusivity is evident by the fact that no Palestinian Israeli has ever been a government minister or a supreme court justice. In the Israeli justice ministry, only three out of a thousand are Palestinians. Israeli Palestinians receive only 6 percent of Israel's development funds although they make up 55 percent of the Israeli families living in poverty.[18] The viability of economic theories of nationalism will be tested with the recently concluded agreements between Israel and the Palestine Liberation Organization: the theory suggests a mass migration of Israeli Palestinians to the previously occupied territories as a result of perceptions regarding enhanced economic opportunities in a more hospitable cultural environment.

While Gellner argues that the conditions of the modern industrial environment give nationalism its life, those advocating political "separateness" often mangle the paradigm such that its self-image and its true nature are inversely related: "Nationalist ideology suffers from pervasive false consciousness. Its myths invert reality: it claims to defend folk culture while in fact it is forging a high culture; it claims to protect an old folk society while in fact helping to build up an anonymous mass society . . . it preaches and defends cultural diversity, when in fact it imposes homogeneity both inside and, to a lesser degree, between political units."[19]

Similarly, Keane views nationalism as an ideology that, rather than a natural order, is a "scavenger" which is an "upwardly mobile, power-hungry, and potentially dominating form of language-game which makes falsely universal claims . . . [and] tends to destroy heterogenity by squeezing the nation into the Nation."[20]

Still, it would be wrong to think of nationalism in terms of amorphous masses of politically aware ethnicities, rising up in a spontaneous demand for cultural and political unity. Nationalist movements require leadership, someone with the ability to mobilize an imagined community and articulate the perceived injustices suffered. In order for nationalism to occur, "there must be at least some elements of a pre-existing shared sense of nationhood that is in turn capable of manipulation and public deployment by power groups taking advantage of [democracy's] openness."[21] Policymakers must begin to recognize that contemporary nationalism is merely a tool, a means to an often unspecified or concealed end, simply a halfway house along the path to political justice. The more important questions regarding the nature of the state to be created by nationalist elites are seldom asked by the movement's followers. The politicization of ethnicity has become, in John Chipman's words, "the ultimate resort of the politically desperate."[22] Thus, the proper focus in analysis of nationalist movements and ethnic strife is not the ideology of nationalism, but the elites who manipulate it for their own purposes.[23]

The elites in the countries of the former Soviet empire, both communist and anticommunist, have all wrapped the robe of nationalism around them: Milosevic in Serbia, Kravchuk in Ukraine, Iliescu in Romania, Gamsakhurdia in Georgia, Tudjman in Croatia, and Yeltsin in Russia. Elites have used the allure of nationalism to motivate "ethnic cleansing" in the former Yugoslavia, consolidate support for reform programs in Russia, and fuel the continuing conflict over Nagorno-Karabakh. Ethnic-based nationalism, as a producer of regional instability in Eastern Europe, is a study in elite theory.

Contemporary elite theorists have built upon the works of Gaetano Mosca, Vilfredo Pareto, and Robert Michels, to develop classification schemes for describing elite characteristics. Of particular importance to nationalist movements is the degree to which the "three C's"—elite consciousness, cohesion, and conspiracy—can be applied to the movement's leaders. The notion of a unified, impermeable, and omnipotent elite should be contrasted with a political environment where elites are fragmented, accessible, and tolerant of competing political policies and processes. In the first situation (typical of totalitarian regimes), elites often impose their political agenda on the masses, seeking legitimacy through ideological or pseudo-democratic rationales, while using the state's power to coerce dissenters. Elites in the second situation, characteristic of many Western democracies, seek utilitarian solutions through open debates on policy alternatives.

Variants of Nationalism in Eastern Europe

It is instructive, then, to examine the problems of nationalism in Eastern Europe from the perspective of "authoritarian" versus "democratic" elite motivation. Nationalist movements in the former countries of Yugoslavia and Czechoslovakia illustrate these two perspectives.

The characterization of the civil war in the former Yugoslavia as principally an "ethnic conflict" driven by centuries-old animosities between Serbs, Croats, and Muslims, has come under recent scrutiny. Ivo Banac argues that "the current conflict among the South Slavs, specifically between the Serbs and the Croats, is not ancient [or] religious. . . . The current conflict is primarily ideological and political."[24] The ideologies and the politics are apparently informed by an elite triumvirate composed of Slobodan Milosevic, Vojislav Seselj, and Zeljko "Arkan" Ranzjatovic.

Reviving the memory of atrocities at the hands of Nazi-backed Ustashe Croats, and warning of the conspiratorial ambitions of a unified Germany, the Roman Catholic church, and Muslims nationalists, "Serbia's Gang of Three" wrap themselves in the rhetoric of nationalist necessity. Yet, according to some observers, nationalism simply provides an excuse for the trio's meglomania and opportunism.[25] Arkan, a bank robber and alleged communist hitman before his Milosevic-sponsored election as, ominously, Kosovo's representative to the Serbian parliament (an election the Albanian minority boycotted), is the best known "enforcer" of the Milosevic regime. While Arkan's interests "seem confined to crime, business and self-glorification," Seselj is a power-hungry demagogue and paramilitary commander who provides a Joseph Goebbels-like propaganda program of ethnic purity from his Milosevic-backed post as opposition leader. Orchestrating the paranoia, Milosevic allows "the small middle class [to] vent steam, [while] the dominant but largely illiterate working class continues to view the world through the hateful filter of state television and its nightly parade of mutilated corpses."[26]

The Serbian experience is typical of the perversion of nationalism practiced by elites whose true motives lie in directions other than the political protection and promotion of ethnic culture. At the other end of the spectrum, nationalist elites may elect to participate in existing, peaceful, and democratic political processes if, in their view, autonomy is perceived as the only effective method of ensuring social and political justice for ethnic minorities. Even though these elites may be fragmented along policy lines, a political culture that includes an elite consensus regarding democratic *processes*, regardless of the outcome, will obviously lead to less drastic forms of political divorce. Such is the case with Czechoslovakia.

On the first of January 1993, the leaders of the Czech and Slovak Republics parted company. Czechoslovakia was divided along ethnic lines into two sovereign countries. Despite public opinion polls that indicated a large majority of both Czech and Slovak citizens wished to remain united, Vladimir Meciar manipulated economic disparities and political power-sharing disagreements into a drive for Slovak sovereignty, the consequences of which will be felt much more strongly by the nation he now leads. As in Yugoslavia, the motivations for separation appear dubious given that Slovakia is bound to suffer more. Fortunately, and unlike Yugoslavia, borders are undisputed and the Czechs and Slovaks have no history of violence; in fact, the attitude of the ruling elites in the Czech Republic has been unusually cooperative. Commenting on Czech willingness to absorb the total external debt of $9.1 billion, the Czech minister of economic policy believes "we can afford to be generous."[27]

Still, the potential for ethnic strife in the Czech and Slovak Republics is high. As in the Balkans, the territory that encompassed the former Czechoslovakia contains various nationalistic groups including Hungarians, Moravians, and Silesians who have had significant, if so far minor, concerns and complaints about their status. Thus, "it is not the danger of armed confrontation between the Czechs and Slovaks that represents the greatest security concern, but the destabilizing consequences of [the] partition of Czechoslovakia into two or more weak states. Such a partition may stimulate a chain reaction of local ethnic conflicts, territorial claims, foreign intervention, and possibly even war in the region."[28]

When the stakes are so high, the risks apparent, and where the immediate costs in blood and quality of life are so visible, the motivations of nationalist elites in both Czechoslovakia and Yugoslavia, and their fitness for national leadership, are suspect. Beyond sovereignty, what form of government does the movement's elites espouse? How will independence affect the citizenry's economic well-being? As was the case in Czechoslovakia, does the populace really want independence? After all, is it not the role of the state in the modern social contract to provide a system of consensual government for its citizenry? Over and above the responsibilities of the movement's elites to its followers, participants in nationalist movements share responsibility for their would-be nation's future. Similarly, just as those nationalist elites who would reject peaceful political processes within the existing political framework are to be held accountable, so too should those ruling elites who would suppress movements aimed at addressing the inequities among the system's ethnic groups. The American response must carefully weigh both sides' commitment to liberal democratic principles and processes.

America's Choice

While American options for the near-term problems in the Balkans discussed earlier are primarily limited to degrees of military intervention, the situation in the former Yugoslavia should serve as a warning to US policymakers who would ignore the complicated problems of resurgent European nationalism. We have seen that Eastern Europe, as part of a larger European community, *is* of vital concern to the US. What is the proper American response, then, to the long-term challenges of European nationalism? We can pursue this answer along two lines: policies of prevention and punishment for nationalism's authoritarian elites versus policies of encouragement and facilitation for democratic elites.

Where structural changes in the international environment produce conditions for the rise of authoritarian opportunists under the guise of national patriots, America's options are limited. In the 1930s, worldwide economic depression combined with a German perception of inequitable treatment as a result of the Treaty of Versailles to facilitate the rise of national socialism under Adolph Hitler. The collapse of the Soviet Empire in the late 1980s provided Serbia's "Gang of Three" a free rein to launch a new round of Nazi-style ethnic pogroms. Other than a "neo-containment" policy of limiting regional spillover effects, policies of war crime responsibility for authoritarian elites, and humanitarian aid for innocent victims, America's best, albeit limited, hope for preventing the rise of violent nationalist demagogues might be centered around programs of elite cooptation.

A variety of such programs exist in the United States today. The Department of Defense has established international officer exchange programs wherein foreign military officers with high military and government leadership potential attend defense universities in the United States (for example, the Naval Command College and the National Defense University) and spend considerable amounts of time touring the country. Of the more than 1000 graduates of the Naval Command College, over half have gone on to become flag officers in some 70 countries. Nearly 100 have led their country's military establishment.[29] The intent, of course, is to provide foreign elites with an appreciation of American political institutions and culture, and to produce ties of friendship and affection toward the United States.[30]

American universities can also play a key role. Education in Western political thought exposes foreign students, especially those being groomed by their countries' elites for future leadership positions, with alternative patterns of democratic development. Programs such as Yale University's Civic Education Project, wherein North American scholars are dispatched to Central and Eastern European universities to teach social science courses, help the democratic reform efforts in this region. Certainly, these kind of educational ties have been helpful in solidifying relations and providing influence with several Mideastern countries (for example, Saudia Arabia), even if immediate democratic reform failed to materialize. Although unsuccessful in his bid for the Serbian presidency, American-educated Milan Panic represents the kind of elite placement that these kinds of cooptation programs can hope to achieve.

Picking foreign elites for American indoctrination is certainly problematic. Moreover, the kind of elite personality that would sanction "ethnic cleansing" is likely to be uninfluenced by Western political thought and cultures anyway. Occasionally, elites chosen for education in the United States return to their countries with a profound antipathy toward anything American. The West, and the United States in particular, will have better success encouraging and assisting those democratic elites who, out of genuine concern for the betterment of the "nations" they lead, look to the West for aid in achieving the transition to stable democracy and political security.

In order for a stable democracy to take root, agreements must be made among competing elites who represent important segments of society.[31] Elites must become consensually unified wherein agreement is reached on respect for a *process* of democratization. This consensus can be achieved through either elite *settlements*, wherein elites suddenly and deliberately negotiate compromises to their disagreements, or elite *convergence*, where rival elites gradually achieve consensus indirectly via results of decisions made over a period of time. Where an elite consensus is not achieved, mass mobilization continues, polarization of elites and masses occurs, and the regime flounders in a pseudo-democracy or, worse, returns to authoritarianism. The US contribution, then, should be to use American diplomatic, cultural, and economic power and leadership to facilitate the construction of a consensus among competing elite factions.

Certainly, long-term strategies of consensus-building would involve the indirect programs of cooptation discussed above. More directly, the United States can use its influence and prestige where competing elites seek a mediator to find workable power-sharing and minority-rights arrangements. As evidenced by the intractable problems encountered by American mediators in negotiating a resolution to the dispute over

Palestinian nationalist rights in the Israeli-occupied territories, the challenges to finding an acceptable agreement can be immense, even when elites are weary of conflict and highly motivated.

Even so, success stories are abundant. Burton, Gunther, and Higley have found empirical support for elite settlements and convergences that led to stable, consolidated democracies in Costa Rica, Italy, Portugal, Spain, Uruguay, and Venezuela.[32] While each solution is necessarily tailor-made, one model that has proven its utility has been referred to as consociational democracy.

Austria, Belgium, the Netherlands, and Switzerland (in its original formation) have used a form of consociational democracy to satisfy competing elite factions in the transition to stable democracy. Where elites are motived to cooperate, consociational democracy is formed around four elements: a grand coalition of political elites, a mutual veto by each member of the coalition, a commitment to proportional allocation of political appointments and financial resources, and segmental autonomy wherein minorities rule themselves for all issues not of general coalition interest. Even where ethnicities are intermingled, segmental autonomy has been shown to work (Austria and the Netherlands) through a "personality principle," wherein each individual declares a nationality.[33] While the viability of this proposition for a state characterized by ethnic violence, such as in Bosnia-Herzegovina, is dubious, other regions in Central and Eastern Europe (and perhaps the former Soviet Union) without such historical baggage may benefit from the consociational democracy approach. The "good offices" of the United States could be offered in pursuit of these ends.

Occasionally, political integration of diverse factions will prove impossible. Although some studies suggest that the size of a potential country is not necessarily an impediment to its viability, some kind of guideline for deciding the acceptability of contested claims to independent statehood for emerging "nations" must be available.[34] Allen Buchanan offers the following criteria: first, minorities must have experienced consistent cultural or human-rights violations and there is no practical resolution for these abuses other than separation; second, the seceding group must be capable of compensating innocent third parties for losses they might suffer; third, the purpose of secession must not be to establish some illiberal state that would only provoke new injustices; and finally, "the sum of the injustices avoided and the rights of the people protected and advanced is deemed politically significant enough to grant title to territory previously held by others."[35] While these guidelines appear to be meant for contested secessions, in cases where the separation is negotiated peacefully, one might add the additional stipulation that the majority of the citizenry should approve of secession, which was not the case in Czechoslovakia.

Certainly, applying the guidelines above would undoubtedly prove difficult. Again, elites leading a secessionist movement could be expected to apply their own "spin" to each of the criteria, advancing those that worked for their own purposes and promising to uphold those that were prescriptive in nature. It will be up to the international community to judge the philanthropic nature of the secessionists' motivations through programs of observation and supervision—what Chipman describes as "incubation." For the first time, the US Department of Defense budget includes money ($300 million) earmarked for peacekeeping operations—money that could be used to deploy teams of American political, economic, and military observers that would report back to the United Nations on the efforts made to adhere to international norms and the guidelines outlined above.[36] The international community might want to delay formal recognition until the new regime successfully completes an adequate "incubating" period.

Because economic difficulties exacerbate nationalistic and antidemocratic sentiments, US monetary aid through grants and beneficial trade practices will often be more useful than Washington's diplomatic and bargaining skills. By contributing its $12-billion share of the planned increase to the International Monetary Fund, the United States could free up another $48 billion from other members that might be used to assist in stabilizing these new democracies.[37] However, allocation of economic aid to the countries of Eastern Europe will be very difficult to sell in the current American domestic environment, where deficit reduction is the priority.

Conclusion

Obviously, not every ethnic dispute can or must involve American aid and diplomacy. More likely, the most effective American strategy might be to polish the "city on the hill" image of functioning and effective liberal democracy. The modern nation state was invented in America around the ideas of individual equality and rights. The system of geographic federalism that evolved, even as the nation expanded across a continent, remained true to the fundamental and founding principle of individualism.

Notwithstanding its ideological foundations, the United States remains locked in an ongoing social struggle to operationalize individual equality. A dialectical process of social progress continues to express itself in contemporary American society (the debates and subsequent social revolutions regarding slavery, treatment of native Americans, and civil rights movements come to mind). Still, while many "interest groups" continue to clamor for special consideration from the central government (the elderly, farmers, business, etc.), calls for special ethnic or racial privileges should not be part of the political agenda. Even the strident black nationalist Malcolm X was eventually converted by the power of the founding fathers' ideology: "In all honesty and sincerity it can be stated that I wish nothing but freedom, justice, and equality; life, liberty, and the pursuit of happiness—for all people."[38]

Still, parochialism is on the rise. The proclivity to accede to group politics over individualism is often counterproductive. Anthony Smith argues that state policies that provide tacit encouragement of ethnic diversity can lead to divisive ethnic political mobilization, where ethnic groups must compete for society's increasingly scarce public resources. This competition and "emphasis upon group mobility rather than individual advancement, inevitably accentuates inequalities between ethnic communities."[39] In this light, the Clinton administration's "policies of inclusion" that seek politically to empower parochial segments of American society, such as ethnic and gender-based cabinet member selections, may ultimately be more harmful than beneficial to American societal harmony, and detrimental to American interests in Eastern Europe.

Instead of the "ethnic federalism" practiced by Stalin and Tito, American emphasis on liberal individualism has produced de facto policies of ethnic integration instead of separation. Rather than empowering ethnic groups, the US model has attempted to provide equal *opportunity* for individuals within society while protecting the individual's rights to cultural freedom.[40] Perhaps the most effective course for American leadership to take regarding the problems of European nationalism would be to continue the process of perfecting the American brand of liberalism, which although far from perfect, represents history's most successful approach yet to the challenges of ethnic politics.

Notes

1. For a complete account of conditions in Armenia, see Margaret Shapiro, "'Welcome to Hell' in Armenia," *Washington Post National Weekly Edition*, 8 February 1993, p. 12.

2. Ernest Gellner, *Nations and Nationalism* (Ithaca: Cornell University Press, 1983), p. 7.

3. Steven A. Holmes, "Backing Away Again, Christopher Says Bosnia Is Not a Vital Interest," *New York Times*, 4 June 1993, p. A12.

4. Guizzi Goerens, "European Union and Developments in Central and Eastern Europe," *Western European Union Document* 1293, 27 November 1991, p. 336.

5. Jan Zielonka, "Security in Central Europe," *Adelphi Paper* 272 (Autumn 1992): 30-31.

6. Ibid., p. 55.

7. Daniel Nelson, "In the Wake of the Revolution: Eastern Europe in the 1990's," *European Security* 1 (Spring 1992): 95.

8. Zielonka, "Security in Central Europe," pp. 56-57.

9. See "US Strategy Plan Calls for Insuring No Rivals Develop," *New York Times*, 8 March 1992, p. 1; and "Pentagon Drops Goal of Blocking New Superpowers," *New York Times*, 24 May 1992, p. 1.

10. "The Generals' Shrinking Threat," *New York Times*, 15 March 1993, p. 18.

11. Part of the US Strategic Principles as discussed in "The Changing Strategic Environment," taken from chaps. 1 and 2 of the Joint Military Net Assessment, *Defense 92*, November/December 1992, p. 11.

12. George Liska, *Career of Empire* (Baltimore: Johns Hopkins University Press, 1978), p. 4.

13. See, for example, Jenonne Walker, "Avoiding the Responsibility: The United States and Eastern Europe," *Current History* 91 (November 1992): 364-68.

14. For a discussion of the varying views on which organization is best situated to handle conflict in Europe, see Walker and Nelson for the CSCE, Zielonka for the EC, and F. Stephen Larrabee, "Instability and Change in the Balkans," *Survival* 34 (Summer 1992): 31-49, for NATO.

15. For a discussion of the European Union's decisionmaking processes, see Philip Zelikow, "The New Concert of Europe," *Survival* 34 (Summer 1992): 12-30.

16. Walker, "Avoiding Risk and Responsibility," p. 364.

17. Quoted in John Keane's "Democracy's Poisonous Fruit: Can European Citizenship be an Antidote to the Perils of Nationalism?" *Times Literary Supplement*, 21 August 1992, p. 10.

18. Donald Neff, "Israel Seen In a New Light," Book Review, *Washington Post National Weekly Edition*, 8 February 1993, p. 35.

19. Gellner, *Nations and Nationalism*, p. 124.

20. Keane, "Democracy's Poisonous Fruit," p. 11.

21. Ibid., p. 11.

22. John Chipman, "Managing the Politics of Parochialism," *Survival* 35 (Spring 1993): 143.

23. See also John Mearsheimer's discussion of the role of elites in hypernationalism in "Back to the Future: Instability in Europe after the Cold War," *International Security* 15 (Summer 1990): 21.

24. Ivo Banac, "Yugoslavia: The Fearful Asymmetry of War," *Daedalus* 121 (Spring 1992): 141-74.

25. See Blaine Harden, "Serbia's Treacherous Gang of Three," *Washington Post*, 7 February 1993, p. C1.

26. Ibid.

27. Nikolaus Piper, "The Slovak Poorhouse," *World Press Review*, November 1992, p. 43.

28. Zielonka, "Security in Central Europe," p. 14.

29. Rear Admiral Joseph Strasser, "President's Notes," *Naval War College Review* (Spring 1991): 5.

30. In announcing the 1994 Department of Defense budget, Secretary Aspin outlined an additional $50-million program designed along these lines. See *News Briefing*, "Secretary of Defense Les Aspin, FY 1994 Defense Budget," released by office of the assistant secretary of defense (public affairs), p. 4.

31. See the introduction to *Elites and Democratic Consolidation in Latin America and Southern Europe*, ed. John Higley and Richard Gunther (Cambridge: Cambridge University Press, 1992).

32. Ibid., p. 325.

33. For a discussion of consociational democracy, see Arend Lijphart, *Democracies in Plural Societies* (New Haven: Yale University Press, 1977).

34. Dahl and Tufte concluded that "a country's chances of survival do not depend significantly on its size." Sawyer found that population size and per capita GNP were virtually unrelated. Lijphart, *Democracies in Plural Societies*, p. 46.

35. Allen Buchanan, *Secession: The Morality of Political Divorce From Fort Sumter to Lithuania and Quebec*, as quoted in Chipman, "Managing the Politics of Parochialism," p. 151.

36. Barton Gellman, "Aspin Sees No Need to Alter Defense Cuts Set for 1994," *Washington Post*, 26 March 1993, p. 17.

37. Walker, "Avoiding Risk and Responsibility," p. 365.

38. As quoted in "Thomas Jefferson and the Character Issue," *The Atlantic*, November 1992, p. 74.

39. Anthony D. Smith, *Ethnic Revival* (Cambridge: Cambridge University Press, 1981), pp. 187-88.

40. Michael Barone, in his review of Senator Daniel Patrick Moynihan's book, *Pandemonium: Ethnicity in International Politics*, and Joel Kotkin's *Tribes*, points out that while Moynihan stresses that ethnic groups seeking political power can be a source of instability, Kotkin shows that ethnic groups seeking economic gain can be a source of national strength. *US News and World Report*, 15 February 1993, p. 55.

6

Germany, the Blue-Helmet Debate, and the Eastern Crisis

Joachim Rabe

Introduction

In his policy statement delivered on 4 October 1990, one day after the reunification of Germany, Chancellor Helmut Kohl said:

> Reunited Germany will have to assume a great responsibility within the international community, last but not least with respect to the maintenance of global peace. We will live up to this responsibility, within the scope of the United Nations, the European Community, and the Atlantic Alliance as well as in our relations with individual countries. To this end, we intend to soon create the appropriate constitutional preconditions.[1]

Since then, more than three years have passed and the German government has yet to change the constitution. During the Gulf War, Germany tried to stay out of direct involvement, resorting to a much criticized "checkbook diplomacy." However, now it faces a potential for conflict in Eastern Europe that threatens Western Europe to a far greater extent than did the Gulf War. This inevitably raises the question as to how Germany intends to contribute to the resolution of the Eastern crisis, and whether it is willing to commit forces to out-of-area peacekeeping operations.

In order to answer this question, one has to examine various factors influencing the German "blue-helmet" debate. Germany's domestic situation appears to be crucial, as well as the nature of the Eastern crisis itself. Several issues are central to an understanding of Germany's current domestic situation, such as its search for a renewed national identity, an ongoing economic recession, a growing national debt, the problems surrounding exploding numbers of asylum-seekers, an increasing crime rate, the relative weakness of the political leadership, and a certain state of depression responsible for a changing attitude of the electorate. An analysis of the blue-helmet debate furthermore requires a close look at Germany's constitutional basis, the positions of the major political parties, and recent proposals for constitutional amendments.

It is my argument in these pages that Germany's precarious domestic situation, currently characterized by social unrest and economic as well as political instability, renders highly improbable a strong commitment by the country to international peacemaking operations. Public opinion and public attitudes, especially important in light of the upcoming 1994 "super election" year, are currently not strongly supportive of risky German foreign-policy ventures. However, an evaluation of the Eastern crisis, specifically in terms of the war in the former Yugoslavia, and the potential for similar events in what used to be the Soviet Union, will reveal that Germany has a fairly strong commitment to nonmilitary solutions and confidence-building measures.

Domestic Crisis in Germany

To grasp the German position with regard to support for out-of-area military operations, it is necessary to understand the German attitude toward war. It is not the purpose of this chapter to scrutinize the German identity, but it is useful, perhaps necessary, to establish some understanding of the relationship between the German people and war. Put at its simplest, in their attitude to war, the Germans have undergone an amazing development. What is the explanation for this particular learning process, and how profound has this change of mind been?

Karl Otto Hondrich identifies five factors designed to effect the disposition toward peacefulness, or what we might label the "irenic impulse": the Christian ethic as the basis for a universal morality; economic cooperation; monopolization and restriction of the application of force; rational fear of war; and suffering in war.[2] He concludes that the physical and psychological impact of suffering experienced during a war constitutes the most effective and direct—albeit the most undesirable—factor for assimilating "peacefulness." There are many causes of suffering during war: widespread death and mutilation, other cruelties, devastation, defeat, and humiliation. Moreover, there is the violation of national integrity as a result of occupation, partition, or annexation of parts of the national territory, or—what is even more severe—the loss of moral integrity owing to an unneglected war guilt. If the commonly experienced suffering reflects all these factors, it can be assumed that they will effect a strong, common desire for peace.

Given Bismarck's successful wars, which brought about national unity, Wilhelminian Germany still found it relatively easy on the eve of the First World War to mobilize collective public support for a new war. In 1939, however, there was hardly any such enthusiasm, as the German population still remembered the dreadfulness of the recent conflict; those soldiers who had survived this war had grown just 20 years older. As a result of the total defeat in 1945, people detested any kind of militarism and belligerence.

During the Second World War, not only the soldiers in the field, but also the civilian population at home suffered from bomb attacks and expulsion. Germany lost the eastern part of its territory, and the rest was occupied and divided into two states that had to assume responsibility for the atrocious crimes committed by Hitler's Germany. Total war and total defeat also totally annihilated the ethic of readiness for war, which has been replaced by the ethic of peacefulness. The Cold War raised among Germans a rational fear both of nuclear war and of conventional war, as either would have been fatal to Germany.

As a result of two world wars, Cold War Germany turned into a model of peacefulness. But psychological factors alone do not account for the irenic impulse; the current domestic situation also plays an important role in the development of German foreign policy. Economic situations change abruptly. While GNP growth rates were relatively high from 1988 to 1991, a decline began in 1992, and for 1993 a negative growth rate was anticipated. As a result of this, the rate of unemployment increased significantly, from 211,000 in 1988 to more than 740,000 in 1991. By August 1992 the ranks of the unemployed swelled by a further 150,000, and by 1993 a full-blown recession buffeted Western Germany.[3]

Initially it was believed that the costs of German unity, estimated at 40 to 60 billion Deutsche marks, could be easily met. However, the actual costs turned out to be much higher. The cause for this was the collapse of both the economic structures in East Germany and the markets in Eastern Europe on which approximately two-thirds of the former East German economy relied.

The decrease of economic output coincided with a dramatic deterioration of the employment situation: in East Germany, the number of employed had dropped to approximately 5.2 million by 1992, as compared to approximately 8.2 million in 1990; 1.3 million are registered as unemployed, 400,000 jobs are subsidized, 225,000 are working on a reduced-working-hour basis, and 500,000 commuters are working in West Germany. The funds required for Eastern Germany are largely covered by new debts: budget deficits amounted to DM10 billion in 1989, DM88 billion in 1990, DM154 billion in 1991, and approximately DM175 billion in 1992.

Given the budget deficits that have to be covered by new credits, the total public debt, which at the end of 1989 stood at approximately DM1,100 billion, is expected to more than double to approximately DM2,400 billion by the end of 1996, an amount equalling nearly 70 percent of the GNP.[4] Germany's rising public debts would, on a per capita basis, exceed the current national debt of the US, which amounts to some $4,000 billion.[5] While the solidarity pact concluded between the German federal and state governments in March 1993 provides for burdensharing at national and state levels during the next two years, it has not effected debt relief, but will produce an increase in the levy and tax rate of currently 43.4 percent of the GNP.[6]

The social tensions caused by the economic recession and a growing national debt are being intensified by the problems surrounding the issue of refugees seeking asylum in Germany. For several months, images of violence committed by Germans against foreigners and that warn against a new aggressive German nationalism have been circulating around the world.[7]

The number of foreigners living in Germany had increased from 506,000 in 1951 to 5,408,000 in 1990.[8] By the end of 1991, the number of foreigners totalled 5,882,267. Among those, 1,483,766 were from within the European Community (EC), 3,324,964 were other Europeans, and 1,073,537 were Africans, Americans, and Asians.[9] Many of these people had been hired as long ago as the 1950s, as a labor force for Germany, and have managed to integrate relatively well with their families.

Current problems stem from the asylum-seekers issue. Between 1953 and 1974, a total of 116,400 individuals were registered and their accommodation caused no major problems. Since 1975, the influx of asylum seekers from Asia, and since 1977, from Africa, has increased to an unparalleled degree.[10]

The costs for their living and social care impose a significant burden on local budgets and reduce the margin for other important social projects. In the state of North Rhine-Westphalia, an average monthly amount of DM1,000 is required for each asylum seeker. Nationwide, the costs for asylum seekers have increased from DM2.0 billion in 1985 to DM5.5 billion in 1990.[11] As the asylum seekers are evenly distributed across Germany, including East Germany with several sensitive areas affected by very high unemployment, it was not difficult to foresee that sooner or later the volcano of social tension would erupt.

By amending the article of the German Basic Law that governs the granting of asylum and promulgating associated legislation in spring 1993, Bonn intended to deter economic refugees, while still providing continuing support for political asylum seekers.[12] Even if these measures may offer a solution to the asylum-seekers issue, there can be no doubt about the fact that politicians for more than a decade had failed to resolve this obvious problem. It was not until social tension escalated, as in Rostock in the late summer of 1992, that the Social Democratic Party abandoned its concerns. Yet, the issue of those asylum seekers who are currently in Germany continues to pose a problem. In response to assaults against asylum seekers during the second half of 1992, hundreds of thousands joined in demonstrations in order to express their conviction that Germany as a nation cannot and will not turn against foreigners.

In addition to economic and social challenges, an increasing crime rate threatens the population's quality of life, as well as their trust in political leadership. Nineteen ninety-two saw a significant growth in crime; while the rate of increase in West Germany ranged from 9.6 percent in Hesse to 18 percent in Lower Saxony, it amounted to 84 percent in the East German state of Mecklenburg-Vorpommern, and 140 percent in Saxony.[13]

That the Christian Democratic/Christian Social group in the Bundestag, for the first time in postwar German history, has called for a "national security conference" designed to enhance domestic security reflects the priority placed on the issue of growing crime rates.[14] Kurt Biedenkopf, until recently an outspoken thinker among the Christian Democrats in the West and now head of the East German state of Saxony, claims the morale of the reunited nation is at its lowest; he is not lacking for company in this assessment.[15] Three-quarters of the German population are concerned about the situation in their country, and they cite as worrisome factors unemployment, recession, the unending influx of foreigners, a growing crime rate, and illegal drugs. Much if not all of the above are seen to be consequences of miscalculations and other unfortunate developments that have complicated the unification process and produced tension and disappointment.

West and East Germans have not yet achieved a smooth division of responsibilities at the governmental level. Eight percent of the West Germans and 33 percent of the East Germans are afraid of losing their jobs. This reflects a depressive mood heretofore rarely (if ever) felt in West Germany. More than a third of adult Easterners feel that they "are no longer needed in this society," and the share of those who "are afraid of the future" has increased from 33 percent in autumn 1990 to 45 percent in late 1992. As well, 64 percent of the Westerners and 74 percent of the Easterners believe that the Germans have drifted apart since reunification and that "a wall in the minds" is being erected. East Germany seems to have developed an identity of defiance: 54 percent consider themselves primarily to be "East Germans," while only 45 percent feel they are "Germans."[16]

It could be suggested that in order to solve Germany's domestic problems and the psychological challenges posed since the day of reunification, Germans will have to develop a renewed "inner" unity and identity. Additional challenges at this time, such as a stronger commitment to UN peacekeeping efforts characterized by questionable success rates and unexpected human losses, could only add to Germany's dilemmas.

In 1994, a record total of 19 elections at local, state, and national levels will be held; hence, there may be a significant shift in the distribution of political power, and the parties will attempt to avoid unpopular decisions that might influence the electorate. This may be another reason for the Social Democrats' continued refusal to agree to an amendment of the Basic Law allowing the use of German forces even for peacekeeping operations.

What is the image of the leading politicians who are to solve the aforementioned problems and compete during the next national elections? In German politics there appears to be a pattern that the authority of a government wears out and its capabilities attained after eight years, or two terms. For instance, the last five years of his 13 and-a-half years in office were an ordeal for Chancellor Konrad Adenauer and his Christian Democrats; Helmut Schmidt had to quit after eight-and-a-half years.

Prior to 1989/90, Chancellor Helmut Kohl barely managed to sustain himself against opponents from within his own party. During the phase of reunification and its consolidation in the arena of foreign policy, he managed to display a strategic vision, energy, and proficiency in leadership that will make for him his mark in history as the "Chancellor of Unity."[17] Today, however, his popularity has sagged to an unparalleled low, and occasionally he has been urged to resign. Contrary to earlier years, the opposition this time shows little sign of being able to take advantage of the weak position of the government by providing promising alternative leadership.[18]

The two world wars and particularly the total defeat in 1945 brought about a fundamental change in Germany's national identity. Besides freedom and democracy, peacefulness and helpfulness in its relations with other countries represent some of Germany's new essential virtues. Any government infringing upon those virtues, for instance by abandoning the principle of peacefulness through the use of German forces for what could be premature and unsuccessful operations, would be doomed to fail.

Besides these considerations, the urgent problems have, of course, a significant impact on political developments. Even when the current economic recession has been overcome, Germany will still have to cope with a higher than normal unemployment rate and its associated social consequences for a long time. In spite of higher taxes, the national debt continues to increase and will, similar to the predicament the US currently experiences, require a debt-relief process extending over years or even decades. Hence, the economic power of Germany will be restricted for years. Financial aid as provided during the Gulf War or such extensive aid as has been provided to the Eastern European countries will have immediate repercussions for Germany's economic capabilities. The asylum-seekers issue, crime increase, continuing housing shortage, higher taxes, and a reduction in the standard of living combine to produce widespread uncertainty and an attitude of discontent among the population, which is reflected by a significant change in their behavior as an electorate.

The government and the opposition which, due to its majority in the Bundesrat participates de facto in the government, are unable to come to an agreement to work together. Only mass demonstrations and electoral defeats seem to be able to persuade the SPD to adopt a more cooperative stance vis-à-vis the ruling coalition. Among the leading politicians, at present, there is no outstanding character who might bring about a change. Both the government and the opposition appear to lack spiritual leadership and longer-term vision. Wherever possible, awkward projects and decisions will be postponed until after the 1994 national election. This fact of political life has to be taken into consideration in any analysis of the blue-helmet debate.

The Blue-Helmet Debate

In the German Basic Law of 1949, or constitution, there is no explicit provision governing the employment of the German armed forces for operations under the aegis of the UN. By means of article 87a, added only in 1968, legislators deliberately provided a strict legal basis for the employment of the armed forces. The objective was to establish clearly that the latter, in keeping with the ban on violence and war of aggression under international law, may only be employed for defensive purposes and never for aggression (articles 25 and 26). Article 87a(2) stipulates that "apart from defense, the armed forces may only be used to the extent explicitly permitted by this Basic Law." Article 25 states that "the general rules of public international law shall be an integral part of federal law. They shall take precedence over statutes and shall directly create rights and duties for the inhabitants of the federal territory." According to article 26(1), "acts tending to and undertaken with intent to disturb the peaceful relations between nations, especially to prepare for war of aggression, shall be unconstitutional. They shall be made a criminal offense." Some clarifying stipulations as to the employment of armed

forces outside the borders of the German territory or in conjunction with
the forces of other countries are missing.

The meaning of the constitutional term "defense" cannot be determined by means of the Basic Law but, according to some scholars, "by
means of the international rules governing the application of armed
force between subjects of international law."[19] Through article 25, these
rules have become an integral part of German federal law.[20] Article 24 is
one of the original articles of the Basic Law proclaimed in 1949; its
paragraph 2 stipulates that: "for the maintenance of peace, the Federation may enter a system of mutual collective security; in doing so it shall
consent to such limitations upon its rights of sovereignty as will bring
about and secure a peaceful and lasting order in Europe and among the
nations of the world."

Given the experience of two world wars, the Bundesrat as well as the
Bundestag recognized the necessity for the Federal Republic of Germany
to contribute to a collective-security system. The United Nations already
existed when the Basic Law was discussed in the three occupation zones
of West Germany, and there was no doubt about the fact that it already
aspired to be a collective-security system.[21] The importance of such a
system for the newly created Federal Republic was to be reflected by an
appropriate wording of the Basic Law, thus providing, from the very
beginning, for the opportunity to practice constructive cooperation
within the framework of the United Nations. However, in 1949 nobody
could take the deployment of military force components very much into
consideration, as the German armed forces were only established in
1955.

In a comprehensive study on the obstacles imposed by constitutional
and international law, Norbert Karl Riedel argues the provocative case
that not only can Bonn deploy forces within the framework of NATO in
a crisis ("in-area") context, it can also participate in "out-of-area" operations if the NATO treaty is amended accordingly. However, with respect
to an employment under the aegis of the UN, Riedel holds that such a
deployment would be unconstitutional, and thus contributions to UN
observer missions and other multinational peacekeeping and surveillance roles are and will remain illegal in the absence of explicit constitutional authorization.[22] This shows that there is no unequivocal
constitutional basis and that a review or amendment is required.

Germany's major political parties take different positions on this
issue. From the very beginning of the debate, the Christian Democratic
Union and its sister party, the Christian Social Union, have advocated
the employment of the German armed forces under the aegis of the UN.
Even before reunification Chancellor Kohl stated: "We, the Federal Republic of Germany, cannot claim international solidarity and, at the same

time, refuse to contribute our share if others call on us for international solidarity."[23] One year later Volker Rühe, then secretary general of the CDU and now minister of defense, explained that there was much more at stake than just Germany's image in the international community; at stake was the fundamental issue of Germany's self-perception and the future of Europe: "It is my firm belief that the unification process in Europe would be severely affected if we, the Germans, permanently attempted to distinguish ourselves from our European neighbors." Consequently he called for the creation of appropriate preconditions for safeguarding, within the scope of a "European security identity," European security interests in conjunction with the European neighbors and for strengthening the role of the UN through appropriate contributions.[24]

The Christian Social Union has always held the opinion that the existing constitutional framework permits the employment of the German armed forces for the purpose of enforcing UN resolutions and safeguarding global peace. A recent hearing of prominent constitutional experts of the CDU/CSU parliamentary group revealed that an overwhelming majority of German experts in constitutional and international law consider an employment of the Bundeswehr under the authority of the UN to be legal under article 24(2). The Social Democrats were warned that if they did not consent to a clarification of the constitution, deployment of forces would be recommended based on the existing constitutional framework.[25]

The position of the Free Democratic Party (FDP) was decisively shaped by the former foreign minister, Hans-Dietrich Genscher. According to Genscher, all German governments have stated that out-of-area operations by German forces are illegal. No government could assume the responsibility of taking such a crucial decision on a shaky constitutional basis.[26] The Liberals have stated on several occasions that they will not accept a clandestine evasion of the constitution by their coalition partners, the CDU/CSU.[27]

Initially, the Social Democratic Party strictly rejected a constitutional amendment:

We reject an extension of the missions of NATO and WEU aimed at the potential use of their forces for operations outside the borders of the NATO area as well as the projected establishment of Rapid Reaction Forces. An amendment to the Basic Law designed to provide for the participation of the German armed forces in those or other military out-of-area operations is incompatible with our peace policy. We reject a German participation in military combat operations conducted under UN command or by authorization of the UN. However, the Federal Republic of Germany must be capable of participating in peacekeeping missions under the aegis of the UN (blue-helmet missions).[28]

During an out-of-schedule party congress held in autumn 1992 the Social Democrats declared their support for a constitutional amendment permitting a participation in blue-helmet missions.[29] Several delegates also supported peacemaking missions. In August 1992, the Social Democratic group in the Bundestag filed a constitutional suit against the government for deploying German naval vessels to the Adriatic. However, the government was unable to provide a constitutional rationale by the deadline in mid-December.[30] As of this writing, the federal constitutional court had yet to announce its decision. The Social Democrats will presumably once again put this issue on the agenda of a party congress scheduled for late 1993.

In early 1993, both the government and the opposition brought forward new proposals for constitutional amendments.[31] Overall, the positions of the political parties can be summarized as follows: the coalition (CDU/CSU and FDP) would like to provide for participation in any operation except for a war of aggression, as well as for emergency relief operations carried out at the German government's discretion. However, the ruling coalition partners differ in their position insofar as the CDU/CSU consider the necessary constitutional prerequisites to be already present while the FDP expects amendments to be indispensable. The Social Democrats would like to preclude any operations save those for the purpose of defense and UN peacekeeping.

To date, the blue-helmet debate, which has been continuing since the Gulf War, has focused on constitutional aspects. Hans Rühe, head of the planning staff at the German ministry of defense from 1982 to 1988, had, on several occasions, raised some practical concerns against the deployment of German forces. For example, he argued, many German politicians insist that German forces cannot be employed in countries occupied by Germany during World War II. This prohibition would also apply to Israel and its neighbors as well as to former colonies. Hence, large portions of Europe, Africa, and the Middle East would automatically become "restricted areas."[32]

Rühe further argues that the German armed forces do not have a single unit (battalion level and above) that could be available as a coherent formation. This would not seem to be an insurmountable problem, for as of 1 October 1993, there are to be two battalions available for peacekeeping missions; moreover, prior German participation in missions below the peacekeeping level, in Kurdistan and Cambodia, has shown that there may be sufficient volunteers.[33] Furthermore, since early 1993, 30 German soldiers have been receiving training in

Niimisalo, Finland, qualifying them as military observers and instructors for UN missions. Another 50 commissioned and noncommissioned officers are to participate in UN training programs in Austria, Sweden, Finland, Denmark, and Switzerland, thus providing for swift support of the United Nations once the appropriate legal prerequisites have been established.[34]

Rühe considers the chief obstacle to be German society. Society has psychologically banished the notion of war, replacing it with trust in a functioning deterrence. Once the first zinc coffins return with bodies of German soldiers, the ensuing public outrage could well reduce the rearmament debate of the 1980s to a mild breeze. The belief that the fate of the German expeditionary force would reinforce solidarity with the populations to be protected by peacemaking missions might turn out to be a fatal fallacy.[35] Nevertheless, as most recent polls conducted by the research institutes Emnid and Allensbach suggest, public consent to blue-helmet missions under the aegis of the UN has increased in recent months.[36]

According to these same polls, consent (32 percent) and rejection (36 percent) with respect to the issue of constitutional amendment were nearly even, with approximately 30 percent undecided. Consent to the missions was greater in the Western than in the Eastern part of Germany. This suggests that public opinion is slowly being socialized toward UN actions by the humanitarian commitments in Iraq, Cambodia, and Bosnia, as well as daily television reports of the civil war in the former Yugoslavia, a tendency that could, in the long term, change the German attitude toward peacekeeping missions. In this context, Germany's recent decision actively to participate in humanitarian relief efforts in

Table 6.1 Consent to Potential Missions (in percent)

	1991	1992
National Defense	90	91
Defense (NATO)	71	70
Blue-Helmet Missions (UN)	65	71
Combat Missions (UN)	44	48

Source: "Immer mehr für UN-Einsätze," *Bundeswehr Aktuell*, 11 March 1993.

Somalia, even in the face of possible involvement in combat, should serve as a testing ground for German public opinion toward further blue-helmet participation.

The discussion on the employment of the Bundeswehr abroad has become murky at times, with the coalition government and the Social Democratic opposition bringing forward contradictory legislative initiatives. The current constitutional situation is hardly simple, and there is much scope for creative interpretation. The constitutional arguments of the government seem no better than those of the opposition, which rejects the deployment of German forces. Even after an amendment to the Basic Law, there would be no *obligation* to deploy, whether under international law or existing NATO understandings. In Bonn it is anticipated that an amendment to the constitution will not be achieved for the time being, and that even the federal constitutional court cannot be counted upon to clarify the issue. The court has already stated that for 1993 no decision, other than a limited reply to the suit filed by the Social Democrats with respect to naval operations in the Adriatic, could be expected, for it maintains that such a decision would relieve the Bundestag from its duty to clarify the options for deployment.[37]

The War in Yugoslavia

On the one hand, the collapse of communism in Central and Eastern Europe has brought an end to decades of crisis; on the other hand, the ensuing transition to democracy and market-oriented economies has sparked yet another crisis, which constitutes a significant risk to the West.

The Central European states seem to have turned the corner in their difficult transition process. For 1993, Poland and Hungary are expecting real growth in their economies.[38] In the former Czechoslovakia the upswing might be delayed as a result of its division into two independent states. Nevertheless, these countries impart on the other Eastern nations a hope that transition can be achieved. The most severe crises requiring close Western attention are the war in the former Yugoslavia and the crisis in Russia; Western security politicians unanimously share the opinion that the greatest hazard lies in the instability and the ethnic conflicts in the post-Soviet successor states as well as in the potential resurrection of reactionary forces in Russia.[39]

For the first time, the post-Cold War European Community has been put to the test. The EC has been unable to resolve a European conflict on its own. The main concern appears not to be safeguarding the principles of self-determination and integrity of national borders but rather preserving the national interests of individual EC member states, which have to deal with autonomy aspirations of their own minorities as well as with a distrust of Germany as the alleged beneficiary of the disintegration of the Yugoslavian state.[40] The fact that some countries historically harbor sympathy for Serbia as a former ally plays a role as well.

When one considers the overall levels of humanitarian aid provided by the European Community, one sees that Germany has covered the bulk of material aid, and has also carried out supply flights. However, it does not participate in UN land operations.

There are no indications that Germany will downgrade or discontinue its humanitarian aid. Exploiting the opportunities available under existing constitutional conditions, Germany has aided the United States during its air-dropping operations over Bosnia. This prompted Bosnian Serb threats that aircraft over Bosnia would be shot down if German aircraft were involved in the relief operations.[41] This is evidence of the

Table 6.2 Humanitarian Aid for the Former Yugoslavia Since 1991: Selected Countries in Comparison (millions of US dollars)

EC Commission (German share)	368.1 (103.1)
US	150.7
Germany	75.3
Great Britain	55.2
Turkey	37.9
Italy	36.0
France	34.0
Switzerland	31.0
Denmark	28.7
Austria	23.5
Canada	23.5
Japan	22.5
Total	621.4

Source: *The Week in Germany*, 29 January 1993.

hatred the Serbs harbor as a result of the occupation by German forces during the Second World War, German cooperation with the then-fascist regime in Croatia, and Germany's eager recognition of the Slovenian and Croatian states. Hence, Serbia will be very hesitant in approving the employment of German forces for peacekeeping operations. For historic reasons, politicians of all major German parties have rejected such a deployment. Even such prominent foreign observers as Henry Kissinger consider German operations in the former Yugoslavia to be inappropriate.[42] Hence, such operations appear to be most unlikely even assuming an amendment of the Basic Law.

Yet, there is another problem calling for a long-term solution—the refugee issue. According to UN estimates, by mid-1992 approximately 2.4 million people had been displaced as a result of the war in the former Yugoslavia. At the same time, the numbers of registered asylum seekers and refugees from the former Yugoslavia were as indicated below.

Britain refuses to accept Bosnian refugees, arguing that they should be accommodated as close as possible to their home. Approximately half of the predominantly Muslim refugees are seeking asylum for political reasons.[43] The majority of these refugees will come to Germany, a fact that might further aggravate the asylum-seekers issue. As yet, there has been no support for Germany's plight from the Western community. A ceasefire alone would not make the refugees return to their former home. Hence, from the German point of view, it is necessary to seek, within the

Table 6.3 Intake of Refugees from the Former Yugoslavia as of mid-1992

Germany	200,000	Italy	1,600
Hungary	60,000	Denmark	1,000
Austria	50,000	France	900
Sweden	41,000	Britain	–
Turkey	26,000	US	–
Switzerland	12,200	Australia	–
Netherlands	3,300	Canada	–
Norway	1,900		

Source: "Eine Million auf dem Sprung," *Der Spiegel*, 17 July 1992, pp. 18-27.

scope of burdensharing, an allocation of refugees to other members of the European Community and also to North America.

Both the misery of the refugees and daily media coverage of the horrors taking place in Bosnia-Herzegovina seem to have had a heavy impact on public opinion. Conny Jürgens, secretary of the Green-Alternative List (GAL) grouping in the Hamburg state parliament calls for a swift intervention of UN forces in order to restore human rights in Bosnia. The former peace movement activist is now regarded as one of the spokespersons of the interventionists within her party. The GAL is the first Green section to advocate intervention, even with German participation, in order to terminate the war. From her point of view, it is time to restore morality in politics.[44]

Until now, many high-ranking military officers in almost all Western countries, among them General Klaus Naumann, chief of staff of the German armed forces, have discouraged intervention in the former Yugoslavia. However, in a speech delivered to a CDU/CSU working group in January 1993, Naumann articulated a radical change of mind.[45] He noted that his generation again and again asked their parents why, during the Third Reich, they had not stood up against the cruelties committed against parts of the German population. Today his own children ask him what he is going to do to terminate the holocaust in Bosnia-Herzegovina. According to Naumann, a point has been reached where it has to be made clear that a revision of national borders by force will not be tolerated. He proposed a series of military and political measures, including full implementation of the sanctions agreed on; imposition of a blockade against Serbia and Montenegro, disrupting supply at sea, on the ground, and in the air by force, if necessary; imposition of a ban on flights over Bosnia-Herzegovina and sanctions against those who violate this ban; interdiction of access to Bosnia-Herzegovina from Serbia and Montenegro by UN forces; provision of full-scale humanitarian aid for Bosnia-Herzegovina, enforcing access to suffering cities and communities, if necessary; and legal prosecution of war criminals. Naumann advocates a clear mandate for the UN with respect to these measures.

It is interesting that in this case a German top official has discussed the employment of ground forces with a combat mission and that enforcement of the flight ban might also imply deliberate attacks, for instance against Serbian airfields. Hence, Naumann by early 1993 was advocating the most extreme option within the scope of the official decisionmaking process.

The German government succeeded in creating consent on the issue of AWACS (Airborne Warning and Control System) operations. The dispute within the governmental coalition on the participation of

German AWACS crew members in case of a military enforcement of the UN flight ban centered around the fact that the CDU/CSU unconditionally approved their employment, whereas the FDP considered this to be unconstitutional. On 24 March 1993, the coalition partners agreed that in the cabinet the CDU/CSU ministers would vote for a deployment while the FDP ministers would abstain; subsequently, the FDP took the issue to the federal constitutional court to obtain a short-notice ruling on the constitutionality of the cabinet decision.[46] The decision by the FDP to choose this rather unusual venue stirred up German public opinion. Had the court rejected the inquiry, the coalition would have been in an awkward position. However, the court decided not to rule on the issue of constitutionality itself, although it did agree to examine that issue at a later date. It did, however, decide that significant foreign-policy disadvantages would accrue to Germany if it distanced itself from international peace efforts.[47] Since this was only a temporary measure, the problematic constitutional situation itself has not changed.

It is difficult if not impossible to predict the future course of the war in the former Yugoslavia. From the present point of view, however, it can and must be said that the employment of German forces seems unlikely. To sum up, Germany has carried the largest share of the material burden by contributing to humanitarian aid and accommodating refugees— even when taking into consideration the recent reform of its refugee policy—and it will maintain an adequate level of commitment. At the same time, though, it will have to insist on adequate participation on the part of the other European countries. Both the misery of refugees arriving in Germany, as well as daily news reports on the horrors of the Bosnian war could possibly cause a change in public opinion. At both ends of the political spectrum, from the Green Party to the chief of staff of the country's armed forces, demands for a military solution to end the war in the former Yugoslavia have been voiced. The constitutional court supports the government's decision to allow German officers to participate in AWACS operations securing a non-flight zone over Bosnia. In spite of this temporary commitment, the constitutional situation remains unclear.

The Russian Crisis

As recent events demonstrate so well, not only outside Russia (in the "near abroad") but also within it violent solutions to ethnic, nationalist, and political conflicts cannot be ruled out. A new constitution will define the final structure of the Russian Federation with its population of approximately 150 million, 80 percent of whom are Russians. Efforts to create a new centralized order are opposed by various forms of separatism and regionalism, and it will be one of Boris Yeltsin's priorities, now that he has suppressed his parliamentary foes, to arrest the decentralization trends of the past two years. During his lengthy struggle with the parliamentarians, Yeltsin aimed to strengthen his position against them by establishing a new institution, the Council of the Heads of Republics of Russia. His policy, or tactic, of compromise and dialogue with the republics was met with increasing criticism—and not just on the part of his foes in parliament. Among the military there were growing numbers of voices advocating the application of force to solve domestic conflicts within the federation.[48] As explained in chapter one of this volume, there has been evolving a hegemonic approach of Russia toward other republics within the Commonwealth of Independent States (CIS), some of which have large Russian minorities; this may be a factor of uncertainty with clear potential for conflict.

This state of uncertainty raises once again the question of peacekeeping forces, not only on the part of Russian forces but possibly involving Western countries and organizations as well. In this context, one has to examine the extent to which peacekeeping concepts already do exist within the CIS, and whether Western countries, including Germany, might be expected to have a hand in this area.

The first discussion of peacekeeping forces took place at the fourth CIS summit meeting held in Kiev on 20 March 1992. At this meeting, ten of the 11 CIS member states signed an agreement on "Groups of Military Observers and Collective Peacekeeping Forces in the CIS." This agreement, which dealt in great detail with the issue of peacekeeping forces, stated that

> groups of military observers and of collective peacekeeping forces of the CIS member states . . . are being created for the purpose of providing each other assistance, on the basis of mutual agreement, in settling and preventing conflicts on the territory of any member of the Commonwealth that may arise on interethnic, religious, and political grounds, and that entail the violation of human rights.[49]

To what extent have these steps been successful? So far, the Russian forces' activities have had an ambiguous relationship to peace in the "near abroad." The Russian army supplied, initially, heavy weapons to Azerbaijan, enabling it to wage an outright war against its Armenian minority in Karabakh; later, it is assumed Russia also supported Armenia, helping it prevail (to date) in its struggle with its eastern neighbor. In Georgia the Russian military has apparently supported several sides, first the secessionists struggling in Abkhazia and South Ossetia, later the government of Eduard Shevardnadze, once the latter took his country into the CIS. In Moldova, the Russian army has protected the renegade "trans-Dniester Republic." In Tajikistan Russian forces brought about a transition of power in favor of the old communist *nomenklatura*.[50]

By contrasting the discussion of peacekeeping with the actual use of forces, a discrepancy between theory and practice has surfaced. Two basic guidelines established in the 20 March agreement on peacekeeping have been neglected: first, peacekeeping forces have been committed in regions where conflicts are still going on; second, rather than being neutral, the peacekeeping forces have been parties to the conflict. The neglect of such fundamental principles would seem to turn the logic underlying the pursuit of peacekeeping missions on its head.

It is most unlikely that non-CIS forces will be deployed for peacekeeping missions on CIS territory. The possibility of intervention on the part of the UN, the Conference for Security and Cooperation in Europe (CSCE), NATO, or other organizations has been increasingly criticized. Russian military sources have not disguised their opposition to the idea of Western commitments of military forces or observers. They also reject the notion of committing non-CIS forces to deal with conflicts at the external borders of the CIS, i.e., between a successor state to the old USSR and a neighboring country.[51] Given the current political parameters, this makes it seem highly improbable that Russia, being a permanent member of the UN Security Council, will permit the employment of Western peacekeeping forces on former Soviet territory or at former Soviet borders. Neither nationally nor internationally has the commitment of German forces been considered for this purpose, even in the most general way.

A more pressing potential problem for Germany is posed by the possibility of a new immigration movement from the East. The desires of a population of German descent, scattered all over Siberia as a result of Stalin's policy of expulsion and resettlement, to be relocated back to the Volga region are not likely to be satisfied, despite the support provided by Germany.[52] As a consequence, resettlement to Germany itself will continue unabated for years to come. Although in the period 1988-92 as many as 400,000 people of German descent arrived in the country every year, in early 1993 the annual acceptance rate was officially limited to 220,000.[53] However, in the case of famine or civil war, these numbers can be expected to increase tremendously, given that there are still between two and three-and-a-half million people of German descent left in Russia itself.

The risks discussed show that the process of reformation in Russia is by no means structurally or personally secured by political leaders and decisionmakers. Germany, like the West as a whole, possesses only limited capacities to respond to the various dangers created by Russian domestic strife. In addition to the obvious option of providing (limited) financial support and advice, more recourse could be had to inviting political, military, and economic leaders to visit Western countries so that they might gain insights into the workings of free-market economies. The employment of German forces for blue-helmet missions within CIS territory is not to be expected, given Germany's current situation. Nevertheless, there may be other, nonmilitary, approaches that are more suitable to Germany in coping with the Eastern crisis.

Ever since the Berlin Wall came down in November 1989 and the Soviet Union broke up in December 1991, an epochal new order has emerged. Its further development, however, is vague and its outcomes are by no means clear. Eastern Europe has, to date, miraculously survived tremendous social, political, and economic transformations without the outbreak of civil wars. We should not so much be surprised to see why violence has sprung up in some cases as to find why it has *not* in other places, and on a much larger scale.

Eastern Europe's contribution to political culture in the twentieth century might be its "self-restraining revolution," which has provided for a negotiated step-by-step transition to a new order.[54] Fortunately, this development is supported by the West in general and Germany specifically, both in economic as well as humanitarian terms. Since 1990 the West has transferred almost DM144 billion to the former Soviet states to support the transition from a planned economy to a market economy. The European share of this assistance has been more than 70 percent, of which Germany's portion is more than 57 percent. More billions can be expected to follow after the events in Moscow of October 1993. However, as Chancellor Kohl has declared, the Germans have reached the limits of what they can afford to contribute.[55] Apart from purely financial support, other forms of assistance (e.g., providing management know-how) seem to be highly important. For example, the Berlin Treuhand has founded a Treuhand Osteuropa Beratungsgesellschaft ("Eastern Europe Assistance Association"), which assigns management consultants for various projects.[56]

Since 1990, the European Community has provided DM3.5 billion worth of food and medicines as well as technical assistance valued at almost DM2 billion. Germany donated more than 10,000 vehicles and hundreds of tons of medical supplies, part of which were taken from the inventories of the former East German army.[57] Moreover, a large number of German relief organizations and private individuals have supported the population, especially during the winter months, by sending millions of food packages. One reason for these food drives, which were promoted by German television and newspapers, was the fact that many

Germans remembered the American "CARE" program of help for Germany after World War II.

Besides economic assistance programs, there is also the question of immediate security guarantees and confidence-building measures. The first results of the CFE (Conventional Forces in Europe) treaty, the withdrawal of the Western Group of Forces (WGF), and bilateral military cooperation all indicate a potential utility of nonmilitary solutions to the Eastern crisis.[58] A new force ratio will be established not only within Europe as a whole but also within the CIS states, with Russia providing 54 percent, Ukraine 27 percent, and Belarus 12 percent of conventional armed forces.[59]

A report on German inspections carried out between 17 July and 13 November 1992 (nine in Russia, eight each in Ukraine and the former Czechoslovakia, seven in Poland, four each in Belarus, Rumania, and Bulgaria, and one each in Hungary, Georgia, and Moldova) shows, in a first assessment, that Russia, Ukraine, and most of the other states had begun destroying equipment and were seeking to fulfill their contractual obligations.[60]

In October 1990, the "Treaty on the Limited Stationing and the Withdrawal of Soviet Forces from Germany" entered into force, requiring not only an enormous logistical operation to move 2.6 million tons of material (including ammunition), but also decisively improving Germany's military-strategic position.[61] During his visit to Moscow in December 1992, Chancellor Kohl agreed with President Yeltsin on an early completion of the withdrawal in exchange for additional credits.[62] Germany supports the withdrawal of forces by paying more than DM12 billion and granting several billions worth of interest-free credits, including DM7.8 billion to provide housing for officers returning to the former Soviet Union. The first of the newly built towns have already been handed over to the Russian authorities, ready for the tenants to occupy.

Having been part of the Soviet forces in East Germany, nearly one million people from the former Soviet Union will have spent a few months or years of their lives in post-reunification Germany. They will have gained some first-hand experience with freedom, democracy, and a free-market economy. Since they receive 80 percent of their pay in German currency, many have already had the chance to purchase consumer goods, such as cars (often used) and electronic appliances. Also, soldiers have been offered professional-development courses, such as management courses, paid for by the German government. As General Hartmut Foertsch notes, "[A] young soldier from Ossetia or Kirghizia is regarded as an expert on Germany once he returns home, which is why for us he could be an important means of advertisement."[63]

Bilateral military cooperation also contributes to mutual confidence and trust. The German armed forces, for instance, share information and experience through staff talks or exchange visits. The Center for Inner Leadership offers seminars and courses designed specifically to address the problem of integrating armed forces into a democratic society, by promoting such concepts as "inner leadership," and the "citizen in uniform."[64]

Further progress toward establishing democracy and free-market principles in Russia will largely depend on the political momentum Boris Yeltsin and the reformers will gain from the successful outcome of the coming election, and the stabilization of the Russian currency. The West can support this development by providing technical assistance and advice.

Conclusion

The blue-helmet debate is likely to remain one of the more pertinent issues in German domestic and foreign policy. Although Germany has strengthened its integration efforts into the West by the Maastricht treaty and the formation of multinational corps, its reluctant attitude toward military participation in United Nations peacekeeping efforts will only add to the apparent indecisiveness of a Europe stricken by domestic problems.

The blue-helmet debate can only be understood if seen in direct relation to Germany's domestic situation, which strengthens the pre-existing consensus against out-of-area commitments of the Bundeswehr. Divergent constitutional positions can only add to the overall confusion attending the blue-helmet debate. Comments and proposals on the part of the major political parties seem clear enough. The governing coalition is prepared to support any operation except wars of aggression and unilateral relief operations. The opposition would prefer to abstain from any operations beyond national defense and genuine blue-helmet missions. A compromise does not seem possible, and a ruling of the constitutional court on these matters is not expected until 1994.

The challenges posed by the Eastern crisis cannot be underestimated. The breakdown of communism and the transition to democracy and free-market principles plunged the countries of Eastern Europe into a deep economic crisis. As a result of the war in the former Yugoslavia, Germany had to carry the highest material burden in the form of humanitarian assistance, including the reception of many thousands of refugees. Allegations of a German "introversion" in terms of a commitment to global humanitarian issues would not appear to be justified.

Germany has taken on a leadership role within the West through its efforts to support peaceful solutions to the Eastern crises. Within the framework of the CFE treaty and the withdrawal of the WGF from Germany personal contacts and relationships based on mutual trust are being established. Even without committing its own forces to UN-sponsored peacekeeping missions, Germany has reached the limitations of its capacity to help solve the Eastern crisis. If forced to take on heavier burdens, Germany itself might fall a victim to that crisis, which in turn could have irreparable consequences for the security of all of Western Europe.

Notes

1. Quoted in Klaus Reinhardt, "Blauhelme—und nicht mehr? Deutschlands Beitrag zur Sicherung des Friedens in einer stabilen Welt," in *Rissener Jahrbuch 1992* (Haus Rissen: Hamburg, 1992), p. 289.

2. Karl Otto Hondrich, *Lehrmeister Krieg* (Reinbek bei Hamburg: Rowohlt, 1992), pp. 7-30.

3. Uwe Möller, "Stehen wir vor einer neuen Rezession?" in *Rissener Jahrbuch 1992*, p. 99.

4. Ibid., p. 100.

5. S. G. Gwymme, "The Long Haul," *Time*, 28 September 1992, p. 18.

6. "Schulden, Schulden, Schulden," *Der Spiegel*, 22 March 1993, pp. 18-20.

7. "Germany's Strains, Europe's Fears," *Economist*, 5 December 1992, pp. 15-16.

8. Heiner Geißler, "'Wir brauchen die Ausländer,' Ein Plädoyer gegen die völkische Renaissance der Deutschen," *Information für die Truppe* (3/92): 39.

9. Mario von Baratta, ed., *Der Fischer Weltalmanach 1993* (Frankfurt a.M.: Fischer Verlag, 1992), p. 302.

10. Helga Hermann, "Ungelöste Probleme: Asylbewerber-Einwanderer-Flüchtlinge," *Informationen zur politischen Bildung* (4. Quarter 1992): 33.

11. Ibid.

12. "Germany Revokes Right to Asylum," *Globe and Mail* (Toronto), 27 May 1993.

13. Heinz Vielain, "Union will Nationale Sicherheitskonferenz," *Welt am Sonntag*, 14 March 1993.

14. Ibid.

15. Kurt Biedenkopf, "Die geeinte Nation im Stimmungstief," *Die Zeit*, 9 October 1992.

16. "Erst vereint, wenn entzweit," Spiegel-Umfrage über die Einstellung der West- und Ostdeutschen zueinander, *Der Spiegel*, 18 January 1993, pp. 52-62.

17. Theo Sommer, "Für Helmut Kohl eine letzte Chance," *Die Zeit*, 18 September 1992, p. 1.

18. Siegmar Schelling, "Die Lage wird für Engholm immer dramatischer," *Welt am Sonntag*, 7 March 1993, p. 4.

19. Christian Tomuschat, "Der Blauhelm ist Bonn erlaubt: Zur Diskussion über einen Einsatz im Dienst der UNO," *Rheinischer Merkur/Christ und Welt*, 4 August 1989, p. 5.

20. Christian Tomuschat, "Deutscher zu den UN-Friedenstruppen," *Außenpolitik* (3/1985): 272-83.

21. Thomas Wandlinger, "UN-Friedenstruppen im Brennpunkt internationaler Friedenssicherung," *Information für die Truppe* (2/1989): 32-46.

22. Norbert Karl Riedel, *Der Einsatz deutscher Streitkräfte im Ausland—verfassungs- und völkerrechtliche Schranken* (Bern: Peter Lang, 1989).

23. *Deutsches Fernsehen*, 16 August 1990.

24. Volker Rühe during CDU meeting on foreign policy held on 15 May 1991.

25. "CDU: Kampfeinsatz der Bundeswehr schon jetzt möglich," *Welt am Sonntag*, 21 February 1993.

26. Interview, *Süddeutsche Zeitung*, 25 August 1990.

27. Bundeshauptausschuß der FDP, 25 May 1991.

28. SPD-Vorsitzender Dr. Hans-Joachim Vogel, *Zweites Deutsches Fernsehen*, 19 August 1990; Saarländischer Ministerpräsident Oskar Lafontaine, *RTL*, 19 August 1990.

29. Ekkehard Kohrs, "Wie sich die SPD an deutsche Blauhelm-Einsätze heranrobbt," *General-Anzeiger*, 18 November 1992, p. 2.

30. Norbert Gansel, "Auf der Suche nach einem Bundeswehrkonsens oder wie kittet man zerbrochenes Porzellan," *Truppenpraxis* (2/93): 130-32.

31. "Und so wollen die Parteien die Verfassung ändern," ibid., p. 129.

32. Hans Rühe, "Und jetzt Krieg?" *Der Spiegel*, 24 February 1992, p. 108.

33. Ibid.

34. "Ausbildung bei Experten," *Bundeswehr Aktuell*, 16 March 1993.

35. Rühe, "Und jetzt Krieg?" p. 108.

36. "Immer mehr für UN-Einsätze," *Bundeswehr Aktuell*, 11 March 1993.

37. "Parteienstreit in Bonn über AWACS-Einsatz," *Welt am Sonntag*, 11 April 1993.

38. Herbert Podlich, "Polen: Wende zum Besseren," *Capital* (2/93); "Gegen die Wand," *Der Spiegel*, 8 March 1993, p. 180.

39. Wolfgang Fechner, "Auf der Suche nach einer neuen Rolle, Die NATO, die Deutschen, die Sicherheit und neue Gefahren—Bericht von der Münchner Konferenz für Sicherheitspolitik," *Truppenpraxis* (2/93): 116.

40. Henrik Bischof, *Die europäische Sicherheit und das Pulverfaß Osteuropa* (Bonn: Friedrich-Ebert Stiftung, 1992).

41. "Bosnian Serb Generals Agree to Ceasefire," *Toronto Star*, 27 March 1993.

42. Manfred Geist, "Der Westen muß wissen, wo er 1995 stehen will," *Welt am Sonntag*, 4 April 1993, p. 25.

43. "Eine Million auf dem Sprung," *Der Spiegel*, 27 July 1992, pp. 18-27.

44. "Sie kneifen, Herr General: Manfred Opel (SPD) und Conny Jürgens (Grüne) über UNO-Interventionen auf dem Balkan," *Der Spiegel*, 1 February 1993, pp. 76-83.

45. Rolf Clement, "Dem Morden ein Ende machen," *Rheinischer Merkur*, 15 January 1993, pp. 3-4.

46. "Kompromiß bei AWACS-Flügen über Bosnien: Bundeswehr beteiligt sich an Hilfsflügen," *Deutschland-Nachrichten,* 26 March 1993, p. 2.

47. "Goverment Expresses Relief at Karlsruhe AWACS Decision; SPD Warns Against 'Carte Blanche'," *The Week in Germany,* 16 April 1993.

48. Henrik Bischof, *Rußland-Machtkampf im Kreml* (Bonn: Friedrich-Ebert Stiftung, 1993), p. 17.

49. Tass, 4 March 1992.

50. Suzanne Crow, "Peacekeeping in the CIS," in *Friedenserhaltende und -schaffende Maßnahmen: Die universale Option (Möglichkeiten, Erfordernisse und Probleme im Rahmen der Vereinten Nationen)* (Ebenhausen: Stiftung Wissenschaft und Politik, 1993), pp. 243-67.

51. *Krasnaya zverda,* 23 June 1992.

52. "Rußlanddeutsche nach Saratow?" *Frankfurter Allgemeine Zeitung,* 22 January 1992, p. 6.

53. "Ein einig Volk von Blutsbrüdern," *Der Spiegel,* 15 March 1993, pp. 50-54.

54. Karl Schlögel, "Die stille Revolution, Umbruch im Osten Europas," *Der Spiegel,* 25 February 1993, pp. 130-45.

55. Heinz Vielan und Siegmar Schelling, "Kanzler Kohl, Deutsche haben für Rußland am meisten getan," *Welt am Sonntag,* 28 March 1993.

56. "Ich habe Bauchschmerzen," *Der Spiegel,* 8 March 1993, pp. 120-28.

57. "Güter für die GUS, Vielfältige Hilfen für die Menschen," *Information für die Truppe* (12/92): 28-30.

58. Georg-Wilhelm von Graevenitz, "Ziel erreicht—trotz mancher Hindernisse," *Truppenpraxis* (5/92): 518-22.

59. "KSE-Vertrag über konventionelle Abrüstung kann in Kraft treten," *Soldat und Technik* (7/92): 442.

60. Heinz Kluss, "Reise nach Utopia," *Truppenpraxis* (2/93): 122-26.

61. Bernt Conrad, "Abzug der Roten Armee ist geregelt," *Die Welt,* 13 October 1990; Hartmut Foertsch, "Eine erste Bilanz: Abzug der Westgruppe der Truppen aus Deutschland," *Europäische Sicherheit* (4/92): 229-31.

62. "Schlüsselfertige Stadt im Kaukasus," *Loyal* (2/93): 21-23.

63. Quoted in Peter Schmalz, "Entspannung zwischen Deutschen und GUS-Armee," *Die Welt,* 29 May 1992.

64. Dieter Francke, "Anleihen im Westen? Ehemalige Ostblockoffiziere am Zentrum Innere Führung," *Beiheft Information für die Truppe* (2/92): 36-39.

7

Between Eurovoluntarism and Realism: France and European Security in Transition

Michel Fortmann and David G. Haglund

Introduction

There is at least one feature that never seems to change on the political landscape of European security: France continues to stake out, as it has done for more than three decades, a staunchly independent policy on defense and security.[1] This constancy aside, there are surprisingly few similarities with the past, for France's security policy, no less than that of other states, is in a period of major transformation. What sets it apart from the others is the degree of criticism and even vituperation it attracts, especially from its allies within NATO. At times it seems the latter have difficulty finding words harsh enough to direct at Paris.

In this regard, numerous examples spring to mind. France, it is said, was caught flat-footed by the events of 1989, and the clumsy efforts of its president, François Mitterrand, to slow the pace of German unification by working with Moscow unleashed a torrent of criticism from across the Rhine.[2] Nor was Paris any more adroit at understanding the political dynamics at work in the collapsing Soviet Union until too late, with French policy continuing to revolve around the need to preserve the "center of power" represented by the Soviet state.[3] From this, say the critics, flowed a set of blunders, the most prominent of them being the inability to discern in the Soviet firmament the rising political star of Boris Yeltsin, and the hasty decision, taken at the time of the August 1991 coup, to recognize the group of conspirators who sought to overthrow Mikhail Gorbachev as the "new leadership" in the Kremlin.[4] Noted one French diplomat, apropos these gaffes: "France may not have been absent from the historical stage, but its diplomatic initiatives had all the appearance of being reactions to, rather than influences upon, the events taking place."[5]

And what could one say about the Prague conference on European confederation, during which the French president clashed so bitterly with his Czechoslovak counterpart, Vaclav Havel? For Mitterrand, what the Central European states needed was to ensconce themselves in the antechamber of the European Community, where they would presumably take comfort in the vague promise of a confederal association with the rich countries of Western Europe. In this, as in so many other regards, French policy differed markedly from that of certain allies, above all the Germans.

To all the above must certainly be added the major aggravation that has been France's policy toward the Atlantic Alliance. Since late 1990 Paris had been conducting a systematic guerrilla campaign against NATO's strategic reform, and particularly against the idea of expanding the alliance's political role. Not content merely to spurn its own rapprochement with NATO, France—through its ambassador to the alliance, Gabriel Robin—sought to block each attempt to initiate a dialogue between the alliance and the countries of Central and Eastern Europe. This same negative outlook characterized French thinking on the issue of a possible NATO peacekeeping mission in the former Yugoslavia.[6]

At the same time, both on its own and in company with Germany, France undertook a series of measures whose goal was to build the foundation of a "Europe of defense," a construction regarded by many of the allies as at best premature, at worst fundamentally damaging to the transatlantic relationship. The creation of the Eurocorps, announced at the Franco-German summit in La Rochelle on 22 May 1992, as well as the bid to link the Western European Union (WEU) to European political union and subordinate the former to the European Council, were poorly received in several alliance capitals, above all London and Washington.[7] Was France trying to wreck NATO by setting up a competing security organization? Some incidents, which at best can only be adjudged to have been ridiculous, characterized the mounting of parallel maritime patrols in the Adriatic by both NATO and the WEU during the summer of 1992, and these tended to confirm the suspicions of the pessimists about French intentions. As the *Economist* wryly noted, "this curious naval operation has achieved one thing: it has torpedoed the theory that the Western European Union is an organisation that will help hold the Atlantic Alliance together. On this evidence, the WEU is an alliance divider."[8]

From this perspective, 1992 marked the low point in relations between France and NATO; several allies even raised the possibility of meeting as a group of 15 rather than have to continue confronting French obstructionism in the midst of the North Atlantic Council.[9] Others were gloomily asking themselves whether Paris had not become Washington's number one enemy. Certain analysts who were fairly well connected to the French policy community were having increasing difficulty justifying a stance that seemed to be progressively isolating their country from its partners.[10]

How can these disturbing developments be interpreted? Like other major powers, France felt the aftershocks of the political earthquakes that marked the end of the Cold War order; unlike them, it suffered a singularly traumatic identity crisis as a result. Some writers attribute the crisis to a loss of status attending the disappearance of the Soviet Union and the end of the East-West confrontation. For more than 30 years, Paris was able to present itself as a privileged intermediary between East and West.[11] As Pierre Lellouche has noted, during the Cold War France's situation was particularly enviable: the German threat had disappeared, and the one from Russia was both far away and mitigated by the American security guarantee to Western Europe.[12] Moreover, France's strategic nuclear deterrent allowed the country politically to "travel first-class with a second-class ticket." Today, its nuclear arsenal can no longer provide the former comfort, and France is left to find its bearings without the old compass of Gaullist doctrine, especially as regards the proper policy toward the states of Central and Eastern Europe.

A less charitable interpretation has it that France is suffering from a crisis of regime, namely a hardening of the political arteries and a calling into question of the entire system. Old notions of right and left, so useful for so long in orienting the country's politics, no longer mean very much, and new parties such as the Greens and the National Front hardly loom as serious alternatives to the aging established parties. Moreover, as Steven Kramer notes, France's political life suffers the traumas of an all-powerful state's demonstrated inability to address the problems that bother its citizens the most: immigration, unemployment, and an overall deterioration in their quality of life.[13] Like their political elites, the French themselves are experiencing an identity crisis, one that counterpoises a national ideal of declining credibility against the political gravity of a Europe that is tolling the knell for the notion of French uniqueness.

The above claims all have a certain validity, but can it really be maintained that the recent blows to the country's foreign policy must be attributed solely to a postulated dual crisis? It is possible to undertake a different, perhaps less-superficial, examination of French policy by revisiting the events of the past four years. We could even state that French diplomacy, in reacting to events that it could not obviously control, did demonstrate a long-term, and well-defined, vision for the country, one moreover that gave rise to a certain number of choices, themselves clearly established by President Mitterrand. If this is true, however, how should we account for the negative and aggressive turn in French policy witnessed since 1991?

That turn can be explained as a forceful reaction to a situation that was showing itself to be, at one and the same time, more politically complex, fluid, and competitive. In this sense, rather than representing the whims of a prima donna or constituting a rudderless drifting, France's policy might instead be regarded as a coherent set of arguments that, despite its weaknesses, is worthy of serious study.

France's Security Policy Adjusts to the End of the Cold War: François Mitterrand's Choice

Three fallacies currently characterize the analysis of French reactions to the ending of the Cold War: (1) that French diplomacy was taken by surprise and thrown into panic, especially in respect of Germany; (2) that as a general rule, French reactions were dominated by short-term concerns; and (3) that as a result French policy demonstrated neither a vision nor anything resembling a plan of action.

Each of these claims can be refuted. Moreover, while it may be true that France, like other major powers, was surprised by the rapidity with which events unfolded in the summer and autumn of 1989, it is inaccurate to maintain that its elites were blind to the transformations under way. Speaking in Bonn in November 1989, Mitterrand observed that "with the way things are going, I shall be astounded if in the coming decade we do not have to confront the reality of a new European structure."[14] From the start, the president indicated what was in fact going to occur, albeit his perspective was a more long-term one than events would allow. Nonetheless, as Jérôme Paolini has stressed, "it is only in light of the long-term reconstruction of the European order that it makes sense to analyze French policy during the 1989-92 period."[15]

In that light, some conclusions were drawn, starting in the spring of 1990, when defense minister Jean-Pierre Chevènement proclaimed that "the decolonization of the last empire [the Soviet Union] represented a leap into the unknown for all Europeans, who would henceforth have to organize their security relations on a radically new basis."[16] From that moment on, there began in France a searching reappraisal, which goes on today, of the new requirements of security. The minister's remarks also triggered a fundamental restructuring of French defense, one evidenced by the unveiling, on 1 July 1992, of the military program law for the 1992-94 period.[17] But what is the conceptual foundation of this reorientation of French security policy?

Certain gravitational fields can be identified. The principal threat envisioned by French elites is the creation of a strategic vacuum in the heart of Europe. In that case, the countries of Central and Eastern Europe, as well as Germany and the EC, totally absorbed in a slow and difficult period of reconstruction, would be exposed to the dual menace of reemergent hegemony and proliferating nationalisms. This is what some writers have in mind when they speak of the "return of history."[18] To this can be added, to be sure, the peril represented by the countries on the southern periphery of Europe—a region characterized by the volatile admixture of extreme poverty, overpopulation, political instability, and excessive armaments.

What are these reemergent hegemonies that the French fear? In 1990, Russia surely found its place high on the list, given its indisputable military power; but even more so than Russia, it was Germany—economic superpower, dominant political force—that served as a referent for a France suddenly reduced to the status of diplomatic runner-up.

Given the way in which they assessed the situation, French elites —especially the president and his advisors—carved out a policy whose object was to avoid or to minimize the "risks of a return to the balancing games and reassurance pacts of a bygone era, which had proven so costly for Europe."[19] The goals of this policy, designed at least for the medium term, were the following: (1) to preserve, to the extent possible, France's security status as well as its autonomy and margin of maneuver; (2) to guarantee that Germany would remain firmly integrated within the EC, as well as within NATO and a variety of European organizations (e.g., CSCE, WEU, and Council of Europe); (3) to safeguard France's role as European leader, particularly in the EC context; (4) to preserve the American commitment to European security, even if the US troop presence was going ineluctably to be reduced; (5) to encourage a process of political and economic stabilization in Central and Eastern Europe through the spread of democracy and economic liberalization; (6) to promote, through the CSCE and other regional and international organizations, respect for human rights and minority rights; and (7) to protect the EC from the danger of dilution and the risk of loss of momentum resulting from a premature expansion.

Out of these goals would emerge a policy that President Mitterrand would begin to implement in 1989-90. Its postulate was the acceleration of European integration and the consolidation of the Franco-German "marriage." In this sense, the start of the 1990s presented a unique opportunity to forge the core of a European political union that might guarantee the existence of a continental center of gravity in security matters. That center would, of necessity, be composed of the

Franco-German tandem, in relation to which other states would have to find their place.[20]

France could thereby appease its fears of having to watch Bonn affirm its political independence and at the same time satisfy its hunger for status through what Dominique Moïsi called "the merger of the Deutschmark and the bomb."[21] Germany, for its part, lashed tightly to its French partner and to the EC, would be able to avoid being branded as anyone's threat, and at the same time be able to ratify its leadership within EC institutions. The price France was prepared to pay for all this was a portion of its sovereignty, both economic and political; in return, it expected to retain the status bequeathed to it by Gaullism, on the European level.

Several interesting corollaries were linked to this approach. To begin with, the maintenance if not reinforcement of the Atlantic Alliance was held to be a complement to the anchoring of Germany within the EC. France thus had to reassess its traditional position vis-à-vis NATO, and to seek an eventual rapprochement with it. Moreover, emphasis was given to the necessity of deepening the EC before it could be widened. As a result, it followed that France would be unable to satisfy the wishes of those Central and Eastern European countries seeking immediate entry into the EC.

The explanation for this is simple. Integrating the former East bloc states into the Common Market would not just present economic headaches; it ran the risk as well of unduly increasing Germany's influence, something Paris could not obviously look upon with favor. For similar reasons, France proved extremely reluctant to go beyond the traditional frameworks of European security and make of the CSCE a collective-security organization, as many in Germany were demanding it become. There was (and is) a fear that Germany might abuse its power and lead the EC to dilute its own influence over events. In short, for Paris the construction of a broader Europe founded upon collective security and the rapprochement of peoples would have to wait.

It is easy to see how, in an early stage, French policy conformed to these assumptions and goals in a methodical manner: the need to "strongly encase the process leading to the end of a divided Europe" and to avoid a German drift to the East was keenly felt in Paris.[22] Since 1988, Germany had been parting company from France in a variety of issues, among which was arms control, with Germany plumping for the elimination of tactical nuclear weapons in Central Europe. Bonn was even suspected of conducting a separate diplomacy toward Moscow—a suspicion bolstered by the Kohl-Gorbachev summit of 1988 and the German-Soviet declaration of 13 June 1989. Several observers noted, as well, that certain of the accords leading to German unification were negotiated directly between Bonn and Moscow, with the "two-plus-four" talks being reduced to marginal importance. France complained of a lack of consultation that it saw characterizing certain German decisions. Among these were Kohl's ten-point plan of November 1989, envisioning a united Germany; this was not even discussed in advance with Germany's French partner.

It was hardly surprising, given this drift so apparent by 1988, that Washington should begin to direct a charm offensive toward Germany; this constituted a second danger for the French.[23] In effect, since the summer of 1988, the Bush administration had been touting a new German-American "partnership in leadership" for the alliance. The enthusiasm with which James Baker welcomed the prospect of German unity, in December 1989, and the celebration by the secretary of state of a "new Atlanticism" signalled, for Paris, that the US was maneuvering to attract German sympathies and to assure its continued influence in the new Europe. François Mitterrand's trips to Kiev and East Berlin in December 1989 appear in this light to be what they really were: not diplomatic blunders, but warnings to Kohl. The latter would understand only too well that a Germany that spurned its partnership with France would thereby deprive itself of a dynamic—and essential—element in the building of Europe, and would soon find itself diplomatically isolated.

The message was not lost on Bonn; by March 1990, France and Germany would once again be singing in the same chorus. On 29 March Kohl made an appeal, on French television, for the creation of a United States of Europe by 2000. Within less than a month, on 19 April, a joint Franco-German initiative would be launched, asking the EC 12 to start working immediately to perfect political union. This route would be prepared by two intergovernmental conferences that laid the groundwork for the Maastricht treaty of late 1991. In the sphere of defense, in particular, France got German assent to including security policy within the mandate of political union. Such an inclusion might lead, it was felt, to the creation of a common defense policy over the long term.[24] It was in this context that Germany and France would commence resuscitating, in April 1990, the Western European Union, which was envisioned as a future component of political union—namely its military arm.

France's attitude toward the alliance also stemmed from the same policy context that motivated French behavior toward Germany and European political union. Because of the good relationship between Mitterrand and the US president, George Bush, there was growing in the spring of 1990 an expectation that Paris would rethink its traditional approach to NATO. From Washington's perspective, French involvement in post-Cold War European defense initiatives was regarded as a welcome development. In Paris, French officials expressed their desire to be more involved in alliance debates over the elaboration of a new strategy. They were especially preoccupied by the issue of multinational forces, as well as by the questions of NATO's assumption of new missions and the future of nuclear strategy. That France should make its voice heard in the formulation of a new NATO strategy was taken for granted in Paris, and welcomed. To do so, however, would require that those strategy discussions occur in the alliance fora in which France enjoyed full participation.

As an essential element of that full-blown debate, France was prepared to open up everything for discussion. Mitterrand would even go so far as to suggest that the alliance consider taking up *all* the security problems relating to the European equilibrium, and the possibility of nuclear cooperation with the British and naval collaboration with the Americans was broached.

France, it was said by some during that spring of 1990, would even be prepared to reintegrate itself militarily with the alliance if the latter could be fundamentally transformed. Every wish seemed capable of fulfillment in that season when the French and American presidents were preparing for their summit at Key Largo, on 19 April 1990. This Franco-American rapprochement, it bears stressing, was taking place at precisely the same time as EC integration was accelerating.

If Paris was supporting a fairly circumscribed European security organization, comprising on the one hand the WEU and EC, and on the other NATO, French officials were showing themselves to be much less enthusiastic about the CSCE or the Gorbachev vision of a pan-European collective-security system. This latter, which caught the fancy of many in Germany, would be foreclosed by Paris in favor of a very limited "institutionalization" of the CSCE, which took place in November 1990.[25] Significantly, the CSCE would not be endowed with a security council, which Bonn had sought, but would remain instead essentially a forum for political discussion. It should be noted that this French stance—so curious if judged *a posteriori*—was in harmony with a regnant conception of a benign European historical evolution, one characterized by a belief that an integrative dynamic was at work that predisposed Europe toward peace.

The final element in the French policy approach of that initial period, namely the deepening of EC political and economic union, meant that there should be no expansion of the Community eastward. This clearly reflected Paris' determination that it should be able to control the forces of change unleashed in the old continent, a task that would become virtually impossible in an enlarged EC with France as a necessarily reduced presence. On the other hand, a Europe of the Twelve that was dedicated to greater Western unity would be a Europe in which France's voice could be expected to resonate. Moreover, the EC would be a useful framework for channeling German economic assistance to the East.[26] Thus, as a natural outgrowth of policies adopted in late 1989 by the EC, France would be able to advance a series of initiatives toward the countries of Central and Eastern Europe that would at one and the same time address the clamant needs of those countries without in the process requiring the EC to clasp them to its bosom.

Thus, by the end of 1990 accords were reached between the EC and the three "Visegrad" states (Poland, Hungary, and Czechoslovakia), as well as with Bulgaria and Romania. These accords carried with them associate status in the EC, on the same basis as that granted by the Community to the members of the European Free Trade Association (EFTA).[27] By the same token, France was supportive of such assistance programs as PHARE and TACIS, as well as of such friendship and cooperation accords as those signed with Romania, Poland, Hungary, and Czechoslovakia.[28] The creation in 1991 of the European Bank for Reconstruction and Development (EBRD), headed by Jacques Attali, coupled with the Porto accords, which were sold as a kind of waiting-room for the Community, served to shore up the same policy.[29] So, too, did Mitterrand's hazy scheme for a European confederation, unveiled at Prague in June 1991.

From Eurovoluntarism to Realism:
The Evolution of French Security Policy, 1990 to 1992

If in 1989 and 1990 the above-sketched French approach to policy demonstrated all the hallmarks of coherence and careful thought—and this, it needs repeating, in a situation of continual flux in Europe—the ship of state would nevertheless soon approach a barrier of reefs that may not have been able to capsize it, but could certainly force it to alter its bearings. The "Eurovoluntaristic" euphoria of 1990 would cede position to a new policy that, much as it might have retained some of the tenets of the one described in the previous section, would turn out to be much more pragmatic and realistic.

Starting in the summer of 1990, a series of events occurred that would demonstrate to Paris that things were not going to take place as planned. First of all, the Persian Gulf War reshuffled the cards in the European political deck. During a period of several months, priorities simply changed, as decisionmakers turned their gaze from the East to the Middle East. Even more importantly, the resolution of the Kuwaiti crisis would have paradoxical consequences for the European dynamic. Moreover, the collapse of the Soviet Union the following year, along with the outbreak of the Balkans crisis, would serve to reinforce some of the "lessons" of the Gulf War.

The flames of crisis that burned in 1990 and 1991 threw into question some of the postulates of French policy. The war for Kuwait and the Yugoslav conflict demonstrated clearly that: (1) the transition from the bipolar world of the Cold War era to a new international order would be chaotic and dangerous; (2) American military power and political will would be irreplaceable during this transition period; (3) French military power, at least in the conventional sense, was nearly nonexistent, and could hardly hope to sustain a mooted European pillar of defense; (4) Europe was ready neither to assume regional and international security responsibilities nor even to speak with one voice about these topics; and (5) the EC and WEU, as a result, remained far from constituting the hard core of European defense.[30]

Added to the above, at least as far as the French were concerned, was a series of disappointments that struck at the heart of three important elements of the country's policy. During this critical transition phase Germany turned out to be powerless and floundering (the Gulf War), introverted (the process of reunification), or unpredictable (the Yugoslav crisis)—in short, it was most often a burdensome and scarcely reliable partner for France. Many criticisms were directed by Paris at Bonn concerning the latter's lack of solidarity (viz. an inward-looking political economy, high interest rates, and an ambiguous attitude toward both the alliance and the US), and its tendency toward unilateral initiatives.[31]

After the enormous amount of effort invested in the intergovernmental conferences on political and monetary union, to say nothing of the Maastricht treaty itself, the "construction of Europe" began to stall as a result of the first Danish referendum on Maastricht and the narrow margin of the French vote supporting the treaty. Coming as they did at a time when the EC was reeling from woefully inadequate responses to both the Gulf War and the crisis in the Balkans, they had a magnifying effect on the Community's malaise. But the cruelest blow of all, from France's standpoint, was landed in the alliance ring. Paris had shown itself ready to engage, in the summer of 1990, in a fundamental debate over the future of NATO; instead, the French government found itself being put in a position of taking or leaving the NATO strategy review that culminated with the July 1990 London summit. At Washington's insistence, NATO had begun a process of deliberation that, to the French, had all the trappings of a plot against their interests. France believed, especially, that the alliance's future purposes had not been sufficiently debated, whether those related to the notion of multinationalism or the continuing role of nuclear forces. The details of the dispute that erupted between France and its allies are still shrouded in haziness, but there can be no mistaking the fact that, from the London summit on, there was a Cold War raging in the midst of the alliance, whose principal antagonists were, on one side, Ambassador Gabriel Robin representing the foreign ministry, and on the other, all the other NATO delegations.

This masked struggle did not prevent the strategic reform of the alliance, but it did mean that the latter would take place under German and British leadership, without the participation of France, which suspected its European allies as serving as cat's paws for the US. Given this development, it is hardly surprising the NATO's new rapid reaction forces would be dominated by the British, or that its policy of rapprochement toward the East should have a strong Germanic flavor.

France, like Achilles, retired to its tent to sulk. Mitterrand succinctly summed up his government's view of the London summit: "France does not share the ideas of its allies insofar as NATO's new concepts are concerned. It remains as estranged as it ever was in the past."[32] This negativism, which lasted throughout 1991 and 1992, irritated all the allies, none more so than the Americans, who retaliated for each French ambush at NATO with dagger thrusts of their own. Following the WEU's extraordinary session of 21 February 1991, which resolved that that organization would be reformed in parallel with NATO, the Americans responded with the "Bartholomew memorandum," a vigorous diplomatic initiative that threatened the Europeans with reprisals in the event their reforms competed with NATO's own reform.[33] A few months later, in the spring of 1991, the Dobbins demarche reinforced the earlier warning. This latter was followed by the surprise adoption, in May 1991, of a new force structure for NATO, something that would bring Paris up short, and block a similar WEU undertaking. Beginning with the second half of 1991, the battle lines would be drawn over a new topic, the expansion of NATO's missions, something to which France was virulently opposed, above all as it related to the new North Atlantic Cooperation Council (NACC) and the issue of possible alliance peacekeeping missions.[34]

The biggest question raised by France's diplomatic change of direction, starting in 1990, touches upon its very nature: if it is clear that France's initial adjustment to the changed strategic context demonstrated, as we have argued, a long-term vision, can the same be said of the *second* phase? Jérôme Paolini cautions that it would be wrong to conclude that France's security policy has of late become purely reactive and introverted, as a result of the series of disappointments described above. According to him, this most recent phase of French diplomacy also displays a certain logic, albeit not the one that shaped the earlier phase; it is instead a logic that derives from the central dynamic of European security today. If the first post-Cold War vision developed in

Paris was animated by the goal of integration, the second draws strength
from a perception of reemerging nationalisms—in the West as well as
the East—as the determining factor for the coming decade in Europe. In
this context, European integration will not become a self-fulfilling dynamic, but rather will, as it has in the past, suffer setbacks as well as
experience accelerations, all in keeping with the circumstances of the
day and the various national interests of the EC members. In fact, the
logic of egoisms and particular interests of states will constitute the
central mechanism of European politics. In the background will be the
ever-present reminder of an unstable and indeed chaotic periphery to
the East.

It would be both foolish and dangerous, in this case, to count on the
"small" Europe of the EC Twelve to control this vaster environment.
Moreover, to paraphrase Paolini, France from now on will need not to
deny or combat the return of sovereignty as a major political given, but
rather adapt to it, and in so doing maximize its margin of strategic and
diplomatic leeway.[35] Does this mean that France will plunge headlong
into a "realist" foreign policy, taking direct inspiration from John Mearsheimer's celebrated thesis of three years ago?[36] Not completely, for
Mitterrand's diplomacy has been and remains rooted in a few powerful
universalistic values. As the president stressed, in April 1991: "Proof is
given today that states must define the common rules that govern their
relationships only within the midst of the international community. This
was the choice made by the founders of the United Nations, a choice
inspired by the failures of the League of Nations before the war, and by
the horrors of the Second World War itself. For the past 45 years, in their
bid to avoid the greatest danger—not a negligible consideration—states
have followed, willingly or not, crossroads that little by little have
distanced them from the founding principle of international society,
which is to say respect for the law."[37]

Stated otherwise, it was not a question of returning to the fragmented
Europe of the nineteenth century, but rather of applying to the new
Europe the norms established with the UN Charter and, more recently,
the Charter of Paris. The goal of this reassessment was clear: Europe and
the international community required a basis of legitimation that could
permit them, preferably in a preemptive sense, to intervene in situations
or crises such as those we have witnessed in the past two years. The
CSCE and UN, which were of lesser importance to the first phase of
French post-1989 policy, both suddenly found themselves elevated to
central positions as sources of legitimation and preservers of world
order. In the case of the CSCE, especially, notions of the inviolability of
frontiers against change by force, and of protection of human rights and
minority rights, took on a new significance in view of the developments

in the former Soviet Union and the Balkans.[38] This explains the French about-face on the CSCE, as well as France's new activism on the Security Council.

Nevertheless, the return of history did not just involve the new political actors in Central and Eastern Europe; for Paris, the friction to which both NATO and the EC were subject demonstrated the extent to which national egoism was at work even in the West. The US, for instance, was seen by Paris as lacking the slightest interest in seeing emerge a politically strong EC, an entity that it felt must turn into an even greater economic competitor to America. For the Americans (again, according to the view from Paris), the objective was to encase and marginalize the European security and defense identity in an institutional "architecture" dominated by the alliance, at the same time as Europe's foreign and security policy was diluted in a community stretching "from Vancouver to Vladivostock."

Insofar as Germany was concerned, Franco-German relations during the 1989–90 period very soon demonstrated that the two countries were responding to multiple but sometimes different marching orders. Their behavior seemed to take its inspiration from game theory as utilized by international-relation specialists, and especially, as François Armand observed so trenchantly, from the prisoner's dilemma: "Both countries have an interest in long-term collaboration, but each has an interest in short-term deception."[39] And what could one say about the rest of the European political actors, who did nothing but add to the general cacophony?

In such a fluid and complex environment, it was apparent to the French that they had to safeguard their autonomy in foreign-policy decisionmaking. Even if they continued to support a quickened pace of economic and monetary integration, there was no question of forcing the march in the political sphere. As Nicole Gnesotto, deputy director of the WEU's institute for security studies, has noted, Mitterrand envisioned a federal Europe on the economic and monetary scale, but an intergovernmental one on the level of foreign and security policy.[40] Especially as concerned its relations with Germany, the US, and the other European actors, France would follow a more traditional policy, one that was both pragmatic and realist, and that did not lose sight of a number of fundamental objectives. Bonn was at times turning into such an unreliable partner that, as Lellouche has emphasized, it looked incapable of being "contained."[41] Suppose this was so, replied French policy shapers; this need not prevent either collaboration or courteous relations. However, collaboration with Germany need not stop France from deploying a dual German policy, based on the concepts of anchoring in the West and balancing in the East.

Insofar as concerned the United States, a similar pragmatism emerged. France did not hesitate to participate in the anti-Iraqi coalition, nor did it shrink from placing its forces under American command, but it would continue to work feverishly in pursuit of a European defense entity. This latter did not mean France wanted to kick the Americans out of Europe; quite the contrary. The events we highlighted at the beginning of this section reinforced the idea, in Paris, that an American political and military presence remained essential for European stability. Moreover, Mitterrand's generation needed no reminding that on two occasions in this century the Americans had come to the aid of France. It is the persistence of this memory that accounts both for the importance attached by France's leaders to a strong security relationship between North America and Western Europe and for the feeling of solidarity that flows therefrom each time there has been a serious crisis facing the West. From this perspective, the French opposed neither the existence nor the reform of NATO, and as Mitterrand himself observed on several occasions, the defense of Western Europe could not, either now or for many years to come, be conceivable outside of the alliance context.

The alliance needs, however, to adapt itself to the political realities of today's Europe; and this means that it has to make room for the emergence of a European security and defense entity. But what would that "room" be? And why will not the alliance's own concept of a security and defense identity satisfy Paris? French rationales remain ambiguous on these questions, but what is not ambiguous is that France continues to demand, as a condition of its full and complete cooperation with the new alliance, that there be a profound debate within NATO, something it does not regard as having happened yet.

It is interesting, in this context, to heed French reticence as it is expressed over the issue of NATO's (and Paris') relations with the countries of Central and Eastern Europe. France in effect deems that the reform of European security institutions has been taking place in a fashion that can only be labeled disorganized and much too hurried. As a result, these organizations find themselves called upon to perform a multitude of tasks, ranging from defense to crisis management to peacekeeping—and all the time in a climate of confusion, not to say competition.

For example, the North Atlantic Cooperation Council would make of NATO the privileged vehicle for security cooperation with the entire group of European states, to the detriment of both the CSCE and EC. This same NACC, at least according to the Quai d'Orsay, suffers from a variety of weaknesses that, together, undermine its credibility as a bridge to the East.[42] It is becoming, little by little, a forum with no capacity to take decisions, on account of the great diversity of its membership and the concomitant inability to achieve consensus. It demonstrates once again the reluctance of alliance members to get involved in the hornet's nest of political, ethnic, and boundary questions raised by the countries of Central and Eastern Europe. In like manner, it lays bare the fact that NATO cannot give genuine security guarantees to the former members of the Warsaw Treaty Organization (WTO) without turning itself into a collective-security organization. The NACC cannot even develop into much of an alliance "waiting room" for the members of the Visegrad group, for the good reason that to do so would constitute a flagrant case of discrimination against its 19 other members.

In fact, for Paris the conceptual fog that enshrouds the NACC demonstrates beyond doubt that certain basal questions have not even been addressed, much less resolved; the French critics call the alliance to account by reminding it that revision of the Washington treaty's zone of application has never been addressed, nor has the issue of the optimal level of NATO engagement in the security problems of Central and Eastern Europe. Concerning the division of labor between the divers European security institutions, there has been more obfuscation than progress, thanks to an overreliance on defective "architectural" concepts and a belief that feckless organizations actually have some influence.

What, then, can be said about the French position toward an eventual peacekeeping role for the alliance? The answer flows directly and logically from the preceding analysis. For France, in effect, peacekeeping has a direct impact on the related question of the alliance's "proper" policy toward the countries to the east. As a result, France may not be against the idea of NATO putting its resources at the disposal of such institutions as the CSCE or UN, but it will be out of the question for the alliance to undertake such missions on its own for as long as those issues that France is keen to have debated continue to be denied an airing in NATO fora.

Conclusion

The record of the past two years shows that French security policy, much as it might stimulate polemics and remain somewhat ambiguous, nevertheless reflects certain clear choices and even a "grand design" on the part of French authorities, above all the president. The second phase of Mitterrand's post-1989 policy also bears the earmarks of a "realist" assessment of the risks now facing Europe, and clearly defines a policy that is at one and the same time more traditional and more pragmatic for France. At the risk of sounding "pro-French," we have to say that there is something healthy about the idea that NATO needs to have a second Harmel report, intended to get its members to think deeply about the organization's mandate, just as it must be admitted that the alliance reacted too hastily for its own good in 1990, as it sought to respond to the cascade of historic events of the previous year.

After the Yugoslav ordeal, the idea that the institutionalization of European security should be the goal of a new transatlantic bargain, one specifying the roles and responsibilities of the relevant players, seems to be only common sense. After all, as Mitterrand remarked in December 1991, "the alliance is good, but it is not the Holy Alliance."[43] Finally, the tensions and acrimony that have marked its relations with so many of its alliance partners remind us that France, with one of the most dynamic economies in Europe (despite the current recession), remains what it has been, a factor impossible to ignore if one is seeking to assure European security.

Lest anyone confuse this analysis with apologetics, it bears stating that the obvious weaknesses of French policy also deserve careful examination. France's diplomatic style, and *a fortiori* that of its president, have hardly aided the country's cause, given its apparent contradictions and peculiar tone. Thus, many of its allies simply cannot understand how the country can, in the same breath, denounce Washington's "imperialism" and yet work itself up over the possibility of an American troop withdrawal from Europe. Moreover, while France might reproach some of its allies about their "evangelism" toward the countries of Central and Eastern Europe, it cannot make them see the merits of its own Gaullist theology, which accords special value to France's "voice," as well as to its "rank" among nations, or its universal mission—all the more so given the long period of time that has elapsed since France truly was an empire, and could have pretended to globalism.

By this latter token, it seems to us high time that French officials developed a vision more in keeping with their country's international influence. France is beyond doubt an essential politico-military factor in Europe, but it can no longer avail itself of that "first-class ticket" derided by Lellouche. The influence of its nuclear arsenal, in today's Europe, is much less than it once was, and the Gulf War demonstrated so brutally to the country that it could only count on 14,000 professional soldiers in a moment of crisis. That demonstration has had a radical effect upon the debate over defense policy, and it is safe to say that the erstwhile 30-year-old "consensus" on these matters has been shattered.[44] National service, to say nothing of the general structure of the armed forces, has been called into question; the problem of resources is posed acutely in the context of a shrinking defense budget; and even the legitimacy of nuclear deterrence is cast in doubt. All this augurs ill for the prospects of a fundamental, if needed, reform, which is likely to become extremely difficult in the current period of transition through which France is going.

On a different level, France's relations with the alliance over the past two years reflect what Yves Boyer has termed the "pathologies of the Franco-American relationship," meaning the contradictions of an historical legacy and contemporary realities.[45] Paris, in this respect, has difficulty with the idea that the forces of Lafayette should have to play second fiddle to anyone in Washington's estimation, while for the American authorities, it remains little short of astonishing that France should demand special treatment from a superpower with a host of global responsibilities. A similar problem is posed by the Franco-German relationship, as it seems that the Quai d'Orsay has clung for too long to the dream of being able to "contain" Germany by dint of its special relationship with Bonn—a dream that today appears utterly unrealistic.

What *is* realistic is that France will have to learn to structure its diplomatic relations in a more multilateral, and therefore less bilateral, fashion. It has to be acknowledged that the emphasis placed by the Gaullist tradition on what Philippe Moreau Defarge calls "privileged networks" has prevented France from playing the role it should have in the leading multilateral organizations, such as the UN, CSCE, or even NATO.[46]

Finally, there exists an enormous void in contemporary French diplomacy, one deriving from an inability to develop a comprehensible policy toward the countries to the East. For the moment, the leadership role assumed by France in peacekeeping in the Balkans is certainly both praiseworthy and significant, but it is remarkable nonetheless to realize that two years after the failed coup in Moscow, France has yet to develop an *Ostpolitik* it could call its own.

What security and defense policies can one expect to see implemented by the Balladur government, elected in March 1993? Two points can be highlighted immediately. French institutions have already experienced "cohabitation," from 1986 to 1988, and that experience gives no reason for anyone to imagine that there must be important differences between the president and the prime minister over foreign policy, all the more so given the likelihood that Mitterrand will complete his second term and in all probability leave the political scene within two years.

Moreover, the change of direction already begun in the autumn of 1992 by the last socialist defense minister, Pierre Joxe, will almost certainly be continued by his successor, François Léotard. What explains this tilt toward NATO?[47] What could possibly have been happening over the past several months to account for this latest tack? We think it can be safely said that French authorities have been coming to appreciate the merits of a vigorous alliance given the crises that have erupted in the East, both in Yugoslavia and in the former Soviet Union. The urgency of the moment has made itself felt inside the Balladur government, where many voices have been raised calling for the immediate opening of a politico-strategic dialogue between France and the United States, so as to clean the slate of the old contentious issues, especially those relating to the alliance.[48] Does it follow that a complete reversal of French policy can be expected? Probably not, but one can at least count on witnessing a marked evolution, perhaps featuring what the French have been longing for these past four years—namely a genuine and profound debate on the future of the Atlantic Alliance.

Notes

1. Ronald Tiersky, "France in the New Europe," *Foreign Affairs* 71 (Spring 1992): 132. For the continuity of French politics and its basis, see Diego Ruiz Palmer, "French Strategic Options in the 1990s," *Adelphi Papers* 260 (London: International Institute for Strategic Studies, Summer 1991). Also see an earlier article by David Yost, "France's Deterrent Posture and Security in Europe," *Adelphi Papers* 194-95 (London: International Institute for Strategic Studies, Winter 1984/85).

2. David Yost, "France in the New Europe," *Foreign Affairs* 69 (Winter 1990/91): 112.

3. Claude Grantu, "1988-1992: la France et l'URSS/Russie: la période des occasions perdues," *Relations internationales et stratégiques* 3 (Spring 1993): 173-80.

4. Ibid., p. 178; and Tiersky, "France in the New Europe," p. 135.

5. Grantu, "1988-1992: la France et l'URSS/Russie," p. 172.

6. For a complete account of French relations with NATO, see "La France et l'OTAN," *Relations internationales et diplomatiques* 2 (Autumn 1992): 41-157; and Fréderic Bozo, *La France et l'OTAN* (Paris: Economica, 1992).

7. See "The Franco-German Corps: The Concept is Everything," *RUSI Newsbrief* 12 (May 1992): 1; Kristina Ikavalko, "The Franco-German Corps, the Seeds of a European Army Are Sown," *Strategic Datalink* (Toronto: Canadian Institute of Strategic Studies, July 1992); and David G. Haglund, "Who's Afraid of Franco-German Military Cooperation?" *European Security* (forthcoming).

8. "When Europeans Unravel," *Economist*, 1 August 1992, p. 38.

9. Interview, Department of National Defence, Ottawa, Spring 1993.

10. Flora Lewis, "Europe: Collective Security Is Taking Shape," *International Herald Tribune*, 21 June 1991.

11. Pierre Lellouche, "France in Search of Security," *Foreign Affairs* 72 (Spring 1993): 122.

12. Pierre Lellouche, "La France et l'OTAN," *Relations internationales et stratégiques* 2 (Autumn 1992): 96.

13. See Steven Philip Kramer, "The French Question," *Washington Quarterly* 14 (Autumn 1991): 94.

14. Speech by François Mitterrand to the Bundestag, 3 November 1989 (Paris: Service d'information et de relations publiques des armées [SIRPA], 1990).

15. Jérôme Paolini, "Les deux politiques européennes de François Mitterrand," *Relations internationales et stratégiques* 3 (Spring 1993): 126.

16. Chevènement address to the Royal United Service Institute, London, 7 September 1990, quoted in Yost, "France in the New Europe," p. 108.

17. "Projet de loi de programmation, 1992-1994: Restructurations" (Paris: SIRPA, July 1992).

18. See, in particular, Jean-Michel Boucheron, *Paix et défense* (Paris: Dunod, 1992), pp. 54-91.

19. Paolini, "Les deux politiques," p. 126.

20. See on this topic, William T. Johnsen and Thomas-Durell Young, "Franco-German Security Accommodation: Agreeing to Disagree," *Strategic Review* 21 (Winter 1993): 7-17. Also see George Stein, "The Euro-Corps and Future European Security Architecture," *European Security* 2 (Summer 1993): 200-26.

21. Quoted in Kramer, "The French Question," p. 84.

22. François Armand, "La relation avec l'Allemagne en matière de politique étrangère et de sécurité, 1988-1992," *Relations internationales et stratégiques* 3 (Spring 1993): 149.

23. See Ronald Asmus, "Germany and America: Partners in Leadership," *Survival* 33 (November-December 1991): 546-66.

24. See the succinct and skillful analysis of the institutionalization of the European defense in René Van Beveren, "Military Cooperation: What Structure for the Future?" *Cahiers de Chaillot* 6 (Paris: WEU Institute for Security Studies, January 1993), pp. 23-25. Also see Peter Schmidt, "The Evolution of European Security Structures: Master Plan or Trial and Error?" in *From Euphoria to Hysteria: Western European Security After the Cold War,* ed. David G. Haglund (Boulder: Westview Press, 1993), pp. 145-66.

25. See *La Charte de Paris pour une nouvelle Europe* (Paris, November 1990), pp. 1-10.

26. *Economist,* 17 April 1993, p. 4. Germany had given the countries of Central and Eastern Europe 46.7 billion ECUs between 1990 and 1992. The EC and its other members, by contrast, gave only 26 billion ECUs during the same period, while the US supplied 11.2 billion ECUs in aid.

27. David Allen, "West European Responses to Change in the Soviet Union and Eastern Europe," in *Toward Political Union,* ed. Reinhardt Rummel (Boulder: Westview Press, 1992), p. 129.

28. "Good Intentions, Poor Performance, EC Aid to Eastern Europe," *Economist,* 10 April 1993, p. 21.

29. Howard Frost, "Eastern Europe: Search for Security," *Orbis* 37 (Winter 1993): 50-53.

30. See, for example, Scott Anderson, "Europe and the Gulf War," in *Toward Political Union,* pp. 147-60; and Michael Brenner, "The EC in Yugoslavia: A Debut Performance," *Security Studies* 1 (Summer 1992): 586-609.

31. See, on this topic, Michel Fortmann, "In Search of an Identity: Europe, NATO, and the ESDI Debate," *Extra-Mural Paper*, no. 58 (Ottawa: ORAE, November 1991).

32. *Le Monde*, 8-9 July 1990, p. 5.

33. Kramer, "The French Question," p. 86.

34. For a discussion of the NACC, see the chapter by William Yerex, this volume.

35. Paolini, "Les deux politiques," p. 127.

36. John Mearsheimer, "Back to the Future: Instability in Europe After the Cold War," *International Security* 15 (Summer 1990): 5-56.

37. Address delivered to the École supérieure de guerre (Paris: SIRPA, 11 April 1991), p. 86.

38. Victor Yves Ghebali, "Towards an Operational Institution for Comprehensive Security," *Disarmament* 15, 4 (1992): 1-12.

39. Armand, "La relation avec l'Allemagne," p. 154.

40. Cited in Kramer, "The French Question," p. 87.

41. Lellouche, "La France et l'OTAN," p. 97.

42. Bruno Tertrais, "L'occident et la sécurité à l'Est: le rôle de l'OTAN," *Relations internationales et stratégiques* 2 (Autumn 1992): 142-57.

43. Quoted in the *Economist*, 15 December 1991, p. 53.

44. See Pascal Boniface, ed., *L'année stratégique 1992* (Paris: Dunod, 1993), p. 3.

45. Yves Boyer, "Les relations entre la France et les États-Unis," *Relations internationales et stratégiques* 3 (Spring 1993): 184.

46. Philippe Moreau Defarges, "La France et l'ONU: le ralliement," *Relations internationales et stratégiques* 3 (Spring 1993): 121.

47. "Joxe in Box," *Economist*, 3 October 1992, p. 56; Alan Riding, "France Moves to Take Bigger Part in Delivering New Role for NATO," *New York Times*, 30 September 1992.

48. See Lellouche, "France in Search of Security," p. 131; François de Rose, "A US-French Key to a NATO Future," *International Herald Tribune*, 17 February 1993; and J.A.C. Lewis, "French Government Looks Ahead to Long Term Change," *Jane's Defence Weekly*, 17 April 1993, p. 14.

PART THREE

Institutional Adaptation

8

The European Community and the Eastern Challenge

Charles Pentland

Introduction

Europe after the Cold War, we have been warned, may make us long for the chilling certainties of bipolar deterrence.[1] In the same spirit, it may now be occurring to Western Europeans and North Americans that, as collective objectives go, deterring and containing the Soviets had an attractive simplicity about it compared to what we now seek to achieve in Central and Eastern Europe.

To the extent that they have been clearly articulated by Western governments, those objectives are: first, to create a reliable framework for managing conflict among, and within, the states of the former Soviet bloc and the former Yugoslavia; second, to foster the development of market economies; and, third, to ensure the growth of stable democratic political systems. The causal links among these three broad objectives remain notoriously complex and obscure. We are nevertheless fairly confident that the lessons of Western Europe's experience are likely to apply to the East: a framework of peace and security is the *sine qua non* of both free markets and stable democracy, while the latter two are in turn necessary, if not always sufficient, conditions for establishment of a security community. To set in motion the "virtuous circle" encompassing security, markets, and democracy is, by most accounts, the challenge the post-Cold War East poses to the governments of the West.

What role might we expect the European Community (EC) to play in the West's response to this challenge? Embracing 11 of NATO's 16 member states (all of which are democracies with market economies), constituting the world's largest and richest single market, equipped with an impressive array of collective economic-policy instruments, and slowly acquiring competence and capabilities in matters of security and defense, the EC seems, on the face of it, well placed to assume the central role in meeting the Eastern challenge. I shall argue, however, that while such expectations are not unreasonable, the EC's role is likely to prove less comprehensive and dominant than is sometimes foreseen by both its promoters and its critics. The 40-year history of its relations with Central and Eastern Europe, and particularly the pattern of developments since the revolution of 1989, suggest that the EC's role in the region will, among other things, be more ruthlessly selective in scope, more narrowly economic in its expression, and more supportive of subregional multilateralism than might initially have been expected.

The EC and the East During the Cold War

For almost ten years following the end of World War II Western Europeans were preoccupied with economic recovery and military security, both of which, they speedily concluded, must be sought collectively within a transatlantic institutional framework. By 1948 it was clear to most that this framework, far from embracing all of Europe, would be confined to the West and confronted by structures purporting in some sense to represent its Eastern counterpart. The reciprocal geopolitical and ideological hostility evident in emergent alliances (or their functional equivalent) on both sides was reflected in a parallel bipolarity of economic institutions.

The Organization for European Economic Cooperation (OEEC) and the Council of Europe, institutions that laid the foundations for the EC, partly through their successes in the recovery program, partly through their evident inability to foster more far-reaching integration, elicited in 1949 an institutional response from the Soviet bloc in the form of Comecon (or CMEA). Ostensibly dedicated to fostering multilateral economic cooperation among the Soviet Union, its European allies and, as time went on, selected Third World clients of the Soviet Union, Comecon was, for its first decade at least, a sort of Potemkin village in the lee of whose empty structures the real business of bilateral economic relationships continued. In the West, tariff reductions and the liberalization of payments accelerated intra-European trade, while in the East state trading governed by managed prices for goods and currencies and by a designated division of labor, led to real but more modest increases in trade. As symbolized by the marginalization of the UN's Economic Commission for Europe (ECE), an institution whose mandate was optimistically pan-European, flows of trade and investment between the two blocs were negligible.[2]

The Soviet Union's reaction to the founding of the European Economic Community in 1957 was predictable, especially in its denial of the

EEC's indigenous European character and its emphasis on the link to NATO and to American commercial and financial interests. The source of this hostility may initially have been more doctrinal than geopolitical, since, like the British, the Soviets did not initially think much of the EEC's prospects.[3]

By the early 1960s, however, there was no escaping the economic dynamism of the Brussels enterprise. While continuing to deny the EEC recognition as an international institution, the Soviets extended to it the sincerest form of flattery in attempting in 1962 to impose a program of supranational integration on Comecon. Overt resistance from Romania and quiet obstruction from others frustrated Khrushchev's plan, although the Soviets continued to promote variants of it while presenting "socialist integration" as a worthy rival of the capitalist version proceeding apace in the West.[4] This claim of equivalence went, in turn, unappreciated in Brussels.

In formal terms, the reciprocity was perfect. The EEC and its members paid no attention to Comecon, while in 1963 the Soviet Union ignored an *aide-mémoire* from the EEC seeking to normalize relations with Moscow. The underlying economic realities were, however, beginning to change. The EEC's economic growth and commercial élan began to make itself felt in East-West relations. Since neither the EEC nor Comecon then had the competence to negotiate on behalf of its member states, trade between the blocs was in fact negotiated and conducted exclusively on a bilateral, state-to-state basis. Here asymmetry was the watchword, both in the contrast of economic systems and assumptions about trade and in the relative importance of East-West trade for the two sides.

During its "golden age" of integration and economic growth, from the late 1950s to the late 1960s, then, the EC as such could not be said to have had a policy toward Eastern Europe that went beyond the search for normalization in relations with the Soviet Union and the studious dismissal of Comecon as a counterpart. With the end of the transition period in 1968, however, marking the completion of the customs union, the EC began to move into new and uncharted domains. First, as required by the Treaty of Rome—and indeed flowing logically from the establishment of the Common External Tariff—the EC in 1971 adopted the Common Commercial Policy (CCP) under which, on a mandate from the Council of Ministers, the Commission negotiated trade and association agreements on behalf of the member states.[5] Not least because of special West German concerns with Eastern Europe, implementation of the CCP with respect to that region was delayed until 1974. The EC then proceeded to offer bilateral trade agreements to each European member of Comecon. Not surprisingly, only Romania took up the offer; extended negotiations led to the signing, in 1980, of the first trade agreement between the EC and a member of the Soviet bloc.

Undoubtedly as a response to the EC's achievement of the customs union and its initiation of an ambitious new program aimed at economic and monetary union by 1980, as well as to stirrings within its own bloc, the Soviet Union proposed, in 1971, a Comprehensive Program for Economic Integration for Comecon. Less overtly supranational than the 1962 scheme, the Comprehensive Program sought to commit Comecon's members to designated areas of specialization in agricultural and industrial production, and to tighten their mutual dependency through trade and joint ventures. It also reinforced the old claims of Comecon's equivalence to the EC, enabling the Soviets to assert more forcefully than ever that, as the EC had become via the CCP, so Comecon was henceforth the exclusive negotiating framework for its members' trade with the West. As in so many things, Romania was the exception that proved the rule.[6]

As they launched the CCP in the early 1970s, the EC's member states also embarked on an attempt to coordinate their foreign policies beyond the economic realms to which they were limited under the Rome treaty. In 1970 they inaugurated European Political Cooperation (EPC), an institutionalized system of regular consultation among foreign ministers and senior foreign-policy officials of the EC states, formally separate from the EC's institutions.[7] Never lacking for critics as it dabbled, with mixed results, in various areas of international high politics, EPC nonetheless proved valuable in orchestrating the EC's policy toward the East during the Helsinki process. The CSCE's three-basket structure fitted nicely with the emerging (if uneasy) division of labor in Brussels between foreign economic policy (the preserve of the EC's institutions) and traditional political matters of diplomacy (the business of EPC). If the EC Commission saw Basket II as a vehicle for opening up East-West trade, EPC was instrumental, through Basket III, in placing human rights on the Helsinki agenda, with long-term consequences no one at the time could have anticipated.

Through the years of détente and on into the early 1980s the EC's relations with the Comecon countries consisted, at the formal, institutional level, of a continuing minuet of fruitless negotiations against a backdrop of increasing economic exchange. The EC continued to resist Comecon's demands for recognition as an equivalent and therefore as the appropriate negotiating partner on matters of East-West trade. Seen from Brussels, the claim was hard to sustain, especially since the Comprehensive Program showed few signs of life, and thus to recognize Comecon would in effect have been to legitimize Soviet dominion over its neighbors.

EC policy toward the East from the mid-1970s to the mid-1980s was driven, in a positive sense, by the imperatives of *Ostpolitik* and the traditional Franco-German commercial rivalry that it revived in the region, as well as by the heightened attractiveness of Soviet raw materials and energy. More negatively it reflected growing concern in Brussels over Soviet and East European exports to the EC of agricultural goods and low-technology manufactures, where protection for vulnerable Western European producers might have to be negotiated. In contrast to the Comecon states, whose exports to Western Europe represented 20 to 25 percent of their total exports, EC exports to Comecon accounted for less than 4 percent of its total.[8] The agenda of any prospective bloc-to-bloc negotiations was clear enough, and substantial: Comecon concerns over assured access to EC markets (less for the Soviets, since raw materials and energy already had duty-free access) and West-to-East transfer of technology; EC concerns to protect vulnerable sectors, to gain privileged access to Comecon markets, and to deploy its "civilian power" of trade, investment, and technology to further Western objectives in détente. It seems, however, that these considerations did not provide sufficient motive to overcome the impasse of mutual nonrecognition and drive the EC and Comecon to the negotiating table.

The revival of European integration with the inauguration, in 1985, of the 1992 program, and the accession to power, in the same year, of Mikhail Gorbachev in the Soviet Union, inaugurated a new era in the EC's relations with its eastern neighbors. In 1986 the Soviets accepted for the first time that the EC could negotiate individual bilateral trade agreements with members of the Soviet bloc. The characterization of this concession as leading to a "parallel" or "double-banking" approach involving both Comecon and its member governments seemed, even at the time, to be a face-saving exercise to mask the devaluation of Comecon. Having got what it wanted, the EC was more than pleased, in 1988, to sign a Declaration of Mutual Recognition with Comecon, under which regular discussions of East-West economic matters were to be pursued. Of much more significance to all concerned, however, was the series of trade and cooperation agreements negotiated between 1988 and 1990 between the EC and a succession of Comecon member states. These agreements, negotiated at the outset of what now seems a long and perilous process of transition in Central and Eastern Europe, were rapidly overtaken by events.

The Continuing Transition, 1989–1993

One of the earliest and clearest consequences of the revolutionary events that swept through Central and Eastern Europe in 1989 was an immediate sharpening of the distinctions among states of the region as objects of Western policy. As early as 1948, of course, Yugoslavia had, by virtue of its break with the Soviet Union, been recognized as a case for special treatment. The EC signed a nonpreferential trade agreement with Belgrade in 1970 and a full economic cooperation agreement in 1980. Nonalignment, the unique elements of Yugoslav socialism, and the considerable flow of trade and labor (in contrast to the rest of the region) made these agreements economically necessary and politically conceivable.[9] Gorbachev's signal that the Soviet Union's allies were free to chart their own course amounted to an invitation to the EC and the West in general to make similar differentiations, first between the Soviet Union and the rest, subsequently among the Central and Eastern European states themselves. The formal dissolution of Comecon and the Warsaw Treaty Organization in mid-1991, and of the Soviet Union itself at the end of that year invited, indeed compelled, the EC to make fundamental strategic choices as to its role in the region and its relationship with a new cast of characters. As the transition has progressed, therefore, it has made increasing sense to consider the EC's role in the region under three headings: first, relations with a Yugoslavia in the throes of disintegration and civil war; second, relations with the Soviet Union and its successor states; and third, relations with the former Warsaw Treaty-Comecon associates of the Soviet Union. The marked differences in the EC's role with respect to each reflect, unsurprisingly, differences in the nature and extent of problems facing it, and, perhaps more controversially, unspoken but deeply held understandings in Brussels and the national capitals as to geopolitical and economic priorities.

Yugoslavia

As the Yugoslav federation began coming apart in the latter half of 1991 the EC's objectives with respect to the conflict evolved from the relatively uncomplicated—mediating a new constitutional accord to accommodate autonomist Croats and Slovenes on the one hand and unitarist Serbs on the other—to the inherently contradictory: recognizing the independence of secessionist states and imposing sanctions on what remained of Yugoslavia while continuing attempts to mediate and keep the peace. The brief history of the EC's involvement in the Balkan imbroglio provides some sobering lessons as to the possibilities and, especially, the limits of its role in the broader region.

When Croatia and Slovenia, despairing of their efforts to negotiate a looser form of Yugoslav federation, declared independence at the end of June 1991, the EC's immediate response was to send a "diplomatic rapid reaction force" to Belgrade, consisting of the foreign ministers of the past, current, and next president-countries of the EC (and of EPC),[10] in an unsuccessful effort to forestall military action. Through the summer and into the fall the EC negotiated, first via the Dutch presidency, later through its special representative, Lord Carrington, a series of short-lived ceasefires between Serbs and Croats. At the same time it suspended arms sales and economic aid to Belgrade, pressuring the Serbian government to accept EC mediation, put in place a small contingent of EC peace-observers (numbering 200 by October), and worked to convene peace talks centered on its draft of a plan for settlement of Serbian-Croatian territorial issues. In its combination of peacemaking under EPC auspices and the flexing of economic muscles this approach seemed the perfect embodiment of the EC as a "civilian power."[11]

From late October onward, however, the EC's assumptions about its role and influence in the Yugoslav conflict began to unravel. The shelling of Dubrovnik and the departure of EC observers from the city, and the Serbs' rejection of Carrington's peace proposals on 5 November 1991, turned the EC from a tacit to an overt partisan of the Croats and Slovenes, complicating, to say the least, its continuing offers to mediate. In November 1991 Brussels contemplated mounting a military peacekeeping force through the WEU, but drew back in recognition of the costs and risks, and in light of German and British reservations. It did, however, take the lead, on 8 November, in imposing selected economic sanctions on Serbia.

This trend did not, however, become truly irreversible until the fiasco of recognition. Under pressure from Germany and against French and other inhibitions, the EC agreed, on 17 December 1991, to recognize Croatia and Slovenia by 15 January 1992. Six days later the Germans jumped the gun and extended recognition on their own. Whatever Germany's motives both for pressuring its EC partners and for then going it alone, the net effect of recognition was to give up something that still had some negotiating power as a promise to one side and a threat to the other, to further undermine what credibility still attached to the EC's role as mediator, and to give the (accurate) impression of disarray in Brussels.[12]

During the first half of 1992 the EC nevertheless continued its efforts to combine the oil of partisanship with the water of peacemaking. In April, Brussels, along with Washington, granted Bosnia-Herzegovina the recognition it had been seeking since December. Later in the spring it reacted to the Serbian-Montenegrin claim to constitute the new Yugoslavia by recalling its ambassador from Belgrade. On 27 May the EC imposed a trade embargo on this rump Yugoslavia in response to the war that had broken out in Bosnia-Herzegovina and urged the UN to impose its own sanctions, which it did on 30 May 1992, in the form of a trade embargo and a freeze on financial assets. At the end of June, the EC's foreign ministers agreed, over Greek objections, to extend recognition to Macedonia.

All this partisan activity coexisted, in early 1992, with continuing efforts to convene peace talks under EC auspices and, increasingly, to draw the UN in to perform some of the tasks the EC had originally taken upon itself. In April, Lord Carrington succeeded in reconvening the talks. By August, however, the United Nations had joined the EC in sponsoring the London conference and the UN's man, Cyrus Vance, was sharing with the EC's man, Lord Owen, the daunting task of negotiating and drafting a peace plan for Bosnia-Herzegovina. Meanwhile, UN peacekeeping forces had made their appearance, first 14,000 in Croatia at the end of February, and then in increased numbers at various points in Bosnia. It seems clear, at least in retrospect, that by mid-1992 the EC had backed away from claims to play the leading role in managing the Yugoslav conflict, preferring instead to support, facilitate, and implicate the UN in many of the tasks it had found itself unable to undertake directly.

The Soviet Union and Its Successors

The tribulations of the Soviet Union from 1989 through 1991, and of its successor states thereafter, have provided a second set of challenges to the governments of the Atlantic community. In this case, unlike that of Yugoslavia, the EC could not contemplate taking the leading role either in the financial support of economic reform or in the management of conflict among or within the successor states. It was clear from the outset that support for reform would have to be multilateral, and orchestrated through the G7, in which American leadership would be critical given the continuing (and useful) formalities of the superpower relationship. As for secession and ethnic conflict, there has never been a realistic prospect of intervention by the UN, let alone by Western institutions, beyond warnings about human-rights violations, threats to decrease or withdraw economic assistance (as the EC did, in January 1991, with $1 billion in emergency food aid, over Soviet actions in the Baltic states), and, more recently, pointed comment on Russia's presumed right of intervention to manage conflict in the former Soviet republics.

Despite (or perhaps because of) its caution and concern about the prospects of *perestroika* the EC signed a ten-year trade, economic, and commercial cooperation agreement with the Soviet Union in December 1989. Like the agreements signed at about the same time with the other European members of Comecon, it provided for the gradual abolition of specific EC quantitative restrictions on Soviet exports by the end of 1995, in return for the Soviets' granting of nondiscriminatory treatment to EC exports. There were also provisions for trade and investment promotion, joint ventures, and other forms of industrial and economic cooperation. Unlike the agreement with the rest of Comecon, the Soviet accord has not been superseded by an association agreement. Indeed, implementation of the 1989 agreement has been bedevilled by problems of succession and by the economic turmoil into which the former Soviet Union has plunged.

In practice the EC's role in that sector of Europe's eastern frontier has been limited since 1990 to the provision of aid, either directly, as donor, or indirectly, as coordinator of the Atlantic community's programs. In December 1990 the Rome European Council (EC summit) agreed to extend 750 million ECU in food aid and 400 million ECU in technical assistance to the Soviet Union; after the suspension mentioned earlier was lifted in mid-1991 most of this aid was disbursed. Early in 1992, after the dissolution of the Soviet Union, Russia's president, Boris Yeltsin, did the rounds of the major Western European capitals, securing aid and credits from Britain and France and, most importantly, a commitment from Germany to support a major multilateral aid program. An agreement in April between President Bush and Chancellor Kohl that the G7 would provide $18 billion in export credits and aid plus $6 billion for currency stabilization to Russia laid the groundwork for a formal commitment by the Munich G7 summit in July 1991.

While the EC has an enormous stake in the future of the former Soviet Union, especially in the Baltics, Russia, Ukraine, and its other more westerly parts, it appears to have recognized early on that its means of influencing events there are limited (especially as German resources have been sapped by the costs of unification). Brussels has therefore stuck to what it knows best—economics—and been content to coordinate strategy with Washington in multilateral fora. The contrast could not be more striking with its aspirations to a "civilian-power" role at the outset of the Yugoslav crisis. The Soviet and the Yugoslav cases thus mark the two extremes between which the EC seeks to define its role in the rest of Central and Eastern Europe—the former European associates of the Soviet Union in Comecon and the Warsaw Pact.

The Former WTO/Comecon Associates

This group of Central European and Balkan states (now numbering six with the breakup of Czechoslovakia, and not counting the special case of the former GDR) has been fortunate, despite the existence of numerous potential ethnic flashpoints, in avoiding the outbreak of Yugoslav-style wars of secession or irredentism. As with the Soviet

Union and its successors, therefore, the EC has been able to concentrate on matters of trade and aid in pursuing its objectives of security, democracy, and free markets in the region. In contrast to the Soviet case, however, the EC has moved aggressively to take a leading role in Western policy, to the point of appearing bent on establishing a sphere of economic influence encompassing some, if not all, of these states.

As noted earlier, once Gorbachev had liberated his Eastern European allies to pursue their own course, the EC was able in short order to negotiate trade agreements with each under the Common Commercial Policy provisions of Articles 113-114 of the Rome treaty. The general pattern, varying slightly from state to state, was a limited-term (five to ten years), nonpreferential trade, commercial, and economic cooperation agreement, embracing both industry and agriculture but usually making exceptions or special provisions (i.e., restrictions) for sensitive sectors (to EC producers) such as steel, textiles, and certain agricultural products. Hungary was the first to reach such an agreement (for ten years) in September 1988. In December Czechoslovakia negotiated a four-year agreement limited to trade in industrial goods, but this was superseded in May 1990 by a ten-year agreement of the standard kind. Poland signed a five-year agreement in September 1989 and Bulgaria a ten-year agreement in May 1990. Within a year or two of signature all these agreements were revised to accelerate the elimination of quantitative restrictions by as much as five years. Romania, finally, began renegotiating its 1980 agreement with the EC in 1987. The EC suspended negotiations in late 1989 because of the Ceausescu regime's human-rights violations, reopening them in May 1990. The accord was finally signed in October.

In 1988 the five countries' exports to Western Europe represented about 20 percent of their total exports, while the EC's exports to them constituted less than 3 percent of its total exports.[13] Given that imbalance of dependency, these agreements were a great deal more important for the Five than for the Twelve. While they were not preferential accords, "nonpreferential" meant, in effect, the achievement of most-favored-nation status (indeed this was later improved upon with the extension to the Five of the EC's Generalized System of Preferences, a scheme hitherto limited to the Third World). And while the provisions for sensitive sectors rankled, it could be argued that negotiated limits were better than unilaterally imposed prohibition. On the other hand the EC saw particular value in the normalizing of trade and investment rules and practices with the Five, and in the prospects for industrial cooperation (e.g., joint ventures).

Even as these agreements were being finalized, however, it was becoming clear that developments in Central Europe and in East-West dynamics demanded a more elaborate, sophisticated response on the part of Brussels. As early as the Strasbourg European Council of December 1989, in fact, the Commission had been authorized to explore the implications of negotiating association agreements with the Five under article 238 of the Rome treaty. Association agreements, of which the EC has many with Third World countries, embrace not only trade and economic cooperation, but technical and financial assistance as well. They generally provide for an institutional framework for consultation and joint decisionmaking. Most delicately, they can in some instances signal the possibility of eventual EC membership (as was the case with Greece) while in others it is clear that association is the closest the associates will ever get. Where there is ambiguity on this point (as in the case of Turkey) no end of trouble ensues.

Just as the strategy of the European Economic Area was originally conceived by the EC Commission to contain and divert the EFTA states' demands for full membership, so the concept of association came forward as a response to statements by the governments of the Five that they intended to petition for membership on an urgent basis.[14] In sketching the outlines of association for the Five, the Commission was, however, forthright on two points: association would *not* automatically lead to membership; and secondly, the fate of the negotiations would depend on continued progress in the Five toward democracy and market economies.

In the latter half of 1990 the EC, having accepted these general principles of association, formulated its own negotiating position with respect, particularly, to issues of market access, financial and technical assistance, and the role of the institutions. In December the Commission received its mandate from the Council of Ministers and began negotiations with Czechoslovakia, Poland, and Hungary. After some last-minute hitches over Polish processed beef—predictably enough precipitated by France—the association agreements were signed on 22 November 1991. Similar agreements were reached with Bulgaria and Romania early in 1993.

These agreements are significant in several respects. First, they underline the importance the EC attributes to stabilizing and "normalizing" its immediate eastern flank: among the Five it has given clear priority to the more developed "northern tier" of Poland, Hungary, and Czechoslovakia (and after separation the Czech Republic is clearly preferred to Slovakia). The closest candidates to joining this select circle—Slovenia and the Baltic states—are probably still some years away. Second, they provide for, to a degree that simple trade agreements cannot, a necessarily asymmetrical process of mutual consultation, surveillance, and economic penetration, which is bound to secure a privileged position for the EC in the region. Third, they are the clearest example of a "civilian power" acting out classic liberal doctrine: interdependence and the promise of market access can be deployed to reinforce capitalism, democracy, and hence, regional stability.

The trade and association agreements negotiated with these former Comecon states over the past five years represent a standard form of relationship for the EC with the rest of the world, albeit applied here to a new category of country, and in record time. With respect to financial and technical assistance, however, the EC's role in the region has seen considerable innovation since 1989, even if its success is less than assured.

The centerpiece of the EC's financial and technical assistance program is PHARE (Poland and Hungary Assistance for the Restructuring of the Economy), initiated by the Commission in September 1989, as the first concrete response to its mandate from the Paris G7 summit earlier that year to coordinate aid to the East from the OECD.[15] By the end of 1990 the program had been extended to Czechoslovakia, Bulgaria, Romania, and Yugoslavia. As with the association agreements, criteria of eligibility include the creation and maintenance of a market economy and a democratic polity, along with satisfactory observance of human rights.

In four years PHARE's funding has doubled to just over one billion ECU annually. In the first two years the largest single allocation went to humanitarian and emergency aid, mainly in the form of food. As Eastern harvests have improved, however, and needs have become more clearly articulated both at the micro- and the macro-economic levels, an increasing proportion of PHARE aid has taken the form of technical assistance, in such areas as private-sector (particularly small-business) development, education, training and R&D, government organization and administration, agriculture, and regional development. By 1992 Albania, the Baltics and selected former Yugoslav republics had been added to the list of clients; nevertheless, the Five accounted for more than 60 percent of all PHARE's disbursements, with Poland continuing as the largest single recipient.[16]

Linked to the PHARE program is a second innovation, the European Bank for Reconstruction and Development (EBRD). A French initiative of late 1989, the EBRD was designed at an intergovernmental conference in January 1990, and inaugurated on 15 April of that year. Its 40-plus members include not only the major Western donor-states (and the European Investment Bank [EIB] in its own right) but also the Central and Eastern European recipient states. Although they are not a majority of the participants, EC member states hold, in their own right and through the EIB, 51 percent of the EBRD's capital of 10 billion ECU. Its location (London), its first president (Jacques Attali, former advisor to

President François Mitterrand, who launched the concept of the Bank), and its policies reflect the EC's dominant influence. The EBRD's role is to promote investment to secure the transition to a market economy; it is, in fact, required by statute to make at least 60 percent of its credits available to the private sector. Financial and technical support of privatization has thus become the principal theme of its activity to date.[17]

The third important instrument of EC assistance is the European Investment Bank, an EC institution whose main activity has traditionally been financial assistance to EC members, with increasing emphasis over the years on regional development. It has, however, been able to make loans abroad (e.g., to Third World associates); since February 1990 it has been authorized to make loans to Poland and Hungary and, since the fall of 1991, to Czechoslovakia, Bulgaria, and Romania. Its priorities remain development within the EC: of the 17 billion ECUs of financing provided in 1992, only 320 million went to Central and Eastern Europe. Since 1990 the EIB has provided 820 million ECU, 595 of which have gone to Poland and Hungary.[18]

Even more pointedly than the trade and association agreements, the EC's assistance programs for Central and Eastern Europe involve both conditionality and a significant degree of penetration of recipients' societies, economies, and policies. In contrast to International Monetary Fund (IMF) conditionality, the EC's demands on recipients are couched in terms of general criteria—democracy, free markets, human rights— rather than specific economic performance indices. And while all aid involves asymmetrical intervention into the recipient's affairs, the EC's technical assistance is of a range and variety that gives it an extraordinary degree of access to domestic processes of reform. The uniqueness of these programs is reinforced by the geopolitical proximity of the recipients, which underlines the connection between economic and political transformation, on the one hand, and the EC's security on the other.

The EC and the East: Reflections on Recent Experience

Central and Eastern Europe have been the focus, in the last five years, of a remarkable intensification and diversification of the EC's external relations. To get some sense of how the EC's role in the region might develop over the next few years it would be useful first to explore some propositions about the forces driving the EC's policy to date. Some of these have to do with the internal dynamics of the EC's economic and political development and apply, in principle, to its external relations in general. Others have to do with the unique characteristics of the Central and Eastern European region and of EC members' traditional links to it.

The process identified in the integration literature as "externalization" has played an important role in the EC's relations with its Eastern neighbors.[19] In the early 1970s, as we saw, completion of the customs union, with its Common External Tariff, necessarily entailed the adoption of the Common Commercial Policy and led to the first serious, if frustrating, attempts to normalize relations with the Comecon states. At the same time the internal agenda of political union drove the EC toward the awkward innovation of EPC, which found an early forum for expression in the Helsinki process.

Something similar occurred in the latter half of the 1980s, as the EC's 1992 program gained momentum. Not only did the drive to complete the single internal market have direct implications for external relations; it also laid the groundwork for Maastricht, with its provisions for an EC presence in security and defense policy. Perhaps most importantly, there is little doubt that the quickening of the EC integration process after 1984 led Comecon regimes to compare their economic policies, performance, and prospects increasingly unfavorably with those of Western Europe and to both initiate domestic reforms and intensify their pursuit of privileged links to Brussels. The result—a textbook case of externalization—was pressure on Brussels to develop a new and more extensive policy toward Central and Eastern Europe.

A second set of motives for EC policy—especially since 1989—is essentially defensive, having to do with efforts to anticipate and counter the potential impact on EC members and policies of developments to the east. The trade and association agreements, as noted earlier, contain important restrictions on Eastern exports of steel, textiles, and agricultural goods deemed "disruptive" to EC markets. In addition, economic and technical assistance is aimed, in great measure, at mitigating the economic conditions in the region that have led to a massive westward flow of refugees and asylum-seekers, especially to Germany, with well-known economic and social consequences. More generally, EC policy is aimed at forestalling economic collapse and political chaos, thus heading off the possibility of more direct forms of political and military intervention, all the more unpalatable in the light of the Yugoslav experience.

Related to this last point is the emergent sense of an EC "mission" in the region, partly an amalgam of long-standing conceptions on the part of certain member states—the big four in particular—of their Eastern roles, and partly an expression of the EC's sense of itself as a security community sustained by liberal values and policies. Richard Ullman has stated the objective: "The ultimate aim of any all-European security order should be the extension to the entire continent of the zone of peace that has come about in Western Europe."[20] In EC doctrine the road to that zone of peace lies through economic exchange, free markets, prosperity, and democracy, i.e., an eastward extension of the Pax Bruxellana.[21] There is, of course, a convenient fit between this mission and the more prosaic pursuit of an economic "chasse gardée" in the region.

To the extent, however, that the sense of mission also implies the eastward extension of national policies under an EC cloak, we are back in the realm of traditional geopolitics in which it is as reasonable to expect rivalry as it is to assume cooperation. France and Germany, in particular, are long-standing commercial and political competitors throughout the region. As reflected in its "Pentagonale" initiative, Italy has aspirations in the southern marches of the old Austro-Hungarian empire.[22] It may, moreover, become an implicit function of the EC to attempt to contain the real or presumed Eastern ambitions of its larger members, in particular a new *Drang nach Osten* once the domestic consequences of German reunification are under control. This is not to minimize the prospects of genuine cooperation, of the Twelve speaking with one voice in many areas of Eastern policy; nevertheless, it is unlikely that the débacle of Slovenian and Croatian recognition will be the last instance of EC policy being victimized by divergences in member states' regional interests.

Still in the realm of geopolitics, finally, some realists have trotted out the hoary concept of the "power vacuum" to account for the EC's increased presence in Central and Eastern Europe. With the Soviet recessional, and America's reluctance to provide an alternative framework for stability in the region (either through NATO or through a commitment to direct intervention), it is argued that the nearest available substitute will inevitably be drawn in. If this is not to be Russia—and, with the partial exception of its links to Serbia, the present leadership has shown few signs of being attracted to any conflict outside the old Soviet territory—it must be the EC or, in some formulations, Germany and its Brussels allies. Intervention would necessarily go beyond its present economic manifestations to embrace the security role for which Maastricht is intended ultimately to equip the EC. Alternatives to direct presence—such as the creation of regional cooperative arrangements or the revival of a "Habsburg buffer zone" between the EC and Russia—could only serve effectively to fill the vacuum if sponsored in some form by an outside power, of which the EC is again the most obvious candidate.[23] While the quaint determinism of "power-vacuum" theories need not detain us, they are a remainder that in the competition for influence and advantage in this relatively unorganized system of smallish states, the EC is well-placed, if only by default, to assume a pivotal role.

Conclusions: Present and Future Roles

To sum up, over the past five years the EC's response to the challenge of change in Central and Eastern Europe has become increasingly concentrated on the subregion consisting of the former Comecon associates of the Soviet Union, and particularly on Poland, Hungary, and the Czech Republic. The preferred instruments of its response have been multilateral institutions to promote and control trade and to allocate technical and financial aid. Whatever its original ambitions to play a comprehensive, regionwide role in the wake of the Cold War, the EC has found itself, chastened by its experience in the Balkans and overmatched by the scale of Russia's problems, reverting to what it does best in the subregion it knows best.

This is not to say, of course, that the EC is entirely out of the peacekeeping and peacemaking business in the former Yugoslavia, but simply to note that it no longer pretends to play the leading role there, and that it has drawn some sobering conclusions about the limits of its economic power in the face of atavistic nationalism. All the same, there is something to Gregory Treverton's observation that "Yugoslavia is a problem without a solution." It is, he writes, "a particular case. Its ethnic antagonisms are especially intense, its borders particularly artificial, its population intermingled, all of its republics' economies—except possible Slovenia's—unviable on their own. And none of its leaders are likely candidates for the Nobel Peace Price."[24] To the extent that Yugoslavia truly is exceptional and that the EC's leaders are committed to put flesh on the bare bones of the Maastricht agreement, the EC will find it hard to resist a peacekeeping and peacemaking role in any future conflict, especially one involving its immediate Eastern neighbors.

On the whole, however, Brussels is best-equipped and most-inclined to promote the "virtuous circle" of security, markets, and democracy by focusing first on markets. As Lawrence Freedman puts it, "influence will largely depend on economic measures—access to Western markets and various forms of assistance to reward political good conduct. . . . The general presumption that the problems in [C]entral and [E]astern Europe are best handled by political and economic measures, with military involvement avoided, suits the EC, for it already has the competence to take decisive political and economic measures. Its economic strength and cohesion provide a major source of leverage over those seeking access to Community markets and, ultimately, membership."[25]

It is thus reasonable, if unexciting, to predict that the EC will not soon risk reliving the international humiliation and internal divisions it experienced over Yugoslavia, by aspiring to the dominant conflict-management role in Central and Eastern Europe, and that the next few years at least will see it continue to pursue the economic diplomacy of association agreements and aid. Less predictable is the outcome of two related issues of growing importance in the EC's relations with Central and Eastern Europe in particular—the issue of subregional cooperation or integration, and the issue of membership in the EC.

Schemes to promote cooperation or integration among the states of the region made their appearance as early as the 1920s, whether based on nostalgia for the Austro-Hungarian empire, on one-world idealism, or on functionalist principles.[26] In the wake of the discredited Comecon, variants of these proposals have reappeared, nourished by a renewed sense of Central Europe as a political and cultural expression. Many of these schemes, especially those extending into the Balkans, seem doomed to futility while others are too blatantly self-serving with respect to one nationality or another to gain much broad support.[27]

The most promising cooperative endeavor is that initiated by Hungary, Poland, and Czechoslovakia at the Visegrad summit in February 1991, and consolidated at Cracow in October of that year.[28] Fashioned during a period of anxiety about the implications of German reunification, the collapse of Comecon and the Warsaw Pact, and the future of the Soviet Union, the Visegrad "Triangle" embodied an unstable and somewhat contradictory mix of objectives. On the one hand, Budapest, Warsaw, and Prague agreed to work toward increased mutual trade, the free exchange of information, publications, and cultural goods and values, coordinated development of telecommunications networks, protection of minorities, environmental enhancement, and a host of other worthy economic, social, and cultural aims. On the other hand, it was clear from the outset, despite denials that the Triangle aspired to become an alliance, that its members were preoccupied with security. Moreover, while the initiative gave the appearance of three small, vulnerable countries pooling their resources to maintain independence and security in a newly turbulent Europe, in practice their prime objective was to transfer their economic and security dependence from a collapsed Soviet system to the EC and NATO, by seeking membership in each as early as possible. The EC's response was the association agreements, NATO's the North Atlantic Cooperation Council, both intended to give the supplicants some reassurance while confining them to an anteroom until future notice.

Whatever the timetable for EC membership, it is likely that both Brussels and the states of Central and Eastern Europe will see advantages in promoting regional arrangements going beyond the Visegrad states to embrace Bulgaria, Romania, Slovenia, the Baltics, and perhaps others as they achieve some minimal capacity for effective cooperation. As was the case with postwar European reconstruction, successful regional schemes of this kind require an external patron, not only to provide massive capital and technical assistance but also to impose, as a condition of aid, disciplines of cooperation and liberalization. The EC has powerful leverage with which to play that role in Central and Eastern Europe. Along with its promotion of free markets, democracy, and human rights, therefore, the EC has increasingly felt compelled to insist, as the US did under the European Recovery Plan, on regional cooperation to allocate aid, and on far-reaching liberalization in trade and payments among the recipient states.

As demonstrated by its policies toward the EFTA countries in the European Economic Area, the EC's recent strategy toward applicants for membership in its immediate neighborhood has been not so much "divide and conquer" as "unite and defer." The strategy did not work in the case of the EFTA countries, several of which are expected to join the EC in a few years. With respect to the Eastern states, however, the EC has until recently resisted conceding the principle of eventual membership, even for the three states—Poland, Hungary, and the Czech Republic—whose economies are the most reformed, advanced, and integrated with the EC. Instead, Brussels has negotiated separate, essentially identical agreements with each to manage the increasingly intense economic relationship and to consult on political issues, while encouraging those (and other) aspiring members to make the waiting room more comfortable by furnishing it with some cooperative institutions of their own.[29] No more than in the case of EFTA (from 1973 on, at least) does encouraging collaboration among neighbors risk creating a rival bloc of any significance.

That said, it is highly likely that by the end of the decade the EC will have decided on a timetable for the admission of a select group of Central and Eastern European states, starting with the Visegrad group and gradually extending offers to other Baltic, Central European, and Balkan states as these meet appropriate criteria of free-market development, democratic stability, and concern for human rights. The governments of all these states have concluded that they have no real choice but to seek EC membership by whatever route, under whatever economic and political conditions Brussels demands. The lure of membership—barely diminished by economic downturns or the vicissitudes of the integration process—is the ultimate source of the EC's influence in Central and Eastern Europe. In Brussels the debate is polarizing between those who argue the need to offer no more than the prospect of eventual admission as a support to Central and Eastern Europeans committed to markets, democracy and human rights, and as an incentive to the hesitant, and those who urge the EC to remove its trade restrictions in short order and commit to a firm timetable for admitting new members, in order to head off the imminent breakdown of reform and a surge in ethnic tensions in the region. In the last year or so something of a compromise has emerged in which it is accepted that "the Community should confirm the perspective of future accession to the European Union and should indicate how best to prepare for this." Preparation would take place within a European Political Area based on cooperation and dialogue, and would require the prospective applicants to meet a demanding list of economic and political conditions.[30] The conditions are such that some present EC members would have difficulty meeting all of them. It is not, moreover, in the power of the Central and Eastern European states alone to satisfy some of them, particularly the last. Indeed, the significance of the reference to the momentum of integration will not be lost on the Central Europeans. It will remind them that however much they move toward democracy, stability, and free markets, and however loudly they clamor to be rewarded for it, the timetable of accession will be a function of the EC's internal, post-Maastricht agenda. The tension between the EC's domestic preoccupation with "deepening" integration and the prospective applicants' obsession with economic and political security ensures that the issue of membership will in the next few years come to dominate the EC's attempts to play a constructive role in Central and Eastern Europe.

Notes

1. John Mearsheimer, "Back to the Future: Instability in Europe After the Cold War," *International Security* 15 (Summer 1990): 5-56.

2. Especially for the Western Europeans. For useful summaries of trade data, see Richard Davy, "The Central European Dimension," in *The Dynamics of European Integration*, ed. William Wallace (London: Pinter, 1990), pp. 141-54. Good overviews are Charles Ransom, *The European Community and Eastern Europe* (London: Butterworths, 1975); and John Pinder, *The European Community and Eastern Europe* (London: Pinter, 1990).

3. Angela Stent, "Economic Strategy," in *Soviet Strategy Toward Western Europe*, ed. Edwina Moreton and Gerald Segal (London: Allen and Unwin, 1984), esp. pp. 231-32. See also, in the same volume, Karen Dawisha, "Soviet Ideology and Western Europe," pp. 19-38.

4. For a Western assessment, see Josef van Brabant, *Socialist Economic Integration: Aspects of Contemporary Economic Problems in Eastern Europe* (Cambridge: Cambridge University Press, 1980).

5. On EC external relations generally, see Phillip Taylor, *When Europe Speaks with One Voice: The External Relations of the European Community* (London: Aldwych Press, 1979); and Jacques Bourrinet and Maurice Torrelli, *Les Relations extérieures de la CEE* (Paris: Presses Universitaires de France, 1980).

6. A useful overview of Comecon in later life is Zbigniew Fallenbuchl, "The CMEA and Eastern Europe," *International Journal* 42 (Winter 1987-8): 106-26.

7. David Allen, Reinhardt Rummel, and Wolfgang Wessels, eds., *European Political Cooperation: Towards a Foreign Policy for Western Europe* (London: Butterworths, 1982); and Simon Nuttall, *European Political Cooperation* (Oxford: Clarendon Press, 1992).

8. Davy, "Central European Dimension," p. 143.

9. For background, see Dennison Rusinow, "Yugoslavia," in *Mediterranean Europe and the Common Market,* ed. Eric Baklanoff (Tuscaloosa, AL: University of Alabama Press, 1976), pp. 89-121.

10. At the time, these were the foreign ministers of Luxembourg, the Netherlands, and Portugal, respectively. The phrase "diplomatic rapid reaction force" is cited in Lawrence Freedman, "Order and Disorder in the New World," *Foreign Affairs* 71 (1991-92): 33.

11. On the concept of "civilian power," see François Duchêne, "Europe's Role in the International System: From Regional to Planetary Interdependence," in *A Nation Writ Large,* ed. Wolfgang Hager and Max Kohnstamm (London: Macmillan, 1973); and Christopher Hill, "European Foreign Policy: Power Bloc, Civilian Model—or Flop?" in *The Evolution of an International Actor: Western Europe's New Assertiveness,* ed. Reinhardt Rummel (Boulder: Westview Press, 1990).

12. Josef Joffe presents the episode as "an absurd replay of yesteryear's battles. As in World War I, Germany and Austria were arrayed on the side of Croatia and Slovenia, the old Habsburg possessions. On the other side stood the United States, Britain, and France, implicitly supporting their old ally Serbia by upholding its claim for an intact Yugoslavia." His account does not mention the contemporary commercial and demographic factors that others have seen as driving the German initiative. See Josef Joffe, "The New Europe: Yesterday's Ghosts," *Foreign Affairs* 72 (1991-92): 32.

13. Davy, "Central European Dimension," p. 143. Davy notes that Western Europe's dependence on trade with Eastern Europe has been declining since 1960, while the East's dependence on the West has risen slightly. For a critique of the EC's restrictive approach to trade with Eastern Europe under the association agreements, see *Economist,* 1 May 1993, pp. 54-56. On agricultural trade especially, see Tim Rollo and Alasdair Smith, "The Political Economy of Eastern Europe's Trade with the EC: Why So Sensitive?" *Economic Policy* 16 (April 1993).

14. Gregory Treverton, "The New Europe," *Foreign Affairs* 71 (1991-92): 98. A good summary of the negotiations for a European Economic Area is Finn Laursen, "The EC and its European Neighbours: Special Partnership or Widened Membership?" *International Journal* 47 (Winter 1991-92): 37-48.

15. Linguists will have noted that this rather contrived acronym means "lighthouse" in French, presumably to convey the image of the EC as a beacon unto the East.

16. Commission of the EC, *Second Annual Report on the Implementation of Community Assistance to the Countries of East and Central Europe,* COM(93)172 final, Brussels, 10 May 1993. For a critical review of PHARE, see "EC Aid to the East," *Economist,* 10 April 1993, pp. 21-23.

17. Jacques Attali resigned the presidency in late June 1993 amid charges of corruption and financial profligacy. For an assessment of the EBRD's record and future prospects, see *Economist*, 24 July 1993, p. 75.

18. European Investment Bank, *Annual Report 1992* (Luxembourg: EIB, 1993), pp. 24, 53, and 112.

19. On "externalization," see Philippe Schmitter, "Three Neo-Functional Hypotheses about International Integration," *International Organization* 23 (Winter 1969): 165.

20. Richard Ullman, *Securing Europe* (Princeton: Princeton University Press, 1991), p. 67.

21. William Wallace cites Pierre Hassner's observation that we are witnessing "not the Finlandization of Western Europe, as the Americans feared, but the Brusselization of Eastern Europe." Wallace himself writes of "the West European model spreading across Eastern Europe, as the nineteenth-century industrial revolution—and the eighteenth-century Enlightenment—spread from west to east." William Wallace, *The Transformation of Western Europe* (London: Pinter, 1990), pp. 94, 100.

22. The "Pentagonale," emerging in 1990 from the loose Alpine-Adria Working Group, originally consisted of Italy, Austria, Czechoslovakia, Hungary, and Yugoslavia, and aimed at functional cooperation in a variety of spheres. Poland has since joined, while Czechoslovakia has split and Yugoslavia has, for obvious reasons, ceased to participate.

23. Proposals—since overtaken by events—for such cooperation in Central and Eastern Europe are in Zbigniew Brzezinski, "Post-Communist Nationalism," *Foreign Affairs* 68 (Winter 1989-90): 18-20. Since the collapse of the Soviet Union Brzezinski has advocated including Russia and other former Soviet republics in these arrangements. See "The Cold War and its Aftermath," *Foreign Affairs* 71 (Fall 1992): 48-49.

24. Treverton, "The New Europe," p. 105.

25. Freedman, "Order and Disorder in the New World," pp. 33-34.

26. For a historical review of such ideas, see Paul Pilisi, "Les Pays socialistes de l'Est et l'unité européenne: la tradition dans le socialisme et le socialisme dans la tradition. I. Le fédéralisme en l'Europe de l'Est," *Etudes internationales* 10 (June 1979): 251-83.

27. Hungary, for example, floated the idea of "Tisza-Carpathian" cooperation with regions of Ukraine, Slovakia, and Serbia which, as Kovrig drily notes, "not coincidentally all have Hungarian minorities." Bennett Kovrig, "Moving Time: The Emancipation of Eastern Europe," *International Journal* 46 (Spring 1991): 262.

28. See Joshua Spero, "The Budapest-Prague-Warsaw Triangle: Central European Security After the Visegrad Summit," *European Security* 1 (Spring 1992): 58-83.

29. The EC Commission cites approvingly the project for a free trade agreement among the Visegrad countries as a stimulus to trade and investment in the region. See Commission of the EC, *Towards a Closer Association with the Countries of Central and Eastern Europe.* SEC(93)648 final, Brussels, 18 May 1993, p. 9.

30. Ibid., pp. 3-4. The conditions refer to (a) the capacity of each country to assume the obligations of membership; (b) the stability of its institutions guaranteeing democracy, the rule of law, human rights, and respect for minorities; (c) a functioning market economy; (d) endorsement of the objectives of political, economic, and monetary union; (e) capacity to cope with competitive pressures and market forces in the European Union; and (f) the EC's capacity to absorb new members while maintaining the momentum of integration.

9

The North Atlantic Cooperation Council: NATO's *Ostpolitik* for Post-Cold War Europe

William Yerex

Introduction

Twenty-five years ago, during the period of détente, Willy Brandt launched his famous *Ostpolitik* designed not to end the division of Europe and his own country, but to accommodate those divisions in hope of avoiding a catastrophic clash between East and West. Détente was, however, short lived and the obituaries then being written for the Cold War proved to be decidedly premature. The real ending of the Cold War has allowed the North Atlantic Treaty Organization, through the North Atlantic Cooperation Council (NACC) to undertake a new *Ostpolitik*. It is, to be sure, a different kind of reaching out to the East. But, as discussed below, this current policy, as with its predecessor, is not without its own difficulties, contradictions, and dangers.

It is somewhat ironic that the end of the Cold War does not find Europe dismantling security organizations but rather heightening the activity of existing ones and even developing new institutions. The product of the Helsinki accords, the Conference on Security and Cooperation in Europe (CSCE), is striving toward greater structure, and the Western European Union (WEU) is seeking to become the true pillar of European security, while the European Community—founded to foster trade and economic development—is moving, however fitfully, toward a common security policy. Not to be outdone, the grandfather of Cold War collective-defense organizations, NATO, has created an offshoot, the NACC, wherein the Western allies gather around the same table with their former Warsaw Pact adversaries and newly independent republics of the late Soviet Union.[1]

There is no shortage of critics for Europe's plethora of security organizations, especially in view of the alleged failure of any of them to do anything about the continent's first crisis of the post-Cold War era, the conflict in Yugoslavia. Some argue that the new structures will not only fail to provide security, but might themselves foster discord, and perhaps unnecessary conflict.[2] Others might complain that these new organizations are simply complex and redundant international bureaucracies that provide havens for otherwise unemployable civil servants. But a strong case can be made for the benefits of plural institutionalism and thus for the NACC.[3]

The end of the Cold War did not eliminate the need for an institutional security system. It did, however, complicate the issue of defining relevant roles for existing security structures.[4] NATO, as a successful military alliance, is a logical nucleus for coordination of European security issues and has the distinct advantage of North American participation to offset the parochial interest of any European state wishing to dominate the security scene. The Soviet threat formed a point of focus that subordinated other interests to efforts of collective defense. Those interests are now higher on political agendas and are pulling states in different directions. NATO, with a transatlantic rather than purely European perspective, can retain an emphasis that will foster cooperation more effectively than institutions with only European membership. The transatlantic link is also seen as a critical factor by the emerging new republics of Eastern Europe as they search for a secure niche in an unstable environment.

Institutions are developed and succeed only because it is in the collective national interests of their members. It may not be seen to be in the collective economic interests of many European countries to have Turkey as a member of the European Community, but it is important to have Turkey on-side from a security point of view, and as Stephen Page's chapter argues, Turkey is increasingly trying to be effective in dealing with problems in new (formerly USSR) republics to their east. NATO continues to be a forum where these collective interests can be addressed.

The same sort of logic has led the North Atlantic Assembly and the North Atlantic Council to develop the concept of the NACC. Despite divergent national interests, security issues could therewith be tabled and discussed in a cooperative and constructive forum.

Development of the NACC

The London Declaration of 5-6 July 1990 invited President Mikhail Gorbachev and representatives of the Central and Eastern European countries to Brussels to address the North Atlantic Council and to establish regular diplomatic liaison with NATO.[5] Thirteen months later the coup in the Soviet Union caused the more pessimistic soothsayers to question the advisability of NATO's open-door policy; nonetheless, NATO did not renege on its offer. Vaclav Havel was the first head of state and government from the new democracies of Central and Eastern Europe to take up the invitation of the London Declaration.[6] He was followed by the Polish and Hungarian heads of government as the spirit of the London initiative became reality.[7]

The NATO summit in Rome on 7-9 November 1991 continued the theme of cooperation and institutionalized the process with the announcement of the formation of the North Atlantic Cooperation Council, whose inaugural session was scheduled for 20 December 1991.[8] The first meeting comprised NATO's 16 members plus foreign ministers from Bulgaria, the Czech and Slovak Federal Republic, Estonia, Hungary, Latvia, Lithuania, Poland, Romania, and a representative of the Soviet Union. The historical impact of this meeting was punctuated when the Soviet Union's representative, Ambassador Afanassievsky, announced the dissolution of his own state and indicated his wish to have agreements from the process made valid for the Soviet successor republics.[9] As a result, the 10 March 1992 meeting in Oslo saw the addition of representatives from Armenia, Azerbaidzhan, Belarus, Kazakhstan, Kyrgystan, Moldova, Tadzhikistan, Turkmenistan, Ukraine, Uzbekistan, and Russia.

That inaugural meeting was little more than a symbolic "get-acquainted" effort to enunciate the collective goal of "a Europe whole and free." It set out a schedule for meetings of the Council at different levels of representation and for subordinate committees to focus on specific policies and issues. Ambassadors were tasked to develop a work plan, which was issued at a meeting on 10 March 1992, and covered a range of topics: political and security related matters, defense planning and military matters, defense conversion, economic issues, science, challenges of modern society, dissemination of information, policy planning consultations, and air-traffic management.[10] The 5 June 1992 meeting in Oslo coined the "Vancouver to Vladivostok" phrase and welcomed Georgia and Albania as members. Finland attended as an observer.[11] But what specific objectives did NATO have in mind when forming this new institution? What group of national interests are being served in this rather unwieldy collection of former adversaries? The concept of stability seemed to be the key theme in every major statement concerned with the NACC. As the communiqué of the first NACC meeting issued on 20 December 1991 observed: "in the new era of European relations where the confrontation and division of past decades have been replaced by dialogue, partnership and cooperation, we are determined to work towards a new, lasting order of peace in Europe. Aware of NATO's positive influence as a source of stability, our common objective is to contribute to the enhancement of European security by promoting stability in Central and Eastern Europe."[12]

It is not just for the member states of NATO that the success of the Atlantic Alliance will be important, but for all the 51 members of the CSCE as well. In the past, it has been difficult enough fashioning a consensus among NATO's 16 members. With so many more national interests to reconcile, the challenge of building new security regimes in Europe will be all the more exacting, particularly since even within the NATO club national interests are not nearly as convergent as during the 40 years of the defensive alliance. Nevertheless, the NACC represents one of the first initiatives to meet the requirements of NATO's new role.

Contrary to the claim articulated in Christopher Conliffe's chapter, NATO did respond quickly to the incredible rate of change in Central and Eastern Europe, especially in comparison to other European institutions. The vocabulary of internal NATO documents was changing well before events that made world headlines as even the word "threat" was banished from military intelligence assessments. The Harmel doctrine, which had guided NATO since December 1967 through its twin pillars of defense and dialogue, had also created strong ties to the latter element that would prove invaluable.[13] The third pillar of cooperation was soon to be added.

The Rome summit on 7 and 8 November 1991 put the heads of government seal of approval on efforts to change NATO that had been advanced through the Military Committee, Defence Planning Committee, and the North Atlantic Council during the 1988-90 period. During the Council meeting in Turnberry, Scotland, the ministers extended the hand of friendship and cooperation to the then Soviet Union and in the London Declaration a month later, the heads of government formally ended the adversarial relationship that had existed since NATO's formation.

In the first months of the post-Cold War era optimism about the "new world order" abounded and Francis Fukuyama's essay, "The End of History," became the most widely quoted paper in academic, political, and even military circles.[14] The absence of the "threat" signalled for many the end of any need for a military alliance and resulted in numerous predictions about the early breakup of NATO. Academics and strategists at NATO argued whether the requirement for defense against "risks" and "instability" was appropriately a NATO mandate.

A European Security and Defense Identity (ESDI) was emerging as the new focus for dealing with European problems. France saw the

opportunity to make the EC and Western European Union more dominant as the centers for discussion of European events, thereby marginal-
izing American influence. France consistently blocked any attempts by
NATO to move toward any new or expanded role.[15] The United States
viewed the European pillar more in the burdensharing sense but seemed
willing to adopt a lower profile on European issues.

The August 1991 coup attempt in Moscow, the Gulf Crisis, and the
violent disintegration of Yugoslavia made it clear that "history" had not
yet ended. The risks and instability that NATO had identified in its new
assessment became clear to all, yet no mandate had been given to the
alliance to deal with such events. The EC, WEU, and CSCE proved
woefully incapable of any effective action, yet some alliance members
(particularly France) still frustrated any NATO action on even basic
contingency planning in response to these crises.[16]

Ironically, it was the new governments from Central and Eastern
Europe that clearly identified NATO as the focal point for security and
stability. Leaders such as Vaclav Havel came to NATO with specific
requests for membership and protection. The EC and WEU were not seen
as institutions that could offer any real comfort in terms of security. This
left NATO with a real dilemma: internally no agreement to expansion of
membership was achievable, yet encouragement, cooperation, and assistance to the new democracies was considered to be in the interest of
all members. The NACC was seen as a vehicle to retain the momentum
of democratization without jeopardizing the solidarity of the defensive
alliance. The NACC could be the forum in which to continue the themes
expressed in the London Declaration and provide an institution for the
development of new initiatives. The many paradoxes that resulted (for
example, former Warsaw Pact states as members, but neutral countries
such as Sweden or Finland only granted observer status) were accepted
as bureaucratic anomalies that would gradually sort themselves out.[17]

Successive failures by the EC and WEU, particularly in dealing with
the Yugoslavia crisis, and the renewed credibility given NATO by the
Eastern Europeans tempered the early enthusiasm for an exclusively
European approach and shifted the focus of discussion back to the
NATO tables. NATO had proven itself to be a stable, well-respected
institution that provided for high-level consultation and was thought to
be the only institution with the means to take any real action if the
situation so dictated. The CSCE was recognized as the key institution in
which all Central and Eastern European countries could have equal
access to a platform for discussion, but it, as its name suggests, was
purely a conference and had no "teeth" to enforce or even verify provisions adopted by consensus. Institutionalization of CSCE was a step

strongly supported at Turnberry and in the London Declaration, but the means of doing this proved elusive.

What the NACC Is and Is Not

In light of the uncertainty surrounding the future of European security, the creation of the NACC has not been an insignificant achievement. It brought former adversaries into a consultation forum on security issues. Those countries that had belonged to, and rejoiced in the dissolution of, the Warsaw Pact, at the same time felt naked and vulnerable. The NACC provided scant cover, but some temporary comfort nonetheless. But, in the longer term, the NACC has the potential to foster European security by providing a meeting place where smaller bilateral/multilateral arrangements may begin. To be sure, the process is not fully developed and it is far from evident how the NACC will cope with its membership anomalies. It will remain heavily dependent on the momentum provided by strong personalities that direct their energies to its success. Of particular importance will be the development of a close relationship between the CSCE and NACC in order to enhance the utility of both institutions.

While seeking to foster a sense of security, the NACC does not provide any security guarantees to the Central and Eastern European states in the same way that NATO does to its members. And despite the pleading of Havel and Poland's president, Lech Walesa, NATO membership is not likely to expand in the very near future. Yet, both Czech and Polish senior politicians have set definite timetables to become full members of the alliance. Both governments put a great deal of emphasis on meeting human rights standards and Western economic stability norms in the hope that they might better ensure future membership in the alliance.

At the same time many Central and Eastern European countries see the NACC merely as another source of financial and technical handouts. These expectations have not been fulfilled. While advice and assistance have been offered freely, financial aid has not been an item on the NACC agenda. Still, some delegates from the East show up for nearly every meeting sponsored by the NACC. They simply change titles, ask for air fare and hotel accommodation at NATO expense and appear at meetings more as spectators than as sources of any real intellectual input. This assessment may seem somewhat harsh but it is one of the realities of dealing with some states where institutions are still seen simply as a means for collecting bureaucratic perks.

Where the NACC has been able to make a modest beginning is in its outreach programs from senior political level to junior military officers. In the way that the CSCE process and in particular the Stockholm agreement on inspections of military exercises brought down barriers simply through confidence building, the NACC has spawned interactions such as the Oberammergau courses, the Rome staff college meetings, and other fora that have removed barriers of mistrust purely through exposure and education.

To illustrate the types of initiatives that the NACC can take to assist in resolving current problems in Central and Eastern Europe it might be useful to examine briefly a seminar held in NATO on defense industry conversion. Not solely a NACC initiative, this seminar used the NACC and NATO's Economic Committee to generate discussion. Significant world expertise was concentrated in Brussels to focus on the restructuring problems in the East. Parliamentarians, economists, academics and representatives of industry prepared and presented a series of papers on the subject that admittedly defined more problems than solutions, but clearly enunciated those problems from a wide range of perspectives. Countries such as the then Czech and Slovak Federal Republic, Poland, and Bulgaria were able to identify specific problems that threatened their national economies and thwarted any attempts at responsible budgeting. Consultants who had begun work with these governments were able to outline various approaches and obstacles to success such as transfer of technology issues. While delegates may have returned home wondering if any success had been realized in terms of moving toward solutions to the massive problems that existed, a new framework had been created that, if nothing more, raised awareness and moved the perspective of many from a parochial point of view to a more global approach. At the same time, bilateral and multilateral contacts provided many new long-term alternatives for Central and East European countries. While some might have been disappointed with the lack of financial commitments, the collective intellectual resources of many were now concentrated on the real problems at hand.[18]

Another major role for the NACC might be in furthering nuclear arms control and nonproliferation. With NATO's ties to CSCE and the various arms-control processes that have occurred during the past decade, the NACC is a natural forum to follow up on the various issues regarding nuclear weapons. Verification, destruction, accountability, and processing of fissile material would appear to be natural extensions of the NACC agenda.

The NACC has already spawned parallel committees at the Defence Planning Committee and Military Committee levels. Defense ministers first met on 1 April 1992 and the Military Committee in chiefs-of-staff session later in May 1992. From these meetings various initiatives on the role of the military in a democratic society have been generated.

While earlier meetings of the NACC discussed little but the structure of how meetings will be organized, the potential for significant dialogue is apparent. As the countries of Central and Eastern Europe evolve into new democracies they constantly seek advice on civil-military relationships and the new democratic institutions that have never before existed in these countries. The education element cannot be underestimated. Long-entrenched misconceptions about NATO and Western European military organizations must be eliminated through face-to-face contact at middle and lower levels of government and military personnel.

The experimental nature of the NACC, as it attempts to foster consultation without offering participants full NATO membership, presents significant new challenges. Within the alliance, consensus is required for any action to take place. Will the NACC operate on a similar basis or will NACC members gradually become full members of NATO as they meet a check-list of prerequisites? How will duplication of efforts between the CSCE and the NACC be avoided and consistency of approach be achieved? There is a large divergence of opinion on these issues, with some NATO members viewing NACC as a temporary fixture that will disappear with the institutionalization of the CSCE and the development of conflict-prevention mechanisms therein. Others view the NACC as a conduit for eventual formation of NATO as a security arm for the CSCE and/or the United Nations. The lack of clear roles at this time should not, however, be seen as a weakness of the process, but rather as a natural feature of a new and experimental organization.

In the past, NATO has demonstrated a reluctance to act in any situations or extend security guarantees in any manner that would upset Russia. In order to avoid adopting policies that would fan anti-Western forces within Russia and potentially derail the move toward democracy and a market economy, a "tread-softly" approach seems to have been advocated. The NACC offers a forum in which Russia can play an integral role in consensus building for any mandate that would see the employment of NATO forces on security missions. Peacekeeping roles would be completely transparent to Russian officials, avoiding the possibility of interpretation as provocative actions. Similarly, Russian activities in former Soviet republics could be the subject of discussion and examination within the NACC. There is some concern that Russia might attempt to legitimize actions against "unruly" republics by token discussions in the NACC as a prelude to actions that might be viewed by the West as suppressive. The presence of such a wide cast of former USSR republics within the NACC would augur for collective condemnation for any such actions by Russia and the transparency element could be further developed in the NACC and the CSCE to guard against such activities.

Cooperative Versus Competitive Institutionalism

There is a new phenomenon affecting plural institutionalism, however, that threatens both collective and individual success. Institutions seem to be competing for prominence in some undefined hierarchy. During the period immediately following the breakup of the Soviet Union and in particular the move of relief supplies to Estonia, Latvia, and Lithuania, there was an almost ugly competitive air to the provision of relief. Canadian flights that were offered through NATO auspices were rejected by the EC, despite the lack of any alternative plans. France's apparent obstructionism in NATO become frustrating for states trying to use NATO as a rallying point for relief operations. The very parochial approach to a world problem was symptomatic of institutionalism at its worst, with bureaucrats caught up in competition for media attention rather than in reassessing the priority issues that required decisive actions. NATO managed to avoid becoming involved centrally in these competitive tussles. While the EC insisted on its primacy and leadership in Eastern Europe and then in Yugoslavia, failing miserably at every turn, NATO showed a measure of maturity and character by offering to help wherever and whenever the bickering Eurocrats could decide help was needed.

But this reluctance to compete with other European organizations also stemmed from the very nature of the Atlantic Alliance. The Rome summit defined three future risks for NATO: a resurgent Russia, Islamic fundamentalism, and instability in Central and Eastern Europe. Of these, the third is the real point of focus, as Yugoslavia clearly demonstrates. However, NATO, under its current charter, cannot act in such situations. Unless that mandate is changed to allow NATO to use its vast resources to address such new "risks" head on, the large expenditures that have been invested to run the alliance could be withdrawn by members desperate to balance budgets. In the past, NATO fulfilled its role just by being there. With the Soviet threat gone that is no longer enough. NATO has substantial resources that it can offer. The problem is that as an institution it cannot make them available. As an arm of another institution, or in response to the request of an institution in which all its members are included, it may, however, discover a formula by which it could become more effective.

The NACC can form a core element from which the institution of NATO can expand to take on a new mandate. As members of the NACC fulfil the standards of NATO full membership through human rights criteria, plural democratic values, and economic reform, NATO might grow to become the real bastion of European security. Even now NATO should be looking to provide peacekeeping resources not just from existing military forces but by including elements of the entire NACC community. This would constitute cooperation beyond the purely bureaucratic level.

In sum, the NACC should be seen as more than just an effort by NATO to extend its useful life by moving into policy areas now claimed by other European institutions. It is more than weak glue being applied by bureaucrats desperate to perpetuate the alliance and their jobs. Rather, the NACC can help NATO find its proper niche within the network of European institutions. If this can be done in a cooperative, synergistic manner rather than in the competitive atmosphere now prevalent, it can be a valuable institution in Europe for a long time to come. It can become a strong adhesive for the entire framework of European collective security.

For the NACC truly to succeed it will require US membership and active participation. American military hegemony is a fact of life and will continue to be so for some time. If the United States is the reluctant global policeman, its reluctance comes from weariness and frustration in dealing with allies more than from a lack of responsibility. Washington has given no indication that it wishes to disengage entirely from European security matters that would still be of vital interest to America's security. As with NATO, the United States is redefining how those interests can best be achieved. In a major policy address at the dedication of the George C. Marshall Center in Garmisch, Germany, on 5 June 1993, Secretary of Defense Les Aspin outlined the character of a "new strategic partnership" between the United States and Europe. He declared that the US could not "hold itself aloof from the instability and conflict in Europe. US involvement in two world wars in this century demonstrates that beyond doubt." He stressed that Washington was prepared to join in new security arrangements for Europe:

> How then is this new security system for this vast space to be created? Not by undermining the strength and solidarity of NATO and the strength and solidarity of bilateral relations with its members . . . Not by the announcement of some grand new architecture. Not by fruitless arguments about which of the current institutions shall have the right to do what. My belief is we should proceed pragmatically and patiently and seek to weave a seamless security web across this space—thread by thread. The US effort to do this envisages three complementary initiatives. First we seek to strengthen and extend institutions that are now working: NATO and the North Atlantic Cooperation Council . . . the CSCE. Second, we should thicken bilateral relations between each of the nations . . . Third, we favor the growth of regional understandings and associations among neighbors.[19]

For their part, the new NACC members see their membership in the NACC as the sole means of tying themselves institutionally to the world's only hegemon. A stronger NATO, gradually expanded through the movement of NACC members to full membership in a newly defined institution, would hold US interest and involvement.

As for NATO's other North American member, Canada, the NACC also offers certain advantages. It can afford Ottawa an important forum in which to pursue long-standing Canadian European interests relating to arms control, peacekeeping, human rights, and trade policy.

NATO Peacekeeping and the NACC

At the North Atlantic Cooperation Council meeting on 18 December 1992, ambassadors decided to establish an ad hoc group, chaired by the deputy secretary-general, Amedeo de Franchis, to study areas for cooperation in peacekeeping and make specific recommendations. Several meetings of that group have taken place and proposed frameworks for an initial program of cooperation in the area of peacekeeping were presented to the Council at its meeting on 15 March 1993. Peacekeeping has been at the top of the agenda in meetings of the Defence Planning Committee, the Group on Defence Matters, and the Military Committee. There is a strong sentiment in certain quarters that the future utility of the alliance rests in its ability to undertake peacekeeping roles. On its own, NATO cannot initiate peacekeeping operations—the present mandate does not include such initiatives and it is unlikely that agreement could be reached to give NATO such freedom of independent action. However, the UN and the CSCE (in accordance with the document agreed in Helsinki in July 1992) might well call upon NATO to provide forces, infrastructure, and resources to support such operations. The UN or the CSCE would have to lay out a clear mandate to which NATO would be asked to respond. With current misused and misunderstood terms such as "peacemaking" and "imposed peace," the mandate element is extremely important.

Once given a clear mandate NATO has the capability to be very successful in a peacekeeping role. For several years now the structure of NATO's forces and its crisis management procedures have been under significant revision to take on such a role. The interlocking and overlapping institutions of Europe are beginning to draw back from their previous confrontational stances and adopt a more cooperative and synergistic profile. The crisis in Yugoslavia and the "CNN factor" (resulting from extensive media coverage) have heightened public awareness and forced senior officials in all institutions to look for the most effective approach to meeting public demands to "do something."

The CSCE, at its summit in Helsinki, 19 July 1992, established a forum for security cooperation. This forum could initiate, under the CSCE chairman-in-office, consultations with NATO regarding cooperative and supportive efforts in peacekeeping activities. The CSCE has adopted a "consensus-minus-one" principle that would apply in such circumstances.[20] (NATO requires consensus before taking any action.) NATO Headquarters has the advantage of instant access to senior defense and military expertise. NATO's situation-center and crisis-management structure can support 24-hour consultations, if necessary, with current information and expert evaluation.

The UN is also studying procedures by which it could call upon NATO resources to assist in peacekeeping missions. The Persian Gulf conflict employed doctrine, structures, and procedures developed in NATO, as well as NATO-designated forces. In Yugoslavia, NATO command and control doctrine has been in place and a functioning headquarters element has been made available to United Nations Protection Force (UNPROFOR) II in Bosnia-Herzegovina. NATO naval forces and Advanced Early Warning aircraft have supported UN operations. NATO planners have travelled to UN Headquarters in New York to examine potential resources and relevant procedures for additional NATO contributions.

Formerly, NATO concentrated several important member countries in frontline military formations such as the Allied Command Europe (ACE) Mobile Force, to ensure total commitment as early in any conflict as possible. Peacekeeping operations do not require the same sort of organizations. The flexibility of the new rapid reaction forces would permit members to contribute according to their best abilities. Forces could be tailored by the military experts within NATO with some countries providing ground forces, others logistic support or infrastructure and the myriad of additional resources needed for successful operations. Any such peacekeeping force would be backed up by the largest military structure in the world. Compared to the rather frail UN military coordination elements and the embryonic conflict-prevention resources of the CSCE, NATO has the potential to be significantly more effective and efficient.

Peacekeeping experience and expertise exists within NATO with countries such as Norway and Canada. The military, financial, and command structures are currently being fine-tuned within NATO to allow alliance forces to take on this role. Meetings of military experts will look at the planning, technical, procedural, and training issues over the next few months. These meetings are taking place not only in Brussels but also in such places as Bucharest and Cesky Krumlov.

The NACC could act as a consultation forum in which to garner maximum support for both CSCE and NATO efforts. It would be a useful forum for the development of clear understanding of the principles and concepts necessary for collective peacekeeping efforts. By including all 38 members in the process and by including representatives from other institutions at key meetings, the NACC can become a focal point for resolving any roadblocks to this new role for NATO.

Conclusion

With the creation of the NACC, the Atlantic Alliance has begun to develop an *Ostpolitik* to meet the extraordinary circumstances of post-Cold War Europe. It has responded to the Central and East European countries who would not accept "no" for an answer when they asked for NATO membership. The NACC has gained a momentum beyond that generated by NATO's 16 members. Given the political will to see it succeed, the NACC can become the dominant new institution that could well be the glue for all of Europe.

The NACC also has the potential to be effective in the long term by bringing clearer understanding and intellectual synergy to a vast array of issues. While the CSCE addresses continued movement to foster and guard the ideals of the Helsinki Final Act of 1975, the NACC can coordinate alliance resources on specific problems in a complementary rather than a duplicative or competitive manner. NATO does not have the authority to initiate solutions to problems directly, but it does have significant human and material resources that can assist the Central and Eastern Europeans in establishing democracy within their borders and security along them. For this new *Ostpolitik* to succeed, however, it will be important that both East and West understand not only NATO's capabilities but its limitations as well.

Notes

1. See Brigadier-General B.A. Goetze and Captain E.C. Sloan, "The New European Security Architecture," *Canadian Defence Quarterly* 22 (March 1993):26-34.

2. On the dangers of new collective-security arrangements, see Richard K. Betts, "Systems for Peace or Causes of War? Collective Security, Arms Control and the New Europe," in *America's Strategy in a Changing World*, ed. Sean M. Lynn-Jones and Steven E. Miller (Cambridge, MA: MIT Press, 1992), pp. 199-237.

3. A strong case for plural institutionalism and the reduction or avoidance of conflict through overlapping security institutions is made by Arlene Idol Broadhurst,"Forward to the Past: A Long View of the Long Peace," in *From*

Euphoria to Hysteria: Western European Security After the Cold War, ed. David G. Haglund (Boulder: Westview Press, 1993), pp. 45-68.

4. For a more complete examination of the complex issues facing institutional security systems in Europe see Michel Fortmann and David G. Haglund, "Europe, NATO, and the EDSI Debate: In Quest of an Identity," in ibid., pp. 21-44.

5. The text is available as: NATO, "London Declaration on a Transformed North Atlantic Alliance," Issued by the Heads of State and Government participating in the meeting of the North Atlantic Council in London on 5-6 July 1990 (NATO Press Communiqué S-1 [90] 36). See also Henning Wegener, "The Transformed Alliance," *NATO Review* 38 (August 1990):1-9.

6. For documentation on Vaclav Havel's visit to NATO on 21 March 1991 and his address to the NATO Council, see *NATO Review* 39 (April 91):29-33.

7. For documentation of Lech Walesa's visit to NATO and text of his address to the NATO Council see *NATO Review* 39 (August 1991):33-35.

8. The Rome summit is well documented in *NATO Review* 39 (December 1991).

9. For the text of the final communiqué, including Ambassador Afanassievsky's statement, see NATO Press Communiqué M-NACC-1(91) 111(Rev), 20 December 1991.

10. The complete work plan for dialogue, partnership, and cooperation is available in Guido Gerosa, "The North Atlantic Cooperation Council," *European Security* 1 (Autumn 1992):273-94.

11. See Oslo Communiqué, 4 June 1992.

12. North Atlantic Cooperation Council, "Statement on Dialogue, Partnership and Cooperation," issued at NATO Headquarters, Brussels, 20 December 1991.

13. NATO, *Facts and Figures* (Brussels: NATO Information Services 1989), p. 31.

14. Francis Fukuyama, "The End Of History?" *National Interest,* no. 16 (Summer 1989), pp.3-18.

15. For a discussion of France's position and reasons for the seemingly obstructionist approach, see the essay by Michel Fortmann and David G. Haglund, "Between Eurovoluntarism and Realism: France and European Security in Transition," in this volume.

16. Ibid.

17. See Hilmar Linnenkamp, "The North Atlantic Cooperation Council: A Stabilizing Element of a New European Order?" in *The Former Soviet Union and European Security: Between Integration and Re-Nationalization,* ed. Hans-Georg Ehrhart, Anna Kreikemeyer, and Andrei V. Zagorski (Baden-Baden: Nomos Verlagesgesellschaft, 1993), pp. 219-28.

18. See papers on NATO-Central and East European Countries Seminar on Defense Industry Conversion, Brussels, 20-22 May 1992, available from NATO Information Services.

19. United States Embassy, Ottawa, "Aspin Outlines New Strategic Partnership," *Text* 93-19 (8 June 1993), p. 2.

20. See CSCE Helsinki Final Document, *Challenges of Change,* 1992.

10

Discovering Westminster: The Transformation of Civil-Military Relations in Central Europe

Douglas Bland

Introduction

"Allies," noted the British chief of the general staff during the First World War, "are a troublesome lot." Europe's Eastern dilemma is centered on its appreciation that on the one hand the security of Europe and the Atlantic area is dependent on stability in the East, but on the other that Western Europeans are reluctant to entangle themselves with the troublesome—and for the moment, nonallied—lot that lives there. The Western public's aversion to becoming engaged with the regimes in the East is not merely due to the fear of the security problems that Easterners will bring with them. Westerners are also apprehensive that the Atlantic security community, which is held together by the glue of "like-mindedness" and liberal democratic traditions, might be damaged if it allied itself with new governments that are not credible democracies. The perception in the West that Central European states lack reliable civil control of their military forces is an important part of these concerns, and is the focus of this chapter.

Civil or parliamentary control of the military is a defining characteristic of liberal-democratic societies. In the East this concept is untested, at least as it is understood and operationalized in the West. It is true that the military forces of the Soviet Union and member states of the Warsaw Pact Treaty Organization (WTO) were under the civil control of the Communist Party but that tradition did not leave a legacy of structures and processes that are compatible with those in the West. In any case, the collapse of the party apparatus has made the relationship between the current civil authorities and the military problematical. In

Poland, of course, the transition from the party to the present democratic government by way of a military dictatorship exposes a more complicated set of questions. Until there is clear evidence that the governments of the East have established relationships that are compatible with those in the West, NATO's Eastern dilemmas will continue.

This chapter's purpose is to explore the relationship between conceptual and structural development in Central Europe, all within the overall context of general European security. It is premised on the idea that the formation of an effective European defense community that includes the Central European states will require the establishment in those states of national-security structures that are compatible with those in the West. As a fundamental condition, this goal will necessitate the confirmation in Central European states of civil-military relations based on Western ideas and norms. Furthermore, these ideas and norms will have to be revealed in the structure and functioning of each state's defense ministry. This convergence of norms of behavior and structure is the sine qua non for any defense community that might embrace all states in Europe.

Institutionalized Security

It is widely believed that institutions will provide the foundation for future European security. François Heisbourg was partly right when he declared that the great question facing Europeans was "how to organize a new [security] system in Europe from the debris of the old order."[1] Unfortunately, not much of the old debris scattered about the rubble cluttering the Central European security environment can or will provide suitable materiel for constructing a pan-European security structure.

Among the "debris of the old order" in Western Europe, however, are building blocks that could provide the materiel for building a new security structure, even if these construction artifacts of a bygone era must remain inappropriate foundations in and of themselves. Each entity, including the Western European Union (WEU), the Conference on Security and Cooperation in Europe (CSCE), and the North Atlantic Treaty Organization (NATO), was built on a conceptual framework that explicitly or implicitly acknowledged an antagonistic relationship between East and West. Western leaders will have to make substantial adjustments to their security assumptions and the political and military leaders of Central Europe will have to import from the West's rich political heritage many things that may be unfamiliar, and even disturbing, before any stable structure can be constructed to maintain peace and security throughout Europe in the coming decade.

Recent attempts in the West to build a new order have not been overwhelming successes, as the current history of the Maastricht process suggests. Similarly, French and German efforts to create an "alliance within the [NATO] alliance" have stumbled over national sovereignty and the inability of the partners to find a shared strategic assessment or even a consensus on the purpose of the partnership.[2] Faith in the salvation of Europe through union as illustrated by Michel Rocard, who recently asked, "what could be more eloquent than a European army?"[3] must be answered by the cold-blooded reality of Europe's ineloquent failure to respond to the carnage on its Balkan doorstep.

There is not much with which to build in the debris in the East. The Warsaw Pact alliance was irretrievably discredited even before it expired, and can hardly serve as an inspiration for a new security order in Central Europe. The armed forces of all the states in the region are in various degrees of disorder. Each force suffers from the shocks caused by the loss of its supporting allied structure, the collapse of its raison d'être, and the continued decline in its once-assured share of national resources. Politicians in the East, though nominally democratic, have yet to confirm that they have complete control of the policy agenda in each state, nor indeed, can anyone know whether the present desire for democratic methods can be sustained.[4]

No one can predict the future of the process of state building now underway in Central Europe. Therefore, NATO's dilemma is likely to continue indeterminately. The inability to see clearly into the future, however, does not excuse us from trying to anticipate it, at least in some of its aspects. Not a few observers see the outcome in dark shades. David Owen, for one, is essentially pessimistic and has concluded that "Europe is starting to breed attitudes that are profoundly antagonistic to the continuance, let alone the development, of the Atlantic partnership."[5] These attitudes could wreck the one structure, NATO, that enjoys some coherence, at least in the West, and which most Central European politicians hold to be the solution to their security problems. Other observers are more optimistic and predict a growing interdependence among all European states based on the acceptance of "traditional political ties, institutions, and cultural patterns" that will inevitably increase the security of all.[6]

For his part, Stanley Hoffmann perceives an emerging approach in which Europe, "thanks to a combination of democratic regimes, diffuse threats, and extensive institutionalization, may be on the threshold of a new kind of politics that goes beyond such traditional categories as balancing alliances or alignments, loose cooperative concerts, or jungle-like anarchy. Whether Europe will cross this threshold by extending and deepening its institutionalization, depends on the chief actors inside and outside the continent."[7] Hoffmann's view reflects Kenneth Waltz's notion that institutions are the most appropriate instruments for controlling the "immediate causes" of war.[8] But Hoffmann's hopefulness is reminiscent of Karl Deutsch's faith in the power of the idea of community in encouraging the development of "security communities" in which there would be a high expectation that problems within the community could and would be solved by peaceful means.[9]

Building a new security structure in Europe will not likely be a tidy project and it is hard to imagine how the final edifice will serve every player and every issue perfectly. The factors are simply too dynamic. Too many peripheral issues are poised to sabotage nice plans and rigid structures. Some might ask, Why any structure at all? Why not allow the issues to form the debate and to motivate appropriate responses through the power of the "invisible hand" of national self-interest? The reality is that uncertainty breeds fear and mistrust prompts a search for international institutions that will assist competing states to control, if not to eliminate, war. The invisible hand may usefully guide economic decisions, but in this situation it can be too murderous.

Enriching Europe's current institutions and creating new ones to manage a broader security regime will require more than the will of the main actors. Institutions "find policy" in a dynamic process of debate and consultation; and this process, in international relations, requires a high degree of compatibility among the concepts, structures, and policy expectations of all the participating national and international institutions. Just as international railway systems work most efficiently when the roadways are of the same gauge and schedules and communication networks are common, so too does the effectiveness of international security institutions depend on their capability to address critical security issues in ways that "mesh" community and national interests.[10] The usefulness and survival of future European security institutions will depend on the acceptance by all the actors (and the publics for whom they act) of the steadfastness and the appropriateness of the concepts that underpin these institutions.

Compatible civil-military relations are at the heart of the Atlantic Alliance, an international security structure that ensures civil control while allowing for the effective aggregation of allied military power. It is an evolved structure that is derived from the West's liberal-democratic traditions. No Western government would be allowed to surrender the safeguards inherent in this structure merely to enhance European security. In fact, many people expect Western politicians to champion Western ideas (and idealism) in the East and would react with anger if political leaders sought security by compromising these notions. Resolving NATO's (and Europe's) Eastern dilemma(s) and meeting the security objectives of Central European leaders, therefore, is dependent on the successful transfer of Western norms of civil-military relations into the Eastern community and its governing institutions.

The Westminster Legacy

Common and fundamental concepts drawn from the military and civil history of Western Europe are the foundation of civil-military relations in all Western states. Answers to such questions as who stands guard, who is responsible for the national security, what is the "referent object" of national security, and when and under what constraints will force be used in the name of the state are not in themselves policy so much as they are philosophical and cultural guides to policymaking. The federation of defense policies in the West required at the outset a strong consensus on these philosophical signposts.[11]

War has no logic in the absence of political goals and political direction. This Clausewitzian dictum provides the keystone to Western civil-military relations and institutions. It is wed to the notion that the power to establish and to modify a state's policies flows from the people as expressed in parliaments. Military leaders, the "managers of violence," may be charged to command the operational resources of the state, but they are always conditioned by the authority and direction of parliament. There is, therefore, in all Western states a type of shared responsibility for national defense: politicians set goals and determine resources; and soldiers organize and direct campaigns. When either group strays too far into the other's domain, civil control is diminished.

Civilian control of the military can become civilian abuse of democracy. Kings, party autocracies, and civil dictatorships that use the military as the instrument for their power are as abusive of parliamentary control of the military as is any military dictator. "It is always necessary to ask which civilians are doing the controlling."[12] Controlling the use of military forces in the interests of democracy, therefore, requires more than the obedience of the military to its political master.

Huntington argues that "civilian control decreases as the military becomes increasingly involved in institutional, class, and constitutional politics" and that "objective civilian control" of the military requires the "militarizing of the military." That is to say, the military must acquire a high degree of professionalism and society must value and support the "recognition of an autonomous military professionalism" that is "politically sterile and neutral." For its part the professional military leadership must insist that it "stands ready to carry out the wishes of any civilian group which secures legitimate authority within the state."[13]

Political neutrality can, however, clash with the military's own view of its responsibility to defend the state if, in its opinion, political leaders are negligent in their duties to national defense. This situation could prompt some officers to attempt to seize power in the name of national defense. That has often been the case in Latin American states. In Western states this difficulty is overcome by the constitutional convention that places responsibility for determining the national interests and for defining national security goals in the hands of political leaders and not military officers. It is an important divide that eliminates any legitimate military involvement in national politics and policymaking. Officers may inform politicians of military threats and risks but they have no responsibility to insist that political leaders address the threats or redress the risks.

This slim conceptual framework has important structural consequences. Parliamentary control, political leadership, shared responsibility, and professional neutrality are inherent in the political and military institutions that formulate and direct the security policies and the military operations of Western states. In all Western societies military forces are under the direct control of political leaders responsible to parliament. Political direction may come directly from a head of state, as in the case of the United States, or indirectly through some type of minister of defense. In all cases the military is restricted from acting without political authority and has no right of access to the policymaking levels of government, although some military leaders may routinely be invited to participate in high-level policy meetings.

Political authority is given meaning in several ways but the most obvious and important is through the control of resources that are at the disposal of military officers. Military leaders have no right to any national asset and can only recommend what they considered to be prudent expenditures for national defense. Parliament will decide.

Political control through resource allocation goes much further than the control of the doors of the treasury. In mature democratic states political leaders have come to understand that their responsibilities include the auditing of the expenditure of military resources in the broadest interpretation of that term. Politicians in Western states are routinely involved in the technical consideration of weapons procurement, infrastructure development, force design, and operational deployments. The divide between policy and administration is blurred and the political supervision of operational decisions has become more pervasive as political sensitivities increase and communications capabilities advance.

Western organizations for defense, both national ministries and international staffs such as NATO, are constructed around the need for political control, continuous audit, professional military neutrality, and shared responsibility. Defense ministries typically include a ministerial office, a civil service office, and a military headquarters. The three sections are joined conceptually and politically by the office of the minister—always a civilian—who may or may not have sole authority over military affairs. The minister provides political direction to the military and civil-service staffs, supervises the major aspects of operations, and carries military opinion and advice to the cabinet or parliament legislature.

Most governments maintain some type of civil service-staff to provide for the continuous interaction of the defense ministry with the other elements of the civil government. Some senior defense officials may be influential in their own right and have responsibilities for providing defense-related political advice to the minister and the government and for overseeing the preparation of defense estimates. Officials often act as the internal auditors for ministers and supervise the expenditures of funds allocated to departments and services. In a few ministries, civil servants may have considerable influence on defense programs and may aid their ministers in evaluating military opinion by acting as a counter-expert group and by establishing their own strategic assessment and policy advising bodies.

Military headquarters in Western states have evolved into two main types. The first is the traditional command headquarters responsible for the preparation, deployment, and command of forces. This type of headquarters might be formed around army, navy, and air force services, or on "functional" commands, that is formations with distinct or special tasks such as submarine commands. The second type of headquarters, and usually the senior of the two, is the national command. This headquarters most often has a joint, and sometimes integrated, staff with representation from each service and functional command. It is typically responsible for developing national policy and for controlling joint or integrated operations.

National command headquarters may be presided over by a joint committee of senior officers or by a national chief of staff. While there are several similarities between these two broad types of national command organization, the actual functions and responsibility of the officers and committees in them may vary to some degree. At one end of the spectrum of command is the Canadian model with a single chief of defense responsible for all aspects of a single service. At the other, more typical, end is the "chairman" model in which one officer acts as the coordinator for some central functions of defense policy and shares responsibility with other officers, often service chiefs, for other aspects of policy and operations. Most national commands are evolving toward a unitary organization and more authority is concentrated in one officer who becomes identified as the military advisor to political leaders.

Concepts for Change

From this brief description of general conditions in Western societies it is possible to define a few critical concepts that may be used to guide and measure the development of Western precepts of civil-military relations in Central Europe. That is not to say that every experience and decision in the West has to be replicated in the East. Rather, the concepts that will be described here have provided Western governments with a high degree of control over armed forces and defense policy and the suggestion is that if they were to be applied in the Central European states, then those states ought, other things being equal, to achieve similar results.

The Active Minister. Defense ministers are confronted always by complex and difficult problems layered in domestic and international factors and concerns. From whom are ministers to get their advice? If they are dependent for advice upon only one source, the military staff for example, how are they to maintain credible political control of military policy? Huntington's assertion in 1957 that "the problem in the modern state is not armed revolt but the relation of the expert to the politician" would ring true for any Western minister today, even though most ministers have had some indoctrination into defense issues before they take office.

Politicians often confess to feeling trapped by the advice they receive from expert staffs. There is no easy answer to the "expert" problem in any modern society but in the West some governments have found that a clue lies in the effort ministers take to involve themselves in the details of policy and their insistence that officers and officials explain their advice in terms comprehensible to political leaders. As in other fields, the application of this discovery to defense planning depends on the assumption that ministers will perform their duties energetically and that is not always a reliable assumption on which to base critical policy.

The notion of an "active defense minister" who has unlimited access to all managerial and operational information and an unlimited right to promote and set any policy has become the standard model for civil-military relations in Western ministries of defense. The degree to which ministers can enter routinely into the details of defense policy planning and impose their will on the decisionmaking process is a primary indicator of the extent of parliamentary control of the military in any state. In the East military resistance to ministerial intrusions into the defense policy process will continue to menace civil-military relations until such time as the new democratic system promotes political leaders who are confident in their understanding of the issues and of their relationship with the military and defense establishments.

Political control of this vital and expensive segment of government, therefore, requires the constant attention of ministers and their active involvement in the details of civil and military policy and plans. In some societies military officers would be alarmed by such intrusiveness, but Western military officers have come not only to expect it but often to demand it of their political leaders and citizens. One price of Huntington's autonomous military professional is constant attention by informed politicians. Gaining the acceptance of both politicians and military officers of the need for such close cooperation is the first demand of Western concepts of civil-military relations.

Lines of Authority. Control of defense policy and the armed forces requires clear lines of authority. Military leaders need to understand what constitutes legal authority and from whom they are to receive their orders. If there are doubts or ambiguities concerning either of these two points, then there will always be room for officers to circumvent parliamentary authority and for civilians and subordinate military officers to subvert the armed forces' chain of command and perhaps the will of parliament. Either situation could lead to a breakdown of discipline and civil control. In the absence of constitutional or other legal definitions of the lines of authority the armed forces might be encouraged to establish its preferred chain of command and relationship with government, which is only a short step from enforcing its own preferred policies.

Integrated Ministry of Defense. Most ministries of defense in the West are highly integrated structures intended to bring political, civil service, and military staffs together and thereby force a close coalition under the minister. They serve also to reinforce the elected minister's right of access to the decisionmaking process and to direct military operations through the military staff in the name of parliament.

There is a tendency among some officers in Central Europe to build an artificial dichotomy between political and military responsibilities and to see security and defense policy as being separate administrative and operational activities. It is an attitude that stems in some respects from the monarchist tradition in armed forces (and the habits of the Communist Party and the former Soviet armed forces) and from a belief among officers that the nation's defense is above politics and cannot be trusted to mere politicians.

Officers, and others, who hold to these ideas, while professing allegiance to parliamentary control of policy, reconcile this contradiction by attempting to limit a minister's access to information and decisions or by creating multiple lines of authority for different defense situations. For example, commanders might be satisfied to receive "administrative directions" from ministers but would only accept operational direction from the president. This attitude is sometimes further manifested in defense ministries when ministers and their civilian staffs and the issues they deal with are separated—sometimes physically—from the command headquarters or general staff and their plans. Observations of the transformation of civil-military relations in Central Europe, therefore, ought to focus particularly on the internal organization and functioning of defense ministries and command headquarters in order to ascertain the degree to which elected ministers have control of the policy process and operations in all circumstances.

Shared Analysis. Parliamentary control of the military is concerned not only with controlling armed forces but also with controlling the defense agenda, its goals, and the resources applied to them. Defense administration is "about defining problems and choosing solutions to address them." It is a process that requires the development of an operating consensus, a shared analysis, between political leaders and military commanders concerning ends and means. The acceptance of shared responsibilities among politicians and military officers provides a firm base from which the complexities of defense choices can be controlled. In the absence of this understanding the directing and operating arms of defense policy will be in turmoil continually.

While there can be no question but that the government is responsible for national defense, it is equally clear that no government can effect that defense without professional military cooperation. This cooperative and sensitive aspect of civil-military relations can be facilitated by the development of a policy process directed and audited by parliament but which allows each stakeholder access to the policy process at appropriate levels. Most Western states have established some form of defense committee system that is intended to allow for debate on the issues and to provide a forum for the coordination of policies and operations. It is important that such a system demonstrate that it is responsible through elected politicians to parliament and that it is not merely the puppet of any person or group within the defense establishment.

Public Awareness. All aspects of defense policy in the Central European states (and elsewhere in the former Warsaw Pact) were closed subjects outside the ken of the public. By contrast, in the West, although some operational aspects of defense policy may be classified, there is typically still a wide range of interaction and debate among members of parliament, the defense establishment, and the public. This interaction is an essential element of civil control of the military insofar as it allows for the transmission of information and for public audit of governments and armed forces alike. Reasonable access by opposition parliamentarians and the general public to defense issues and decisions is a key criterion of democratic control of civil-military relations. Free societies encourage open debate, routine communication to the public, and some challenge process for access to classified information.

Protection for Military Professionalism. If military forces are to be apolitical instruments of duly elected governments, then it is necessary that soldiers be protected from political abuse and the partisan demands of government leaders. An important measure of democratic civil-military relations is the degree to which the military is by law disengaged from the political process. Strict disengagement might demand that no member of the armed forces take part in any political activity, including voting. Most states, however, have been satisfied to restrict military personnel from active campaigning while in uniform and to separate military and political activities on bases and so on.

More critical is the extent to which commanders and their units are free from partisan political direction. Most Western states have some safeguards that guard against such occurrences. For example, national defense laws might direct that only the chief of staff can issue orders to the armed forces and provide a politically neutral arbitrator, such as a supreme court, to adjudicate for a chief of staff facing a manifestly illegal demand from government.

Governments must have some control over the military promotion system, but it is important that they exercise that control independently of partisan political interests. Governments should approve the promotion of senior officers who are to hold sensitive ranks or appointments but they ought to be required by law to select such officers from a list of candidates prepared outside the political system. Anything less than a politically neutral promotion system would destroy the neutrality of the officer corps and would only tempt politicians to use military promotions for their partisan benefits, an act that would irretrievably corrupt the armed forces.

There is no formula that will assure parliamentary control of the military. Each state must devise its own norms, laws, and procedures from its own constitution and history. In the West the institutionalization of these few concepts, active political supervision, integrated defense ministries, clear lines of authority, shared analysis, public access, and protection for military professionalism form the basis for civil-military relations. They are also the sentinels that every Western observer or critic ought to look for if they are hoping to find compatibility between Western and Eastern defense structures.

The Problems of Transformation

The transformation of the defense structures of the Central European states to match Western norms is complicated by several factors but especially by the significant differences in civil-military relations. None of the Central European states' military or political traditions are founded on Westminster or on anti-Cromwellian concepts. No aspect of their recent history has prepared publics, politicians, or soldiers for the demands of Western style civil-military relations or to act within a Western-style defense structure.

These Central European states are suffering still from a transition hangover that thwarts most attempts to confirm new relationships. The atmosphere of mistrust and uncertainty that is characterized by purges, conflict between members of the old and new regimes, broken relationships, and quarrels about who did what under the former system and who was responsible for the relatively nonviolent transition period creates significant difficulties for governments attempting to construct new structures and policies.

In Poland there has been a significant falling-out between various members and factions of the Solidarity trade union. Although the army has been cleansed of certain officers who were leaders of the previous military government, the army always had a reputation even at the height of the Cold War of being "red on the outside but white on the inside." Today the army's loyalty to Poland (and the people's growing frustration with the confusion in the Sejm) allows it to claim a high standing among the Polish people that is only second to the church.[14] The military leadership, therefore, has a relatively strong position, but it has so far resisted any temptation to throw its weight behind any political leader or party.

In the Czech Republic the situation is both more chaotic and perhaps dangerous. There was never a strong national allegiance to the Warsaw Pact among the people, but the professional army was proud of its central place in the Group of Soviet Forces and the alienation of the people from the armed forces continues today. Nevertheless, the army played, according to its commanders' accounts, a central role in maintaining peace and harmony during the last days of Soviet control in Czechoslovakia, but it was rewarded only with purges and mistrust.[15]

Even in 1993, the Czech Republic investigates officers and subjects them to loyalty checks. It is an atmosphere filled with difficulties compounded by the January 1993 separation of the old state into two independent countries. This "regrettable political failure," as one senior officer termed the loss of Slovakia, caused another round of confusion and cynicism in the armed forces as personnel and equipment were redistributed between the new states.[16]

The situation in Hungary is in some respects more stable than in the Czech Republic, but relations between the population and the army are strained. There is no support among the general population for the continuation of conscription and many of those called to the colors never hear the bugle. Observers note that the Hungarian officer corps is poorly trained and seems unaware of the magnitude of the changes it must undergo in the next few months. More ominous is the not-too-subtle relationship that still exists between senior army commanders and reactive politicians newly won from communist to democratic ways.

The sudden collapse of the Soviet presence and the communist parties in Central Europe left most states without a constitutional basis for government. As a result, each state is attempting to confirm a constitution, build political parties, and address serious policy issues, while they are confronting the difficult process of transition to democracy. Not many of them consider civil-military relations to be the most important concern of the day. This fact, and the confusion in government relationships and the political infighting between levels of government and among politicians, has stranded the military leadership without giving them clear lines of authority.

The civil-military turmoil in Poland is most noticeable at the constitutional level where the president and the government are fighting to establish their positions on most issues including the control of the armed forces in peace and war.[17] Lech Walesa has even hinted loudly that he would form a "presidential guard" to give the president an armed force capable of defending his interests during any conflicts with the government.[18] This type of internal friction confuses the military leadership and it may yet sour its attitude toward democratic methods.

In Hungary, uncertainty and the struggle for control of the army caused a confrontation between the prime minister and the president (an opposition member). It was accompanied by at least two reorganizations of the defense staff which has resulted in a significant denigration of the minister's ability to manage defense policy because of the wholesale transfer of responsibility for issues from the ministry to the strictly military high command.[19] Although there is some evidence that the leaders of the Hungarian defense forces would like to see an integration of the ministry and the command headquarters, parliament is not now in the mood to encourage such a move.[20] The Czech government, on the other hand, has taken firm control of its ministry of defense but the nascent ministry in Bratislava is struggling to find its feet.

Central European governments, military staffs, and bureaucracies, without exception, lack political, military, and civil-service experience and expertise. In most cases, no state has had sovereign authority over its foreign or defense policies since before World War II. First German and then Soviet officers and officials dictated the policies and decisions of these states. Although some officers and officials rose to high rank within these foreign-controlled structures, they were never allowed to develop sovereign policies and their association with the Soviet machinery has only served to qualify most of them for dismissal by the successor governments.

Today, this absence of experience and expertise across Central Europe is most telling especially when one compares the situation in the West with that in the East. Whereas their Western counterparts have long-standing policies and mechanisms that provide a starting point for defense and security reforms, officers and bureaucrats in the East have few policies to follow. Indeed, they sit before blank sheets of paper and under the direction of untested and unsteady government arrangements.

Central European military forces and their officer corps, have, moreover, been subordinates of the Soviet Union. Not only were officers trained in the Soviet Union's techniques of warfare, but also the military forces of most of the Warsaw Pact countries had no military reality in structure or strategy except as part of the war plans of the general staff of the Soviet Union. In fact, they were incorporated into the Soviet military sphere in ways that grossly transgressed national sovereignty. Furthermore, most officers were loyal to the communist party and the armed forces as a whole were dedicated to the salvation of the party and not necessarily the state. The military profession of the Central European states, therefore, has little tradition of acting as a politically neutral or even national armed force.

The lack of trained officers and officials affects the external functioning of these governments as well. Few officers speak English or other Western languages well and only those officers and officials who have had access to the West through foreign postings are even scantly familiar with Western defense structures, ideas, and relationships. Thus, for example, when they are required to attend NATO sessions they are unfamiliar with the substance and the bureaucratic nuances of these meetings and have difficulty drawing useful conclusions or inferences from their visits.[21]

This lack of expertise is matched by the lack of any defense civil service as the term is understood in the West. During the Warsaw Pact era ministries of defense were shadow organizations with no real function and all staff positions were held by military officers. When the successor governments came to power intent on establishing civil control of defense affairs they were not surprised to find that the only individuals who were competent to advise them on defense matters and to make the changes they demanded were military officers.

In some states there has been a determined attempt to form politically directed ministries of defense and to take over from the command headquarters such functions as financial management and personnel development. However, in most cases these new "civil" departments have been staffed by ex-officers. This does not imply that these departments and officers are corrupted, but only that their norms and attitudes may not be focused on the demands of parliamentary control and that the governments face a particularly acute "expert problem" that has few immediate remedies.

In some ministries politicians have attempted to move civilian analysts into strategic-assessment positions, but the opposition of military leaders has made the attempts difficult. Most officers believe that strategic direction is their responsibility. Furthermore, the legacy of the militaries' association with the officer corps of the Soviet Union established and reinforced the notion that national security is predominately a military problem and that "professionalism" is concerned with high levels of technical competence and the employment of forces on a large scale in an alliance strategy. The high commands have defended their "turf" by insisting on a separation of ministerial departments from the command staffs and by ignoring the civilian analysts. In one case, the command staffs simply coopted the civilians by making them reserve officers and subordinating them to the military staff.

Finally, the lack of competent civil servants also hinders relationships with Western states and with international organizations such as NATO. Most Western ministries of defense have very experienced civil staffs that act together to manage certain aspects of national or alliance defense polices. Few of the Central European states have any qualified individuals to send to these meetings and, therefore, they often send military officers in their place. These officers, unfortunately, often find themselves at a disadvantage negotiating complex issues with individuals and groups operating within a well-understood set of management parameters.[22]

This lack of public expertise is matched by a lack of private expertise and opinion. No Central European state has a defense community of interested citizens, academics, media, or nongovernmental organizations ready to act as watchdogs or counter-expert groups. Few politicians have developed any interest in international affairs or military matters. There are no Sam Nunns in Central Europe.

The reason for this absence of public interest is easy to understand, but it does handicap political leaders and can leave the definition of states' defense needs in the hands of the military or under the control of "inexperienced dabblers." The difficulty for civil control is obvious and it will take a considerable time before it can be redressed.

If the Central European states have any advantage in terms of establishing parliamentary control over the military, then it is in the fact that by and large they confront single-service armed forces led by the army. The army is (and has been) the dominant force in all the Central European states not only in terms of numbers but also in the military and political history of these states.

This condition makes the civil job easier because it eliminates policy and resource distribution problems that are often associated with tri-service rivalries in other countries. Defense ministers and their civil service supporters will be able to focus their attention on the relationship of the army to the government without the distraction of having to accommodate the needs of the navy and the air force at the same time. Insofar as interservice rivalries are the cause of conflict and inefficiencies in national armed forces, this is at least a small blessing.

Conclusion

An efficient defense structure built on the concepts, norms, and principles of Westminster could provide the instrument for close political control of the armed forces of Central Europe, but a faulty structure could provide the instrument for military subversion. The question then is not whether the military is subordinated to the political authority but how the military subordination to the civil power is to be effected. How has the government attempted to develop a "normal pattern of behavior" between itself and the military and to what degree has that attempt been successful?

The analysis of behavior or the influence of groups and institutions in government is notoriously difficult and often subjective. The accurate assessment of the influence of particular political and military authorities over security and defense policy outcomes (as opposed to policy declarations) is complicated by national security sensitivities and by the complex nature of the policy field. Although Western security models do not guarantee civil control of the military, they have evolved certain common features that provide strong incentives for political attention and checks and balances that allow for a high level of control when politicians sought to impose it. The absence of these incentives and checks and balances within a civil-military structure might suggest that control is weak, if not totally absent.

Measuring change in Eastern defense structures will not be easy, but it can be made manageable if Western researchers and policy advisors take advantage of an appropriate research framework founded on

Western concepts and institutions. The democratizing process and the control of military forces is accomplished through a (usually) slow assimilation of appropriate ideas and the construction of effective institutions. Not all segments of society will advance or accept the consequences of democratic norms equally or at the same pace.

It may not be true that the armed forces of the Central European states will be the last institution to accept democracy. However, the acceptance of democratic notions by the military may not have penetrated below the uniform's surface because military leaders mistrust democracy's capability to provide for national defense. For this reason, research that is also focused on the concerns of military leaders would provide a distinct and useful measure of their attitudes to civil-military relations and might provide an indication of the depth of democratic sensations in the armed forces.

The West's self-interests demand that it either assist the incorporation of Central Europe into a wider pan-European security community or that it prepare to live with the consequences and uncertainties and expenses created by the so-called security vacuum in the East. That is not to say that the establishment of a cooperative security community would eliminate threats from the East. But insofar as institutions can ameliorate such threats, the West would be well served if it continued actively to promote concepts and structures that have served it well in the past.

The Atlantic community, however, cannot and does not need to beggar its constitutional history in order to provide a mechanism to secure its future. On the contrary, the West must insist that true democratic reforms and institutions will be the currency for entrance into its world. Western leaders, and especially national and international officers and officials from the North Atlantic Alliance, must continue to define the currency and to assist the East to accept it. The establishment of civil-military relations in Central Europe built on Western norms will be a critical part of this new paradigm.

These tasks will require Western leaders to act as coaches and guides for their Eastern counterparts. Before they can undertake that role, however, they will need to confirm in specific terms how the Westminster model of democracy functions and how civil-military relations operate at practical levels in the West. States in the East want to know how, in fact, defense ministries function and how officials and officers relate to politicians in matters of policy. How can democratic states ultimately entrust their national security to elected civilian politicians, the majority of whom have no practical experience or understanding of complex defense issues? In some central states many officers and some politicians believe that the intrusive political control of the military preached in the West is indeed a sham and they can point to situations and histories in the West that seem to support this cynical view. Western scholars and others had best be prepared to explain the context and implication of this sometimes shaky history.

Policy cannot escape the consequences of concepts and structure. Western security policy and the evolution of a European security community are defined by a framework founded on liberal-democratic concepts that encompass and condition all aspects of civil-military relations. Therefore, the key that will allow Central European states to open the gates into the Western security community is the implanting and maturing of the West's concepts of democracy and civil-military relations in those societies. If the concepts that have sustained the West's security so well for so long are adopted by Central European states, then those states will inevitably form and support institutional arrangements that will enable them to function as credible members of a new broader European security community.

The degree to which a security regime can manage the ever-present immediate causes of war so as to produce nonviolent outcomes is the main criterion for determining the success or failure of such a regime. Institutions are the chief instruments for managing international regimes and their competence is the key to regime success. Any future pan-European security community will be built not as Heisbourg suggests "on the debris of the old order" but rather, as Huntington's understanding of civil-military relations implies, on a new institutional framework standing on the democratic traditions and concepts of the Atlantic states. Whether the Central European states will share the benefits and contribute to this security arrangement will depend on their willing adoption of Western norms. The resolution of Europe's Eastern dilemma in a manner congruent with the West's interests demands that Western leaders continue to assist the leaders of Central Europe to find their way to Westminster.

Notes

1. François Heisbourg, "From a Common Security House to a New Security System," in *The Shape of the New Europe,* ed. Gregory Treverton (New York: Council on Foreign Relations Press, 1992), p. 35.

2. See David G. Haglund, *Alliance Within the Alliance? Franco-German Military Cooperation and the European Pillar of Defense* (Boulder: Westview Press, 1991). Also, Michael Stürmer, "Germany in Search of an Enlightened American Leadership," in *The Future of U.S.-European Relations: In Search of a New World Order,* ed. Henry Brandon (Washington: Brookings Institution, 1992), p. 86.

3. Michel Rocard, "Towards a Redefinition of Transatlantic Relations," in *Future of U.S.-European Relations*, p. 46.

4. Ralf Dahrendorf suggests that states will have to go through five electoral cycles or successful transfers of governments before a democratic system could be confirmed. See Ralf Dahrendorf, *Reflections on the Revolution in Europe* (New York: Random House, 1990).

5. David Owen, "Atlantic Partnership or Rivalry," in *Future of U.S.-European Relations*, p. 16.

6. Stephen Larrabee, "Democratization and Change in Eastern Europe," in *Shape of the New Europe*, p. 136.

7. Stanley Hoffmann, "Balance, Concert, Anarchy, or None of the Above," in ibid., p. 194.

8. Kenneth Waltz, *Man, the State and War: A Theoretical Analysis* (New York: Columbia University Press, 1954).

9. Karl Deutsch et al., *Political Community and the North Atlantic Area* (Princeton, NJ: Princeton University Press, 1957).

10. Michael Ward, *Research Gaps in Alliance Dynamics* (Denver: University of Denver Press, 1982).

11. For a history of the evolution of federated defense relations in Western Europe and North America, see Douglas Bland, *The Military Committee of the North Atlantic Alliance: A Study of Structure and Strategy* (New York: Praeger, 1991).

12. Samuel Huntington, *The Soldier and the State: The Theory and Politics of Civil-Military Relations* (New York: Random House, 1957), p. 81.

13. Ibid., pp. 83-84.

14. Interviews, Warsaw, May 1993. See also Andrew Michta, *East Central Europe After the Warsaw Pact* (New York: Greenwood, 1992), p. 95.

15. Interview, Prague, May 1993.

16. Ibid.

17. See *Tenets of the Polish Security Policy* (Warsaw, November 1992).

18. Interviews, Warsaw, May 1993.

19. Alfred Reisch, "The Hungarian Army in Transition," *Radio Free Europe Research Project* 2, 10 (5 March 1993). Also Michta, *East Central Europe*, pp. 151-52.

20. Reisch, "Hungarian Army," p. 50. Also interviews, Budapest, May 1993.

21. Interviews, NATO Headquarters, Brussels, June 1993.

22. Interviews, Warsaw, Prague, Budapest, and Brussels, May 1993.

PART FOUR

Conclusion

11

NATO's Eastern Dilemmas: Flexible Response Redux?

David G. Haglund, S. Neil MacFarlane, and Joel J. Sokolsky

The story is well known. When the representatives of the original 12 countries stepped forward to sign the North Atlantic treaty on 4 April 1949, the US Marine band played two selections from George Gershwin's *Porgy and Bess*, "It Ain't Necessarily So" and "I Got Plenty of Nuttin'." As the Cold War years went by, NATO, despite its growth and apparent success in containing and deterring Soviet power in Europe, could never quite shake the suspicion that behind the burgeoning bureaucracy, the elaborate military command structure, and the carefully crafted nuclear and conventional strategies, all was not necessarily so and that in a real confrontation, the alliance would be shown to have plenty of nothing. These suspicions seemed well founded. For from its very beginnings the alliance has had to cope with a never-ending series of dilemmas and seemingly insoluble contradictions about how it dealt with the threat from the East all the while holding itself together.

Above all, there was the "nuclear dilemma." How could the United States extend its nuclear deterrent umbrella to cover allies in Europe when if deterrence failed, either the bluff would be called and Washington would in fact not sacrifice New York for Paris, or the threat would be made good and both cities perish? Flexible response was supposed to solve this dilemma, but as an agreement to disagree over strategy, it contained its own inconsistencies and imponderables. Did it provide a more credible deterrent or simply make Europe safe for conventional war, thus increasing the chances of nuclear war? If the Soviets believed the NATO threat to use nuclear weapons first, would this only encourage them to contemplate a first strike?

Apart from the military questions there were the uncertainties about the proper political approach to the East. What was the right mixture of consistency and compromise, of determination and détente, of confrontation and co-existence? Should the Warsaw Pact be dealt with simply as a front for Soviet domination of Eastern Europe, or should the countries be treated individually?

If NATO as a whole confronted dilemmas, the alliance itself was continually coping with internal divisions on its military and political approach to the East. As a collection of first 12, finally 16, states, it was not surprising that different governments adopted varied policies.

Washington and its European allies did not always agree, while Ottawa often felt it had to serve in the role of consensus builder. Even within Europe itself, Bonn, Paris, and London were not in accord as to how to deal with Warsaw, Prague, and Sofia—let alone Moscow. Issues such as defense burdensharing, nuclear weapons, arms control, and trade all occasioned disagreements within allied councils. Like its critics, NATO's Eastern challenges were legion and they arose both from within and without the organization.

The alliance never resolved its Cold War Eastern dilemmas. As it turned out, it did not have to. What it had to do, and what it did do, was never let those dilemmas obscure the seriousness of the threat from the East and the need to maintain fundamental allied unity in meeting that threat. Indeed, it might be argued that if the alliance had tried to solve each and every one of its dilemmas to the intellectual satisfaction of its critics, the process itself would have torn NATO apart. Perhaps there is a lesson here in how best to cope with the post-Cold War Eastern challenges.

At their base, NATO's problems stem from the inability to determine what kind of threats, if any, it now faces from the East. Today's problems are at once less urgent and more complicated. There is no clear and present danger from the East. Rather NATO confronts an eclectic array of ill-defined uncertainties, potential instabilities, and all-too-real ethnic conflicts. Despite worrisome trends, it is not evident that any of the current problems in the former Warsaw Pact countries and in the newly emerging post-Soviet republics pose an immediate threat to the physical security and economic well-being of Western Europe, much less to the United States and Canada.

Even having identified problems, it remains to be determined whether NATO continues to be the proper forum in which to address them. A start was made in this direction with the creation of the North Atlantic Cooperation Council (NACC), which brought together former adversaries. But post-Cold War Europe finds the Atlantic Alliance in competition with other organizations, such as the Western European

Union (WEU) and the European Union (EU), which is what the European Community (EC) became on 1 November 1993. The heightened activity of these collective groupings raises anew the old problematique of the relationship between North America, mainly the United States, and European security. Are the problems of the East to be dealt with only by Europeans? And even if Washington and Ottawa are to have a role, is not the Conference on Security and Cooperation in Europe (CSCE), rather than NATO, the proper venue? On the other hand, is the CSCE both too all-encompassing and too lacking in substance to cope with the myriad of problems arising in Eastern Europe?

Complicating NATO's search for the right niche in the new Europe with its array of organizations are national differences. It will be increasingly difficult to achieve any consensus on how best to approach the problems in the East given that multilateral and unilateral avenues are now open to member governments. In the past, the fear that disunity would play into the hands of Moscow had tempered allied disagreements. Now there appears to be little incentive to follow a collective course that might impose costs that some allies do not wish to bear or foreclose options that other governments may wish to exercise.

As with those of the past, NATO's current Eastern dilemmas can and do seem essentially insoluble, and this has given rise to a sense that finally, despite its successes in outliving the Cold War, the alliance does have only "plenty of nothing" in meeting the challenges of post-Cold War European security. But NATO's current critics and self-doubters, like those of the past, could be underestimating its survivability. On the other hand, the current confusion, if carried too far, could contribute to the premature unravelling of what remains a potentially valuable security organization.

Lost amid the contemporary angst about the future of NATO is the simple thought that for North America, and perhaps even Western Europe, the security situation of today could be the best that it has been in the twentieth century. That may not be saying much, but gone is the bipolar era with all its attendant dangers. Gone is the single power that sought to impose its own harsh mastery over Europe by force of arms and thereby threaten North American security. Gone or subdued, as well, are those older predicaments that continually called into question the viability of the alliance—over nuclear weapons, détente, and burdensharing. It must be recalled that the common overwhelming security threat that helped keep the allies allied also threatened to divide them. Whatever dilemmas NATO now faces in the East would seem to be far fewer than those with which it successfully coped for 40 years.

Operating from a favorable security environment, NATO might appear to have the luxury of choice. It might not have to address each and every problem in Eastern Europe as if the whole future of the alliance and European security depended upon getting all 16 governments to adopt a common approach. Indeed, it might even get by with a new version of "flexible response." This could be a political response, one seeking to employ the alliance's strengths where they could best be put to advantage. It could feature an attempt to cooperate and not compete with the emerging new organizations in Europe, supporting them where possible and always standing by in case they should fail in the face of a renewed threat to Western European security. The eclectic and uncertain character of NATO's Eastern dilemmas suggests that the alliance might be well advised neither to expect nor to try to fashion a new consensus on its place in European security. Efforts to fashion such a consensus could themselves hasten the dissolution of NATO in an atmosphere of recrimination that might only serve to undermine overall efforts to deal with the problems of the East.

The alliance in this new era would, instead, seek to sustain a minimum level of political collaboration and consultation. To be sure, minimalism also carries its risks, the foremost of which being the danger of irrelevance. But set against this danger is the recognition that NATO, warts and all, does constitute the most substantive, legitimate forum for North American involvement in European security, whose retention would make sense even though other European bodies may be assuming more responsibility for security in the old continent. Quite simply, a more "political" NATO requires a less formal military structure. Force levels can continue to be reduced, while combined planning and joint exercises could sustain the ability of allied armies, navies, and air forces to operate together. Here, too, there would be continued benefits for flexibility.

This kind of flexibility would entail a measure of inconsistency on the part of the alliance. It would mean going, as it were, with the flow, and awaiting events and developments. Attempts might be made to deal with some Eastern crises, but others could be left unattended. Yet as Richard Betts has argued:

> Inconsistency is reasonable if we do not yet know when and against whom we will once again need a functioning security system for Europe. Relying on any single scheme is too risky in the new world where the current threat is uncertainty. Yes, the idea that post-Cold War strategy must define itself against "uncertainty" is becoming a tiresome and suspiciously facile cliché. That is unfortunate, but cannot be helped, because it happens to be true.[1]

It could well be that over the course of the next few years, the situation in Europe will evolve to the point where NATO is no longer needed, in which case the alliance might be disbanded without rancor and without engendering intra-European or transatlantic acrimony. Alternatively, the now dominant issue of international trade could make it impossible to continue the kind of transatlantic cooperation to which the West had become accustomed; in that event, NATO would have succumbed not to extraordinary Eastern challenges, but to more mundane Western ones related to farm subsidies and other matters of "low politics."

At this time, there is no escaping the reality that the alliance will be strained over questions of how to cope with the situation to the East. Nevertheless, a case might be made for doing as little as necessary, and doing so on behalf of "flexibility." It was, after all, a profound *lack* of flexibility that doomed the Soviet Union and the Warsaw Pact. Relying upon the renowned mercurial flexibility that helped to prevail in the Cold War could yet enable NATO to avoid a premature, and perhaps even unnecessary, fate in the post-Cold War era.

However, should it maintain its unity at the ultimate cost of utility, then it would assuredly run the risk of becoming the transatlantic equivalent of the Organization of American States, an entity that has shown itself adept at surviving, but little else. NATO, in this sense, might persist, but not mean very much. After all, did not Gershwin also compose a "Cuban Overture"?

Note

1. Richard K. Betts, "Systems for Peace or Causes of War? Collective Security, Arms Control and the New Europe," in *America's Strategy in a Changing World*, ed. Sean Lynn-Jones and Steven E. Miller (Cambridge, MA: MIT Press, 1992), p. 237.

About the Contributors

Douglas Bland is a defense consultant in Ottawa, and a retired Lieutenant Colonel in the Canadian Forces. He was a Visiting Defence Fellow at the Queen's Centre for International Relations during the 1985-86 academic year.

Christopher Conliffe, a Lieutenant Colonel in the Canadian Forces, is currently a senior staff officer for curriculum planning at the National Defence College of Canada. He was a Visiting Defence Fellow at the Queen's Centre for International Relations during the 1987-88 academic year.

Kevin F. Donovan, a Lieutenant Colonel in the US Air Force, was a Visiting Defence Fellow at the Centre for International Relations during the 1992-93 academic year. He is currently teaching at the Naval War College in Newport, Rhode Island.

Ernest W. Fischer, a Colonel in the US Army, was a Visiting Defence Fellow at the Centre for International Relations at Queen's University during the 1992-93 academic year. His current assignment is with the Defense Intelligence Agency in Washington.

Michel Fortmann teaches international relations and political science at the Université de Montréal, where he specializes in arms control and security.

David G. Haglund directs the Centre for International Relations at Queen's University, where he is also a professor of political studies and department head. His current research focuses on European security.

S. Neil MacFarlane is a Senior Fellow at the Queen's Centre for International Relations and a professor in the Department of Political Studies, where his teaching and research focus on post-Soviet foreign and security issues.

Stephen Page, a Senior Fellow at the Centre for International Relations at Queen's University and a professor in the Department of Political Studies, specializes in the foreign and domestic policies of Russia and the Central Asian republics of the former Soviet Union.

Charles Pentland is a Senior Fellow at the Queen's Centre for International Relations and is a professor of political studies at Queen's University. He specializes in Western European political and security interests.

Joachim Rabe is a Lieutenant Colonel in the German Army, who is currently assigned to the Chief of Staff of the German Armed Forces, in Bonn. He was a Visiting Defence Fellow at the Centre for International Relations during the 1992-93 academic year.

Joel J. Sokolsky, a Senior Fellow at the Centre for International Relations at Queen's University and a professor in the Department of Political and Economic Science at the Royal Military College of Canada, analyzes Canadian and US defense and security policy.

William Yerex, a Lieutenant Colonel in the Canadian Forces, is a Visiting Defence Fellow at the Centre for International Relations at Queen's University for the 1992-94 academic years. His previous posting was at NATO headquarters in Brussels.

Index

Adenauer, Konrad, 118
Airborne Warning and Control System (AWACS), 127-28
Albania, 49, 53, 56, 59, 95-96, 170
Aliev, Gaidar, 79
Ankara, 72-79, 86
Antall, Jozsef, 96
Armand, François, 149
Armenia, 70-84 *passim*, 93, 129, 183
Arms control, 26, 30-31, 51-54, 58-60, 142, 165, 187, 191
Arms transfers, 14, 51, 200
Ashgabat, 78
Aspin, Les, 6, 98, 190
Atlanticism, 82-83, 143
Attali, Jacques, 145, 170
Augmentation forces, 31
Austria, 40, 46, 49, 96, 107, 123
Austro-Hungarian Empire, 175
Autonomy, 43-48, 57, 60, 96, 103-7, 124, 141-49
Azerbaidzhan (Azerbaijan), 14, 68-86 *passim*, 129, 183
Azerbaidzhan-Armenia War, 68, 79

Baker, James, 72, 74, 143
Balkans, 3, 5, 95-105, 146, 149-53, 167, 174-75, 197
Balladur, Eduoard, 153-54
Bartholomew memorandum, 147
Belarus, 183
Belgium, 25, 107
Berlin Treuhand, 131
Berlin Wall, 131
Betts, Richard, 220
Bevin, Ernest, 25
Biedenkopf, Kurt, 117

Bismarck, Otto, 115
Black Sea Economic Cooperation Pact, 74, 78
Boban, Mate, 47
Bolshevism, 68-73
Bosnia-Herzegovina, 3-4, 14-19, 37-61, 97, 107,123-27, 165-66, 192
Boutros-Ghali, Boutros, 17
Boyer, Yves, 153
Brandt, Willy, 181
Brioni Declaration, 50
Buchanan, Allen, 107
Bulgaria, 28, 49-56, 95, 132, 145, 168-75, 183, 187
Burdensharing, 5, 21, 116, 127, 185, 218-19
Bush, George, 18, 50, 143, 167

Cambodia, 18, 32, 122-23
    Khmer Rouge, 18
Canada, 20-25, 191-92
    Military, 29-30
Carrington, Lord, 25, 165-66
Caspian Sea Organization, 78
Ceausescu, Nicolae, 168
Cetin, Hikmet, 72
Charter of Paris (1990), 97, 148
Cheney, Dick, 98
Chevènement, Jean-Pierre, 140
China, 82, 98
Chipman, John, 102, 108
Christopher, Warren, 3, 95
Ciller, Tansu, 76
Civic Education Project (Yale University), 106
Clinton, Bill, 98

Clinton administration, 3-4, 37, 56,
    96, 109
Cohen, William S., 5, 55
Cold War, 1-2, 13-17, 27-30, 67, 71,
    76, 80, 98, 115, 139-140, 147,
    160, 174, 181-82, 217-21
Collective defense, 1-2, 6, 11-13, 21-
    31, 132-33, 146, 149, 159, 172,
    181-84, 192, 195, 199-208
Comecon, 160-175 *passim*
  Comprehensive Program for Eco-
      nomic Integration (1971), 162
Commonwealth of Independent
      States (CIS), 70, 82-84, 129-32
  Collective Security Council, 84
Communism, 27, 72, 78, 93, 102, 124,
    133, 207
Conference on Security and Coopera-
    tion in Europe (CSCE), 19, 31-
    32, 50-53, 59-61, 72, 97-99, 130,
    141, 144, 148-53, 162, 181-88,
    191-96, 219
Conventional Forces Europe (CFE),
    26, 30, 132-34
Costa Rica, 107
Council of Europe, 141, 160, 169
Cox, Robert, 23
Critical theory, 23
Croatia, 3-4, 14, 19, 37-61, 103, 164-
    66, 173
  Croatian Democratic Union, 45
Cyprus, 60, 76
Czechoslovakia, 7, 33, 95-97, 103-8,
    124, 132, 145, 167-76, 186-87, 206

Defarge, Philippe Moreau, 153
Defence Planning Committee
    (NATO), 30, 184-87, 191
de Franchis, Amedeo, 191
Demirel, Suleiman, 56, 72, 74
Demokratizatsiia, 81
Denmark, 25, 123
Desert Storm, *see* Gulf War
Deterrence, 19, 26, 32, 81, 123, 139,
    152, 159, 217
Deutsch, Karl, 198

Disarmament, 26

Eagleburger, Lawrence, 54, 57
Economic Cooperation Organization
    (ECO), 74, 77-78
  See also Regional Cooperation for
      Development Organization
Elchibey, Abulfaz, 75, 79
Estonia, 82, 189
Ethnic conflict, 11, 37-66 *passim*, 67-
    70, 81-86, 94-103, 107, 174
  "Ethnic cleansing," 95, 102, 106
Ethnicity, 94-96, 100-102
Ethnocentrism, 94-95, 100, 109
Eurasanism, 82-85
European Bank for Reconstruction
    and Development (EBRD), 145,
    170-71
European Community (EC), 19-20,
    31-33, 49-53, 59-60, 71-78, 99,
    116, 124-25, 131, 138, 141-50,
    159-77, 181, 185, 189, 219
  Common Commercial Policy
      (CCP), 161-62, 168, 172
  Common External Tariff, 172
  Declaration of Mutual Regard
      (1988), 163
  European Political Cooperation
      (EPC), 162, 165, 172, 177
European Community Monitor Mis-
    sion Yugoslavia (ECMMY), 53
European Economic Area, 169
European Free Trade Association
    (EFTA), 145, 169, 176
European Investment Bank (EIB),
    170-71
European Recovery Plan, 176
European Security and Defense Iden-
    tity (ESDI), 184

Finland, 123, 183-85
Flexible response, 19, 25, 30, 217, 220
Foertsch, Hartmut, 132
Forward defense, 26, 30-31
France, 4, 16, 25-29, 34, 49-50, 137-54,
    163-65, 169, 173, 184-89, 197

Green Party, 139
National Front Party, 139
Security policy, 137-47, 151
Franco-German Eurocorps, 30, 138
Franco-German summit (1992), 138
Freedman, Lawrence, 174
Fukuyama, Francis, 184

Gamsakhurdia, Zviad, 102
Gaullism, 139-42, 152-53
Gellner, Ernest, 94, 100-1
Genscher, Hans-Dietrich, 121
Georgia, 14, 97, 129, 132
Germany, 4-5, 16, 26-34, 41, 49-50, 55-
    56, 96-97, 113-34 *passim*, 139-43,
    149, 153, 163-67, 172-73, 197, 208
    Christian Democratic Union
        (CDU), 117, 120, 127-28
    Christian Social Union (CSU), 117,
        120-21, 127-28
    Free Democratic Party (FDP), 121,
        128
    German Basic Law, 116, 118-26
    Green-Alternative List (GAL), 127
    Reunification, 113, 115-18, 137,
        142-43, 167, 173
    Rostock, 117
    Social Democratic Party, 117, 121-
        24
Glasnost, 81
Gnesotto, Nicole, 149
Gorbachev, Mikhail, 80, 82, 137, 144,
    163-64, 168, 182
Greece, 19, 26, 49, 52-53, 56, 59, 95-
    96, 166, 169
Grossman, David, 101
Group on Defence Matters (NATO),
    191
Gulf War (1992), 12, 15, 17-20, 58, 97-
    100, 119, 122, 145-46, 152, 285,
    192
Gunther, Richard, 107

Harmel report, 151, 184
Harutyunian, Khosrov, 93
Hashemi-Rafsanjani, Ali Akhbar, 78

Havel, Vaclav, 138, 183-85
Hegemony, 12, 16, 98, 129, 141, 191
Heisbourg, François, 196, 212
Helsinki Accord (1975), 97, 162, 172,
    181, 191-93
Higley, John, 107
Hitler, Adolph, 105
Hoffmann, Stanley, 197-98
Hondrich, Karl Otto, 114
Hungary, 7, 28, 33, 38, 40, 49-53, 96,
    124, 132, 145, 168-76, 183, 207
Huntington, Samuel, 199, 202-3
Hurd, Douglas, 54, 57
Hussein, Saddam, 60

Iceland, 25
Iliescu, Ian, 102
Immediate Reaction Force, 31
Institutionalism, 189-91, 196-205, 209-
    12
Intermediate-Range Nuclear Forces
    (INF), 26
International Monetary Fund (IMF),
    108, 171
Iran, 56, 67-79, 84-86
Iraq, 71, 77, 98, 123, 150
Iskenderum, 75
Islamic Conference Organization, 51,
    56
Islamic fundamentalism, 67, 70-73,
    81, 84, 86, 189
Israel, 85, 101, 107, 122
Israel-Egypt-US Camp David agree-
    ment, 17
Italy, 25, 49, 107, 173

Joffe, George, 26
Joxe, Pierre, 153
Jürgens, Conny, 127

Karadjordjevic, Alexander, 39, 41
Karadjordjevic, Peter, 39, 40
Karadzic, Radovan, 47, 55
Karadzic, Vuk, 38
Kardelj, Edvard, 42

Karimov, Islam, 75, 79, 85
Kazakhstan, 67-78, 80-85, 183
Keane, John, 101
Key Largo summit (1990), 140
Khomeini, Ayatollah, 76-77
Khrushchev, Nikita, 161
Kissinger, Henry, 126
Kohl, Helmut, 4, 34, 113, 118, 120,
    131-32, 143, 167
Kohl-Gorbachev summit (1988), 142
Kosovo, 14, 38, 42-44, 48-49, 53, 56-
    58, 95
Kozyrev, Andrei, 55-6, 13, 82-85
Krajina, 43-46
Kramer, Steven, 139
Kravchuk, Leonid, 102
Kurdistan, 122
Kuwait, 145-46
Kyrgyzstan, 68-73, 80-85, 183

Latvia, 82, 189
League of Nations, 148
Legge, Michael, 24
Lellouche, Pierre, 139, 149, 152
Lenin, Vladimir I., 93
Léotard, François, 153
Liberian civil war, 15
Liska, George, 98
Lithuania, 96, 189
London Declaration (1990), 2, 24, 183-
    86
London summit (1990), 146-47
Luxembourg, 25

Maastricht treaty, 99, 133, 143, 146,
    172-74, 177, 197
Macedonia, 14, 39-49, 52-53, 56-59,
    95-96, 166
MacKenzie, Maj. Gen. Lewis, 46
Malcolm X, 109
Mearsheimer, John, 27-28, 148
Meciar, Vladimir, 104
Mesic, Stipe, 43
Michels, Robert, 102
Migration, 11, 15, 44, 48-49, 60, 68,
    96, 113-19, 126-30, 139

Mihailovic, Draza, 41
Military Committee (NATO), 184,
    187, 191
Milosevic, Slobodan, 43-44, 47-49, 52-
    56, 60, 95, 102-3
Mitterrand, François, 137-53 *passim*,
    171
Moïsi, Dominique, 142
Moldova, 82, 97, 130-32, 183
Montenegro, 37-53, 127, 165
Mortimer, Edward, 33
Mosca, Gaetano, 102
Multinationalism, 2, 31, 133, 146
Multipolarity, 27
Munich summit (1991), 167

Nabiev, Rakhmon, 70, 78, 84
Nacertanije Plan, 39
Nagorno-Karabakh, 70, 79, 83, 87, 102
Nakhichevan, 75, 79
Nationalism, 12, 42-43, 69-70, 93-96,
    100-9, 113-16, 148, 174, 200
    European nationalism, 99, 105
Naumann, Gen. Klaus, 127
Nazarbaev, Nursultan, 78, 83
Netherlands, 107
Niiazov, Separmurad, 75
Nonproliferation, 11, 187
North Atlantic Cooperation Council
    (NACC), 3, 19, 31-33, 147-51,
    175, 181-93, 218
North Atlantic Council (NAC), 16, 19-
    20, 30-31, 182-84
    Strategic Concept, 30
North Atlantic treaty, 25, 27, 217
    see also, Washington treaty
NATO Airborne Early Warning
    (NAEW), 3, 192
North Korea, 98
Norway, 25, 192
Nuclear proliferation, 28, 31-32, 77
Nuclear strategy, 25, 27, 81, 144, 217
Nunn, Sam, 209

Osh, 70
Ostpolitik, 153, 163, 181, 193

Organization for European Economic
    Cooperation (OEEC), 160
Organization for Economic Coopera-
    tion and Development
    (OECD), 170
Owen, Lord David, 51, 55, 166, 197
Owen-Stoltenberg plan, 37
Ozal, Turgut, 71, 73, 75-78

Paine, Thomas, 100
Pakistan, 85
Palestine Liberation Organization,
    101
Panic, Milan, 52, 106
Paolini, Jérôme, 140, 147-48
Pareto, Vilfredo, 102
Paris summit (1989), 170
Pavelic, Ante, 41
Pax Bruxellana, 173
Peacekeeping, 2-3, 6-7, 11, 16-20, 32,
    50-58, 83, 113, 118-22, 126, 129-
    34, 150-53, 165-66, 174, 188-89,
    191-93
Peacemaking, 17, 114, 165, 174
Perestroika, 166
Poland, 7, 28, 33, 96, 124, 132, 145,
    168-76, 183, 186-87, 196, 206-7
Poland and Hungary Assistance for
    the Restructuring of the Econ-
    omy (PHARE), 145, 170
Portugal, 25, 107
Powell, Gen. Colin, 54, 57

Rakhmonov, Imomali, 79
Ranzjatovic, Zeljko "Arkan," 103
Rapid Reaction Force (NATO), 31,
    34, 147, 192
Realism, 23, 28, 173
Regional Cooperation for Develop-
    ment Organization, 77
    see also, Economic Cooperation Or-
    ganization
Riedel, Norbert Karl, 120
Robin, Gabriel, 138, 147
Rocard, Michel, 197
Romania, 28, 49, 53, 56, 59, 95-96,
    132, 145, 161-62, 168-71, 175,
    183
Rome summit (1991), 31, 183-84, 189
Rühe, Hans, 122-23
Rühe, Volker, 121
Russia, 4-6, 11-13, 19-20, 33, 40, 51-
    59, 67-79, 83, 85, 124, 128-29,
    141, 166-67, 173, 183, 188
    Economy, 69-74, 80-83, 86
    Foreign policy, 82, 84-85, 96
    Military, 13, 80-82, 85, 129-30, 141
    Supreme Soviet, 12, 50, 82
Russian Federation, 13, 128

Sandjak, 53, 58
Sarajevo, 52
Saudi Arabia, 56, 85, 106
Schmidt, Helmut, 118
Security, 2-4, 11, 27-33, 60, 67-68, 73,
    77-79, 97, 100, 159-60, 167, 173-
    75, 181-83, 200-12, 218
    Collective security, 2, 5-6, 11-17,
    21, 25, 28, 84-85, 120, 142, 144,
    150-51, 188
    Economic security, 68
    European security, 5, 11, 21, 30-34,
    96, 99-100, 121, 137, 141-42,
    147, 149-52, 171-72, 181, 184-86,
    189-99, 212, 219-20
    Regional security, 11, 68
Serbia, 3, 14, 19-20, 37-61, 95-96, 103,
    125-27, 165, 173
    League of Communists, 43
Seselj, Vojislav, 103
Shevardnadze, Eduard, 129
Slavonia, 45-46
Slovakia, 14, 95, 104, 169, 206
Slovenia, 4, 38, 41-50, 164-65, 173-75
Smith, Anthony, 109
Somalia, 15, 18, 34, 124
South Africa, 95
Sovereignty, 12-17, 43, 69, 104, 142,
    148, 197, 208
Soviet Union, 2, 5, 11-14, 21, 71-74,
    93, 97-98, 131, 137, 149, 154,
    159-67, 182-85, 195, 203, 208-9

Coup (1991), 33, 185
  Threat, 26-27, 71, 182
Spain, 26, 107
Spector, Ronald, 18
Spillover, 15, 37, 44, 48, 56-59, 77, 105
Stalin, Joseph, 24, 109, 130
Stanford, Peter, 26
Stankevich, Sergei, 82-83
Sunni, 68, 72, 76, 94
Supreme Headquarters Allied Powers Europe (SHAPE), 25
Sweden, 123, 185
Switzerland, 94, 107, 123

TACIS, 145
Tadzhikistan (Tajikistan), 68-73, 76-87, 130, 183
  Tadzhik Communist Party, 70
Teheran, 76-79
Tito, Josip, 41-47, 56, 109
Toffler, Alvin, 23
Transatlantic compact, 19-21, 25, 30-31, 138, 182, 211, 221
Transylvania, 14, 28
Treaty of Berlin (1878), 40
Treaty of Brussels, 26
Treaty of Rome, 161-62, 168-69
Treaty of Versailles, 105
Treaty on the Limited Stationing and the Withdrawal of Soviet Forces from Germany, 132
Treverton, Gregory, 174
Tudjman, Franjo, 46-47, 102
Turkey, 19, 26-28, 49, 56, 59, 67-69, 72-79, 85-87, 95-96, 109, 182
  Foreign policy, 71
Turkmenistan, 68-69, 73, 75-78, 80-85, 183

Ukraine, 53, 59, 69, 83, 132, 167, 183
Ullman, Richard, 172
United Kingdom, 25, 49-50, 57-59, 126
United Nations, 16, 19-20, 25, 31-32, 51-54, 59, 85, 95, 108, 119, 121-23, 127-30, 148, 153, 165-66, 188, 191-92

Economic Commission for Europe (ECE), 160
Security Council, 17-18, 50-52, 130, 149
United Nations Protection Force (UNPROFOR), 46, 50-53, 192
United States, 18-25, 35, 49, 57-59, 72-74, 77, 106, 143-44, 147, 185, 190
  Economy, 95, 99-100, 108
  Foreign policy, 96, 99
  Military, 28-30, 56, 59, 95-100, 105, 146
Uruguay, 107
Ustasha, 41, 48, 103
Uzbekistan, 68-73, 78, 80, 83-85, 183

Vance, Cyrus, 51, 55, 166
Vance-Owen plan, 3, 37, 49, 51-55
Van Evera, Stephen, 28
Venezuela, 107
Vietnam, 17-18, 97
Visegrad summit (1991), 175
Vojvodina, 38-43, 47-49, 53, 58

Walesa, Lech, 186, 207
Waltz, Kenneth, 198
Warsaw Treaty Organization (WTO), 1, 6, 19-20, 26, 30, 151, 164, 167, 195
Washington treaty, 25, 151
  see also, North Atlantic treaty
Western European Union (WEU), 19-20, 26, 31, 50, 53, 59, 99, 121, 138, 141-46, 165, 181, 185, 196, 219
Western Group of Forces (WGF), 132, 134
Western Srijem, 45
Wilson, Woodrow, 94
Wörner, Manfred, 2, 24

Yeltsin, Boris, 6, 12-13, 50, 80-85, 96, 102, 129, 132-33, 137, 167
Yugoslavia, 1-4, 15-20, 28, 37-66 *passim*, 96, 102-5, 114, 125-28, 138,

152-59, 164, 166, 170, 174, 185, 189, 192

Crisis (1993), 3, 11, 15, 32, 37, 43, 53, 103, 123-24, 133, 146, 164-67, 182-85, 191

Communist Party, 41-42

Partisans, 41-42

People's Army (JNA), 43-46

Zielonka, Jan, 96